T *The Cradle of Erotica*

*A study
of Afro-Asian
sexual expression and
an analysis of erotic
freedom in social
relationships*

THE CRADLE

*by Allen Edwardes
and R.E.L. Masters
The Julian Press, Inc.*

 *New York
1963*

OF EROTICA

© Copyright 1962
by The Julian Press, Inc.
Library of Congress Catalog Card Number 62–21126
Published by The Julian Press, Inc.
80 East 11th Street, New York 3
Manufactured in the United States of America
by H. Wolff, New York
DESIGN: Marshall Lee
Fourth Printing

The Threnody of Abu Zayd

O folk! I have a wondrous tale, so rare;
Much shall it profit hearers wise and ware.
I saw in youth's springtime a potent brave
(And stout of stave and sharp of point his glaive)
Who entered joust and list with hardiment,
Fearless of risk, of victory confident.
His vigorous onslaught narrowest places oped;
With easy passage through all straits he groped.
He ne'er encountered foe in single fight
But came from tilt with spear in blood stained bright,
Nor stormed a fortress howe'er strong and stark
(With embattled gates defended deep and dark)
But raised his banner high with battle cry:
"Aidance from Allah and full-fledged victory nigh!"
Thuswise both day and night his part he played,
In power and youthtide's knightly garb arrayed,
Dealing to fair young girl delicious joy
And no less welcome to the beardless boy.
Time never ceased to stint his wondrous strength,
Steadfast and upright like the gallows' length,
Until the nights o'ermatched him with their might
And friends derode him as a weakling wight;
Nor was there wizard but who wasted skill
O'er his case, nor leech could cure his ill.
Then he abandoned arms, abandoned him
Who gave and took salutes so fierce and grim,
And now lies prostrate drooping once-proud crest,
For who lives longest him most ills molest.
Now see him, here he lies on bier for bed;
Who will a shroud bestow on stranger dead?

From *El-Meqāmāt* (The Assemblies)
of Abu Muhammed bin Qasim el-Heriri

CONTENTS

PREFACE

Allen Edwardes' *The Jewel in the Lotus* was an historical survey of the sexual culture of the East. This companion volume is a study of Afro-Asian sexual behavior in more recent times, from the closing decades of the nineteenth century well up into the twentieth.

The contents of this volume will come as a surprise, and as a shock, to many readers. The practices and attitudes here dealt with may seem utterly alien and sometimes appallingly vicious. Vicious they certainly are, in some cases; but seldom are they alien. Such differences as distinguish the erotic life of the East from that of the West are of prevalence and overtness of action, resulting from cultural factors, far more than of natural craving for variety and extremity of deed.

A few words might profitably be said about methods and sources. There is no single method best suited to the study of the sexual psychologies and practices of human individuals and groups. The researcher makes use of one or several of a variety of possible techniques; and he knows that each approach has its limits and quota of hazards.

One method employs personal interviews and/or questionnaires. Some surveys of this type, mostly dwarfish in scope, have been made in recent years in the Middle East. Note has been taken of these, but no use has been made of them. And we have conducted no such surveys of our own.

Another method, more valuable when complementary than when exclusive, is to consult the medical and other relevant literatures of the people or peoples being studied. What have they discovered about themselves? What is to be discovered about them by way of not only their scientific literature but also their fiction, their poetry, their painting and sculpture, and their other serious and popular expressions?

Both the Near and Far East have produced vast and detailed sexologic and erotic literatures. For the purposes of this book, the writings of Arab, Hindu, Chinese, Japanese, and other Oriental erotologists have been liberally consulted. So have the folklore, legends, mythologies, holy books, and other writings and oral traditions been taken into account. Excerpts from some of the erotic classics of the East have been included in this volume, where most readers will encounter them for the first time.

Many of the practices we have described here were first reported by the sexual scientists of the Orient. It should be pointed out, and will be noted again, that the method of these erotologists is often that of exaggeration. Even more is exaggeration the carefully chosen method of the artist and of the writer of fiction, and it characterizes oral as well as written discussions of sexual matters, both scholarly and popular, throughout the whole of the East. Here, it will be most apparent in the writings of the Arabs and the Chinese.

While it is no more possible or desirable to exclude the writings of Eastern erotologists from consideration than it would be to exclude those of the sexologists of the West from a study of the West, some caution is called for. The Arab writer, for example, has traditionally been at the opposite extreme from his American counterpart: He has "played up" the importance and incidence of all things erotic while the American has often "played down" the same subject matter. Here, we should take into account the motivation: The Arab has sought to encourage a gamut of sexual activities, beginning early and lasting long; the aim of the American, conscious or unconscious, has often been the reverse.

Whether the one has been more misleading than the other is questionable; if so, it is probably the American who has been the more misleading. In most cases, it is easy enough to determine the approximate point at which the Arab begins to "let his imagination get the better of him." It is not always so easy to determine where the American has distorted or suppressed data—in the name of a spurious "good taste" and of a bogus "sexual morality." It should be added that the most recent tendency, in both East and West, is to have a somewhat greater concern for factuality than was found in the past.

For the Western reader, another word of caution is required, and in the opposite direction. What may seem to him surely exaggeration is not always anything of the kind. The way of the Muslim, and of other Orientals and Africans, is not at all our way. Few serious students of, for example, Arab sex behavior, have failed to take note of the (to Westerners) abnormal interest in sex; or have neglected to remark that this interest almost totally dominates emotional life. Many sober observers credit the Arab with extraordinary sexual appetites; and many also credit the Arab male with a potency (almost) to match. That everyday speech, as well as literature, reflects the intense and almost obsessive preoccupation with sex is universally remarked.

"Authorities" are more likely to differ about the extent to

which the Arab practices what he so incessantly talks about. It seems safe to say that there exist no worth-while data on this subject of a kind that would fully satisfy both the necessity for accuracy and the statistical and some other requirements of the more demanding Western scientist. However, a near-obsessive preoccupation will certainly be translated into a large amount of action (as this book indicates has been the case). And even where the exaggeration is most obvious, it should usually be understood as faithfully reflecting desires. If the cravings are frustrated in part, it is mainly because they transcend the bounds of human capacities, and the limits of what is possible in even a (comparatively) sexually anarchic society, if that society is to survive.

The reader should always keep in mind how vastly different are the values and customs of Africa and the East, even today, from those of the West. Slavery is still to be found in many places; harems continue to exist; polygamy is supplemented by concubinage; and in India, one of the most ancient of all human institutions, that of sacred temple prostitution, still flourishes despite all efforts to suppress it.

Neither the eunuch nor the emasculated transvestite and transsexualist homosexual prostitute has yet vanished from the scene. In both Africa and Asia there remain tribes where young girls are customarily instructed in and dedicated to whoredom. On the streets of many an Eastern city and town tiny boys offer their mothers and their little sisters—and, failing in that, themselves—to passing strangers. In lands where such persons and practices are to be found, we should scarcely expect to find that sexual behavior in general resembles our own.

A third information gathering method is the time-honored "observation-experimental" one—which demands that the researcher not only be an eyewitness to what he writes about but also that he participate in the practices he has undertaken to study. Unquestionably, when the researcher is knowledgeable in his field, and temperamentally and physically equal to his task, no method can be more fruitful. Such research is time-consuming, and may be hazardous; but when employed in the interest of confirming (or disproving) what has been learned from other sources, as well as for the purpose of acquiring new data, this first-person-participating approach is the final and essential method of sex research in depth.

Fortunately, men have not been wanting who, in the tradition of Sir Richard Burton, "make the experiment, active and passive, before offering any opinion upon the subject." To these dedicated students of human behavior supreme gratitude is due; and to them and to their method this book is above all indebted.

Oriental sexual theory and practice are falling, and to some extent already have fallen, under the influence of Occidental "morality." Wilfred Thesiger, a modern Burton, writes that "like many others, I regret the forces which are inexorably suburbanizing the untamed places and turning tribesmen into corner boys." Every true libertarian has good cause to regret the impact of those forces which are gaining in potency as speed of travel, communications, and other factors shrink the world; they relentlessly and all too successfully seek by way of an imposed conformity the destruction of individuality and freedom.

For what is the essential character and direction of what is termed "progress" in today's world? The most influential voices of American and Soviet societies alike, driven by an authoritarian vision and tugging the world in their wake, have accepted the inevitability of a faceless and uniform humanity, and are in the process of creating a stereotyped collectivistic man, the abject slave of his own "democratic" society, free to fill his belly but fettered in mind and in spirit.

Such a man is the inevitable product, too, of the programs

and activities of the United Nations, biggest and most potent of all meddling institutions that mankind has yet devised. The U.N. octopus has shown itself intent upon poking and prodding into sexual matters with tentacles no less avid than those with which it seeks to probe and embrace all other aspects of human existence.

Insatiable authority feeds on all kinds of suppression; especially is it nourished when enthroned as both withholder and dispenser of pleasures, when the most powerful of cravings, and the most intense of fulfillments, are controlled and meted out in a never quite satisfying, never quite intolerable measure.

Under the old Oriental despotisms, although intellectual pursuits were carefully controlled, a virtually free rein was accorded to the sexual impulses. The caliphs and sultans, by reason and intuition, had concluded that suppression or too rigid regulation of both sexual and intellectual activities would spawn first discontent and finally, and fatally, revolt. Today, that traditional pattern has been almost turned around. Male and female are comparatively at liberty to think and to speak as they will; but they must, under the new grinding social tyranny, increasingly seek their pleasures in hiding and stealth. Like their brothers and sisters in the West (who seem to move eastward to meet them) they have come to be exploited in the manner of the day: on the one hand by the wolves of commercialized love, and on the other by the serpents of psychotherapeutic salvation.

To the old saw, "It's not what you do, it's how you do it," have been added the words "and why." It is because there is so much contention and confusion concerning the "what, how and why" of human sexuality, that many of us, like Pilate, begin to ask ourselves: "What is truth?" Haji 'Abdu'l-Yezdi (Sir Richard Burton) attempts to answer this timeless question in Sufistic terms:

All Faith is false, all Faith is true;
　　Truth is the shattered mirror strown
In myriad bits, while each believes
　　His little bit the whole to own.
What is the Truth? was askt of yore;
　　Reply all object Truth is one,
As twain of halves aye makes a whole;
　　The moral Truth for all is none.
Thy faith why false, *my* faith why true?
　　'Tis all the work of Thine and Mine,
The fond and foolish love of self
　　That makes the Mine excel the Thine.

The constructively fatalistic astronomer-poet of classical Persia, 'Omar-i-Khaiyam, struggles to grasp the raw essence of "truth" and plucks the following fruit from the Tree of Knowledge:

One thing at least is certain—This Life flies;
　　One thing is certain and the rest is Lies;
The Flower that once has blown for ever dies.

According to popular Oriental philosophy, the "illusion of truth" is purely personal: a matter of individual taste and temperament. The Hindu mystic-poet Kabir says: "Illusion dies; dies not the Mind, though dead and gone the flesh" (*Māyā marē, nā Man marē, mar mar gayā sarīr*). Haji 'Abdu'l-Yezdi believes that

There is no Good, there is no Bad;
　　These be the whims of mortal will.
What works me weal, that call I *good*;
　　What harms and hurts I hold as *ill*.
They change with place, they shift with race;
　　And, in the veriest span of Time,
Each Vice has worn a Virtue's crown,
　　All Good was banned as Sin or Crime.

xvii

In a scientific sense, let us substitute "normal and abnormal" for "good and bad" and "maladjustment and adjustment" for "vice and virtue." By so doing, we begin to realize what medieval mentality prostitutes modern reason, how superstition is attendant upon a self-defeating fear of life, and why millions of human beings are in constant conflict with their own consciences and cultures.

Present-day witch doctors and witch hunters, passing absolute judgments on, and setting absolute standards for, human sexual behavior, hissing that mental health is agreement with the aims of the authoritarian state, are true sons of their clerical fathers. Many intelligent persons are beguiled by the sorceries of clever pretenders to omniscience—charlatans, whose sophistication is mere fabrication and whose wisdom is as transient as a flash of lightning. Besieged on all sides by a host of "experts," each artfully albeit blindly manipulating body and soul, the child-like individual stands awe-stricken and obedient. Haji 'Abdu'l-Yezdi addresses himself to the presumptuous prophet:

> Theories for truths, fable for fact,
> > System for science vex the thought;
> Life's one great lesson you despise—
> > To know that all we know is nought.
> The world is old and thou art young;
> > The world is large and thou art small;
> Cease, atom of a moment's span,
> > To hold thyself an All-in-All!

It may be said that one man's perversion is another man's (or woman's, for that matter) pleasure, to which our Haji adds:

> Haply the Law that rules the world
> > Allows to man the widest range;
> And haply Fate's a Theist-word,
> > Subject to human chance and change.

xviii

Since the human creature has so repeatedly proved himself a polysexual being, apt to respond to any and almost every erotic stimulus, and creating new erotic stimuli as his condition in the world changes, only the fool and the fanatic will speak with assurance of the sexually "natural" and "unnatural." "Normality" and "abnormality" appear to be cultural and historical, not fundamental and immutable. Each school of thought is likely to have its own definition of the "perverted"; yet rare is the "expert" who fails to declare his own standards absolute ones. In the time of their greatness, the Greeks would have specimen'd such assumed omniscience in Attic salt; but it seems that moderns have all but forgotten Socrates and the wisdom of the gods: *Gnothi seauton*, Know thyself.

Those who attempt to explode the pet theories of petty dictators risk reprisal and persecution. Subtle insinuation and bare-faced intimidation are birds of a feather, for each has as its aim to turn an individual inside out and make him conform, by refined systems of coercion or methodical brainwashing, to the wonder-worker's concept of normality. Scarcely a medicine man lacks his own therapeutic gimmick, ingeniously designed to remedy all the irremediable idiosyncrasies of the human race, and here's the rub:

> When doctors differ, who decides
> 　　Amid the milliard-headed throng?
> Who save the madman dares to cry:
> 　　" 'Tis I am right, you all are wrong!"?

'Omar-i-Khaiyam, who swilled himself to sickness at the illusionary wisdom wells of doctor and divine, prefers the drunkenness produced by wine to the narcotism of modern "knowledge":

> With them the seed of Wisdom did I sow,
> And with mine own hand wrought to make it grow;
> 　　And this was all the Harvest that I reap'd—
> "I came like Water, and like Wind I go."

xix

The so-called "antisexual conservative" keeps a skeleton in his closet to remind him of how his heretical ancestors were tortured to death for their carnal sins. The so-called "prosexual liberal," whom Aldous Huxley equates with the Marquis de Sade, does "his silly best to rationalize the essentially unrationalizable facts of private existence." That adjunct to the Golden Rule and noble guide to universal as well as self-awareness, "Know thyself," is now cleverly and methodically altered to "Know thyself as the all-knowing authoritarian wishes thee to know thyself."

Our fears and frustrations about sanity, security and existence in general, emerge as concern, almost pathological, about the "well-being" of others. Our preconception of what the human condition ought to be is accompanied by a lust to make all of mankind fit the pattern. But a society of neurotics, pretending to an arbitrary nonexistent normalcy, may not be more natural, even less more desirable, than an anarchy of individuals who follow instinct and inclination and are not at all afraid to admit it.

There is an ancient and honorable lesson to be learned from the East: The world is large enough to contain all kinds of people, and if each respects his neighbor's nature and does not pretend to understand what only the gods know, then there is at least a chance for the world to be relatively peaceful and for everyone to experience happiness on which there is no price tag. The alternative is to browbeat the masturbator into marriage, to brainwash the homosexual into breeding, and to bludgeon the prostitute into whatever least accords with her nature and wishes.

May the authoritarians, be they puritans or hedonists or whatever, keep in mind the words of one childlike philosopher who, although subjected to a disgraceful death for his revolutionary benevolence, did not sit upon a dungheap with the Pharisees while he lived:

Judge not, that ye be not judged. For with what judgment ye judge, ye shall be judged; and with what measure ye mete, it shall be measured to you again.

The Marabouts of North Africa have a cruel but telling method of explaining how man preys upon himself with dogmatism and pride, how he confines and castrates himself with phantom fears and frustrations bred out of ignorance and superstition. The Marabout draws a large circle in the dirt, which represents the world. He places a scorpion, symbolic of man, inside the circle. The scorpion, believing that it has achieved freedom, starts to run around the circle—but never attempts to go outside. After the scorpion has raced several times around the inside edge of the circle, the Marabout lowers his stick and divides the circle in half. The scorpion stops for a few seconds, then begins to run around inside its half of the circle. The scorpion runs faster and faster, apparently looking for a way out but never finding it. Strangely enough, the scorpion does not dare to cross over the line. After a few minutes the Marabout divides the half circle. The scorpion becomes frantic. Soon the Marabout makes a space no bigger than the scorpion's body. This is the "moment of truth." The scorpion, dazed and bewildered, finds itself unable to move one way or another. Raising its venomous tail, the scorpion turns rapidly 'round and 'round in a veritable frenzy. Whirling, whirling, whirling until all of its spirit and energy are spent. In utter hopelessness the scorpion stops, lowers the poisonous point of its tail, and stings itself to death. Its torment is ended.

The Hindus have a proverb: "A scorpion in a corner stings itself to death. A coward blames the gods. They laugh and let it die. A man goes forward."

Haji 'Abdu'l-Yezdi invites us to "abjure the Why and seek the How." He advocates suspension of judgment, for "indeed he knows not how to know who knows not also how to unknow." And he cautions us to be wary of those, both well-meaning and otherwise, who salvage lost souls to the tune of dollars and cents and who sell personal theory for universal truth, adding by way of illumination:

> We live our lives with rogues and fools,
>   Dead and alive, alive and dead;
> We die 'twixt one who feels the pulse
>   And one who frets and clouds the head.

With gay-hearted cynicism an Arab poet follows suit:

> This world is run by two great schools,
> Enlightened rogues and religious fools!

To those who are seriously concerned about dishonesty, exploitation, and stupidity in the realm of sex are available the words of Lao-tze: "Who can clear muddy water? If we leave it alone, it clears of its own accord." In the view of the fatalist: Millions are born, they live and die; the human race continues to exist and expand and the earth forever turns on its axis—and not a hundred million acts of masturbation, adultery, sodomy, or any other such chasings after small pleasures can change ought of what is foreordained. And who knows the over-all design of nature or can define the law, the pattern, the rhythms of the cosmos? Who knows what was intended and what is to be desired?

To which the wise Westerner might reply: "Yes. When we needlessly meddle with freedom, we court sickness and death."

1 *The Cradle of Erotica*

N O T E

This book contains commentaries that run with, and should be read with, the text. They are set in oblique type (like this note) at the bottom of the pages where the references occur and are separated from the text by a rule line and an ornament device, as follows:

$$\text{·T·}$$

Where the commentary continues on the next page, the rule line is used alone.

1. PHILOSOPHY

A man has no better thing under the sun
Than to eat and to drink and to have lots of fun.

ECCLESIASTES 8:15

Khojeh 'Omar Halebi Abu 'Othman, the Turkish author of *El-Kitāb Sheri'et el-Khabbeh fī 'Ilm el-Muhhabbeh*
(Book of the Secret Laws of Love), has written that sensuality,
which is idealized in Islam, may be considered an end in itself.
Allah and Eros are regarded as one and the same under divine
and mundane law.

The vital spirit of El-Islam lies in its unqualified sanctification of sexual passion. The same is true of Hinduism. We find
no unnatural fear of the facts of life among otherwise supersti-
tious Orientals; for while the prayers are still chanted with
fervid and melodious regularity in the mosque, the pleasures
are indulged in with even greater devotion in the whorehouse
next door.

Since "the pendulum of history swings between the penis
and the cunnus," we are bound to encounter a less spiritual
and a more practical appraisal of life's purpose from a sex-
worshiping Oriental:

3

The world is based upon the interaction of the male and female principles, and it is natural for men and women to be drawn together. One cannot say that anything we do is out of depravity and evil passion.*

Under the system of refined fatalism, males and females may freely commit fornication, adultery, and crimes of passion because Allah is compassionate and merciful. Destiny is decreed unto all creatures, and none can avoid it. *El-mektūb mektūb:* what is written is written! It cannot be erased. There is no shame in being a fornicator, a masturbator, a pederast, or a rapist if one is satisfied. Since "there is but a feeble breath between the womb and the grave," and since all morality is man-made and therefore ephemeral, there is no ground for condemnation of personal taste and individual temperament.

Honor among Muslim men and women is virtually unknown. Chivalry is now branded as old-fashioned and effeminate. Women have won their social equality and must accept the sexual consequences. Male and female are generally of the opinion that no matter what you want in the world of sex, get it—no matter how and no matter why. Life is too short and its pleasures are few. *El-ghāyeh tebrīr el-wāsteh:* the end justifies the means!

The gynophilic Prophet Muhammed urged his disciples to respect women and to treat them with kindness and equality; but while so saying, he kept his most prized possessions under lock and key. His disciples wondered how far consideration and compassion could go before women got the upper hand.

Modern Muslims believe that universal patriarchy is dying a rapid death and that universal matriarchy, characterized by women not only competing with but also controlling men, is the cultural pattern of the future. With a single standard of

* Wang Shih-cheng, *The Golden Lotus* (*Chin P'ing Mei*), translated by Clement Egerton. 4 vols. London: Routledge & Kegan Paul, 1957.

4

sexual conduct now in vogue, conservatives lament that females may freely prey upon males with impunity and without
any traditional sense of shame.(1) Siddiqi, for example, writes:

᛫᛫᛫᛫᛫᛫᛫

(1) The Muslim is by no means alone in his lament, or in his fears.
The trend to "matriarchy" has for some time been apparent in
many parts of the world, and it has been widely remarked in the
United States.

The implications of this trend (which begins with a declared and
possibly sincere feminine desire to achieve equality, not dominance)
are most interesting. It would seem that males must dominate females or be dominated by them. The male is powerful enough to
subjugate the female, but he is not strong enough to exist alongside
her on a co-equal basis. Feminine equality may only be achieved by
masculine abdication and at the price of masculine subjugation.

The sexual consequences of the subjugation of the male by the
"equal" female are well defined and have often been described: the
male, in varying ways and degrees, is "unmanned." It would seem
that a great many men, and quite likely a majority of men, are able
to function at peak level sexually only with women who are submis-
sive and who willingly accept, or skillfully pretend to accept, the
domination of the male.

Now it may be that the subjugation of the female is also deleteri-
ous, resulting in varying degrees of frigidity. That is a dubious point,
but it is worth considering. And so far as the over-all well-being of
humanity is concerned, it would seem apparent that the choice between widespread male impotence, along with all its damaging
effects, and widespread frigidity, is not a real one. The effects of the
impotence are much worse than those of the frigidity, which prevents neither copulation nor procreation; and which—if only because accommodations have been learned—is less harmful otherwise.

At the core of the matter may lie the painfully evident fact that
all human beings are as yet woefully immature. Theoretically (and
perhaps wishfully) it would seem that co-equal men and women

5

The woman's movement in Pakistan does not spring from genuine altruistic motives or from a real desire for social and national reformation but from a desire to throw off all restraints, some of which are necessary and salutary, in order that a few fortunate women may be able to enjoy a life of luxurious self-indulgence without inviting social opprobrium. More and more of fashion, more and more of luxury distinguishes those of our women who have stepped out into the threshold of public life and demand equality of rights with men. Material acquisitiveness and pleasure-seeking, not service and social work, seem to be their motto.*

But woman is not yet dominant everywhere; neither is every male emasculate or cowed. Hendrik de Leeuw quotes the characteristic comments of a sophisticated Algerian *shaykh*:

"I could never understand the strange anomalies of the conduct of your people. We Muslims are masters and never afraid of our women. You Americans are actually terrorized by a handful of fluff.

"Your American girls, monsieur. They are chic, decidedly pretty, and very spirited. They are provocative but they are without real passion, though they crave sensation." †

---

should enjoy the most satisfactory sexual adjustment. But, as suggested, co-equality seems to transcend our capacities. The male relinquishes his dominance only at the price of handing it over to the female. To assert that this testifies to immaturity may be to speak truly; but it does not solve a problem that is one of the most pressing of our time.

---

* Muhammad Mazheruddin Siddiqi, *Women in Islam*. Lahore: Institute of Islamic Culture, 1959.
† Hendrik de Leeuw, *Sinful Cities of the Western World*. New York: Citadel Press, 1949.

6

Under the philosophy of sexual anarchy, woman is only good for one thing. *Mek'hhel fī mik'hhaleh:* the kohl pencil in the kohl pot! Allah has predetermined her destiny. *El-qelm ma'mūl li'l-miqlameh:* the pen was made for the inkpot! The Egyptians say:

Upon the door two knocks, then three;
I said, "Who's there?" heard "Coynte for free!"

"Then enter," I said, and turned the key,
"Though even the poison of death you be!"

The most sacred part of a classical Muslimeh's attire was her trouser string, as is noted in this chaste declaration from the *Arabian Nights:* "I am bound by the cord of my drawers never to feel you moving in the depths of me!" A man's trouser string, however, was the least sacred part of his apparel:

There is a thing I cannot keep in jail,
    Being but human,
        Of which my drawers are jailer.*

In the old days, when young ladies were obliged to remove their modesty with their petticoat panties, "laxity in the trouser string" was equivalent to the loosest conduct. Nowadays the situation seems to be reversed, for Muslim women outstrip their menfolk in the coital contest.

Modesty (*el-'ār*) is still a passion with the Bedawin, and were a modern city woman to solicit a true Son of the Desert, she might get her teeth knocked down her throat. The nomads metaphorically say: *"En-nār wa-lā'l-'ār!"* (Hell-flame but never shame). Hasan bin 'Ali, Muhammed's grandson, inverted the

* *The Book of the Thousand Nights and One Night,* translated by Dr. J. C. Mardrus and Powys Mathers. 4 vols. London: Routledge, 1947.

saying. Demoralized by overmarrying, he came up with *"El-'ār ahhsen min en-nār!"* (Shame is better than hell-flame). Hasan, who because of his notorious Don Juanism was known as *El-Mitlāq* (The Divorcer), was finally poisoned to death by his 105th wife, Ja'deh, who was the envy of other women for her revolutionary singlemindedness.

Abu 'Ali bin Sa'id Ibn Hezm, the Cordovan author of *El-Kitāb Tōq el-Hhemāmeh* (Book of the Ring of the Dove), tells us that among the Berbers and Moorish Arabs fornicators and sodomists beg repentance of Allah only if the objects of their desire at once deign to gratify their erotic appetite. They would, with righteous indignation, reproach any man or woman who dared to protest, adding: "What! would you make it impossible for a True Believer to repent?"

Finally, we find gloriously written in the *Arabian Nights:*

> By Allah! your son was not to blame for futtering my spouse, for men needs must lust after women and it is the bounden duty of women to defend themselves from men. So the fault lies with my wife, who played me false and deemed me a fool and did with him these dirty deeds.

In other words, "If a bitch will not have it, the dog cannot get his way!"

The Babylonian Talmud gravely proclaims that nine-tenths of all sexual lust was bestowed upon the Arabs, while the remaining one-tenth was divided among the rest of humanity. We may gain some insight into this extraordinary proclamation by opening a widely read book on marital relations by the celebrated Egyptian historian, Gelaleddin es-Seyuti, entitled *Kitāb el-Īdzāhh fī 'Ilm en-Nikāhh* (Book of Revelation in the Science of Copulation), which begins as follows:

> In the name of Allah the Forgiving, the Forgiver! Praise be to Allah, who bejewels beautiful virgins with bell-shaped

8

breasts and who weaves the thighs of women into anvils for the pounding sledge hammers of men!

A passage from the *Arabian Nights* is also indicative of Islamic eroticism:

> He went into the room where my lady was and passed all the night with her in charges, assaults, and other games. I was able to hear all they did and to count on my fingers the number of nails they drove, because of the astonishing noise which they made in doing it. "As Allah lives," I thought, "they must have built a blacksmith's forge on the bed! The iron bar must be very hot to make the anvil groan so much!"
>
> The noise ceased with morning, and I saw the owner of the sounding hammer go out by the great door.

Even more revealing is an essay entitled "General Contemplation of Carnal Copulation" by Shaykh 'Omar bin Sidi en-Nefzawi, the well-known Tunisian author of *Kitāb Rōdzet el-'Ātir fī Nuzhet el-Khātir* (Book of the Scented Garden Site for Heart Delight):

> Praise be to Allah! who has placed the fountainhead of man's greatest pleasure in the natural parts of woman, and who has placed the source of woman's supreme enjoyment in the natural parts of man.
>
> Praise be to All-Bountiful Allah! who has not bestowed well-being upon the sexual parts of the female, who has not accorded these organs satisfaction and happiness, until they have been penetrated by the sexual parts of the male. Likewise, the sexual organs of the male shall know neither rest nor peace until they have entered those of the female.
>
> When the act of carnal copulation is enacted, a lively encounter is raged between the two amorous actors, who engage in heated and frisky combats of kissing and frolicking and interlocking of legs and belly-bumping. And by the sudden

9

impact of the two pubes, the meeting of man and woman in wondrous collision, the enjoyment is not long in coming. For man, in the pride of his potency, works like a pounding pestle in a mixing mortar; and woman, with erotic wrigglings and rapturous writhings, comes artfully to his aid. At last, the climax of their clash comes and the orgasms arrive in mutual bliss.

Islamic folklore based on historic events bears vigorous testimony to the violence of Islamic passion:

> She now turned to him, bussing and bosoming, locking leg over leg, and said to him: "Put your hand between my thighs, to the place of which you know, so that it may stand up as to prayer after prostration."
>
> So he put forth his hand and felt about with his fingers, and found her thighs cooler than cream and softer than satin. The touching of them pleasured him, and he moved his hand hither and thither till his fingers alighted upon a dome bulging with blessings and pulsing with movement and heated with moisture, and soon his fingertips touched upon her prayer niche and the tiny preacher therein.
>
> Then she said: "O 'Ali Shar! it is the custom of my clitoris that it stands not on end save it be rubbed with the hand; so come, rub it with your hand till it be at stand."
>
> So saying, she lay down on her back, and taking his hand, set it fast to her parts; and he found her coynte to be softer and smoother than satins and silks, white, plumply rounded and protuberant, likening for heat and steam the hot room of the bath or the heart of a lover whom love-longing has wasted.
>
> Said 'Ali Shar to himself: "Indeed, what a wonder of wonders!"
>
> Then red-hot lust got hold on him, and his rod rose and stood upright on end to the utmost of its height.
>
> When Zumurrud saw this, she burst out laughing and said:

10

"By Allah, O my lord, all this betides us and yet you know me not!"

So he kissed her and embraced her, and he threw himself upon her like the lion upon the lamb. Then he plunged his sword completely in her sheath, and he ceased not to play the porter at her portal and the preacher in her pulpit and the priest at her prayer niche; while she with him ceased not from inclination and prostration and rising up and sitting down, accompanying her canticles of praise and of "Glory be to Allah!" with passionate movements and wrigglings and claspings of his member and other amorous gestures and gyrations, till two little eunuchs heard the noise.

So they came and peeping out from behind the curtains saw the Queen lying on her back and upon her 'Ali Shar, who was thrusting and thrashing and slashing away while she huffed and puffed and sighed and cried and wriggled and writhed.

Not a few Muslims, when questioned about their alleged lubricities by those seeking to explain the Talmudic theory, might reply that "Man is only looking for a hole, Woman is only looking for a pole!" Or: "*Ferūj li'l-insān, Zebāb li'niswān, 'Aql li'l-hhaywān.*" "Slits for men, Pricks for women, Intellect for animals." *Māshā'llāh:* It is the will of Allah!

Love, then, is lovely. But even with love, or when there is no love, there is nothing in the world like *nayk* (futtering). Says the pederastic poet Abu Nowas el-Hasan bin Hani:

> These are the words that Abu Bilal,
>> Our elder, was wont to utter:
> "Unhealed is lover by kiss and caress;
>> His only cure's to futter!"

Mardrus and Mathers offer the following variation:

> Lust is not content with blushes,
>> Kisses taken from pure lips,

11

> Not content with wedded glances:
> Lust must have a thing which dances,
> Lust must have a thing which gushes,
> Lust must have a thing which drips.

Colonel Dickson discovered this healthy phallicism underlying El-Islam:

> Sexual intercourse is loved by the ordinary Arab above all
> pleasures in the world. It is the one great pleasure common
> to rich and poor alike, and the one moment of forgetfulness
> in his daily round of troubles and hardships that Bedawin or
> townsman can enjoy. Men and women equally love the act,
> which is said to keep man young, "just like riding a mare."
> The Arab seems to possess strength above the average for
> sexual purposes, as can be seen from the large number of men
> of eighty years and over who still continue to marry and pro-
> duce children.*

And as for his religion:

> To evil deeds the folk suspect we're lent,
> And to this thought their hearts and souls are bent.
> Come, dear, the truth to them let's fain give vent;
> Let's savor one good bout—and then repent!

Our Arab is pious and pure when, having done the deed, he
proposes to repent; and repentance, according to common law,
absolves the guilty from all guilt.

The hearty hedonism and lust-love of Orientals, coupled
with their voluptuous temperament and traditions, explain
much about why Islam has succeeded and Christianity has
failed in Negro Africa. The phony humanism and morality

* Colonel H. R. P. Dickson, *The Arab of the Desert*. London: Allen & Unwin,
1951.

12

characteristic of Western civilization is alien and obscene to the African mind. The unvarnished Negro, whose ancestors patterned their erotic customs and laws after those observed in the animal kingdom, sees nothing controversial in the sexual act.

A favorite theme in Islamic folklore is the conversion of Christian females to the Faith. A young and beautiful Greek woman, after a single session in bed with a young and handsome Muslim, says to him:

> "Indeed, my dear, a religion which inspires its holders to such valiance and virtue must be the best, the most human, and the only true of all religions. Eye of my heart, what must I do to be ennobled in the Faith? I would become a Mussulman even as you are; for the peace of my soul is not among the Christians, who make a virtue of horrible continence and honor the emasculate priesthood. They are perverts who know not life, and are unhappy because they are never warmed by any sun. My soul would stay here, where it can flower with all its roses and sing with all its birds. Tell me how I can become a Mussulman." (2)

'I'
_____

(2) *It is surely obvious that nothing could be more remote from traditional Christian thinking than the idea that a Christian male, inspired and strengthened by his faith, could convert a heathen female by copulating with her. There probably remains to be propounded the view that Christian religion is beneficial to potency; and most educated persons are aware that just the opposite is the case.*

Also largely alien to contemporary Western man, and particularly to the white Anglo-American, is the exuberant and healthy (if blatant and possibly childish) self-confidence in his virile powers that enables the Muslim to consider himself a superior lover.

There are, of course, individual Anglo-Americans boastfully confident of their powers—though usually we must descend the intellec-

Elsewhere this same girl proclaims:

"May the Faithful be forever preserved from chastity, that impure thing; may they never have to repent for ought save harm done to a fellow creature! Amen."

A casual perusal of the Babylonian Talmud will readily reveal why the classical rabbis assailed Islamic sexuality. Since ecclesiastical works are generally monuments of superstition and taboo, one need not wonder at all the exaggerations and

---

tual ladder to its lowermost rungs to encounter many of them. But almost never do we find the English or American Caucasian who believes that his countrymen in general are sexually superior to males of other races and nationalities. This is to be explained as neither modesty nor realism; all too often what we encounter is a belief in our comparative sexual incapacity.

In the United States, and not at all just in the South, there is what amounts to a proverb: A woman who has slept with a Negro will never be satisfied with a white man again. Nor does one have to go far into the Western sexological literature to meet more than once with the view that, as one prostitute put it, "A woman who has tasted a dog will have no more use for a man." Americans also attribute superior potency, or greater excellence of technique (which may be termed "animalism" and "depravity"), to Frenchmen, Italians, Spaniards, Latin Americans, etc. All such ideas are accompanied by profound, though often veiled, feelings of sexual inferiority which cannot fail to be damaging to potency, and which may well have stemmed originally from potency problems—a vicious circle.

While we cannot go into the matter at length here, the Muslim is probably not far wrong when he thanks Allah (and his religion) for the gift of vigor; and if the vigor of the Westerner is insufficient, then certainly his castrating religion is not without blame.

14

obsessions which make the Talmud a treasure trove of fantastic faddishness. Moreover, any free and forthright expression of the erotic impulse is always looked upon with suspicion by those who like to make sex a subject of controversy.

Of course, Eastern Jews are just as prolific in their venereal pleasures as Muslims; but a Mosaic authoritarianism harasses the Israeli, creating a conflict of interest. It is otherwise with the Arab fornicator and homosexual, who can be and is a devout Muslim, relatively free to satisfy his sensuality. He renders unto Caesar the things which are Caesar's and unto God the things that are God's; and in matters of sex what is Caesar's is often also God's.

Dr. Jacobus observed that "the Hindu, one of the oldest of civilized beings, is as lascivious as the monkey." He adds that the Indian woman "is as lascivious as the man, and betrays her husband whenever she can, if she finds pleasure or amusement in it." * Jacobus found very few virgins above the age of ten, the hymeneal membrane having been stretched apart or worn away by the little Hindu girl's repeated contact with brothers, cousins, and other young boys.(3)

---

(3) Dr. Jacobus (Jacobus Sutor) was a French army surgeon and was sent by the French government to serve in the various colonial outposts where he conducted his researches among Europeans as well as the native populations. He is probably best known for his Wanderings in Untrodden Fields of Anthropology (first published at Paris in 1893 by Isidore Liseux as L'Amour aux Colonies). The book was considerably expanded for its 1898 English-language edition. Dr. Jacobus' writings are veritable treasure troves of valuable information, and even today few have rivaled the richness of his sexual researches. Unfortunately, he seems sometimes to have shown little

* Dr. Jacobus (nom de plume), L'Ethnologie du Sens Génitale. 5 vols. Paris: 1935.

15

Turning his attention to China, this observant French physician informs us that "wherever he may come from, and whatever may be his social position, the Chinese shows one common characteristic—his lubricity." Sir Richard Burton writes that "the Chinese, as far as we know them in the great cities, are omnivorous and *omnifutuentes* [all-futtering]; they are the chosen people of debauchery and their systematic bestiality with ducks, goats, and other animals is equalled only by their pederasty." * Mantegazza adds: "The Chinese are famous for their love affairs with geese, the necks of which they are in the habit of cruelly wringing off at the moment of ejaculation,(4) in order that they may get the pleasurable benefit of the anal sphincter's last spasms in the victim." †

Like the sex-worshiping Hindu, the free-thinking Chinese dedicates heart and soul to genital stimulation. Illustrative of

---

capacity for distinguishing between native fact and fiction. *Jacobus* is much quoted in this book, and the reader should approach what he has to say cautiously, though not with undue skepticism or presumption of error.

(4) Whoever would like to think of such cruelly bestial practices as peculiarly Oriental will have to resist the temptation (and relinquish the pleasure). The West has a long and extensive history of indulgence in such activities, including the particular one cited. De Sade, for example, related that the practice was known and provided for in the Parisian brothels of his day, where the act was termed avisodomy, and the bird employed was a turkey. It is still possible to debate the origins of avisodomy, and some have credited the Chinese with being its originators. But even here the evidence is insufficient.

* *The Book of the Thousand Nights and a Night*, translated by Richard F. Burton. 17 vols. London: Burton Club, 1885–88.
† Paolo Mantegazza, *L'Amour dans l'Humanité*. Paris: 1886.

16

such dedication are these excerpts from the classic *Chin P'ing Mei* (The Plum in the Golden Vase):

> The woman touched the warrior. It was very hard and frisky, and she felt pleased and terrified at the same time. They kissed each other and set to work. Hsi-men Ch'ing took her by the legs and thrust forward violently. Heart's Delight gasped for breath and her face became very red.
>
> He grasped her white legs firmly and plunged forward violently again. She murmured softly and her starry eyes grew dim. Soon he told the woman to straddle her legs and lie down like a mare, and he rode upon her like a lusty stallion. He drove his spear in all the way; and with the light shining, he fondled her white buttocks as she raised them to receive his thrust.
>
> "Call me your sweetheart," she said, "and please don't stop. Give me the whole length." Heart's Delight lifted her lovely bottom so that Hsi-men Ch'ing could take her full length, and she called him her darling with a trembling voice. They played together for one whole hour before Hsi-men was willing to withdraw. Finally the woman removed his member, wiped it off with a napkin, and took it into her mouth. "I love you so much," she said, "I will suck all night." *

Riza Bey writes of the Orient in general:

> I think it is symbolic of the East that sex should play a greater part in the lives of ordinary people than it does in the West. For one thing it is referred to much more openly, and there is little that is covert. A girl knows the functions for which she has been born long before her Western prototype has discarded her dolls. . . . A lad, more often than not, is openly encouraged to have intercourse at an early age, in the belief that his powers will thereby be increased but liable to fade if he neglects what is deemed an essential exercise.†

* Translated from the Latin version of Clement Egerton, *op. cit.*
† Riza Bey, *Darkest Orient*. London: Arco, 1953.

It was Burton's belief that "man is by nature polygamic, whereas woman as a rule is monogamic and polyandrous only when tired of her lover. For the man, as has been truly said, loves the woman; but the love of the woman is for the love of the man." This is a widespread Oriental philosophy.(5)

On "The Personality of Amorosity" the doctor and mystic Khojeh 'Omar Halebi writes:

> Love, like most other things, is two-sided by nature, being both organic and spiritualistic and springing from the essence of our ego.
>
> The Eros that emerges from the vital agent which maintains the machinery of our body is much more a sensation than a sentiment. Physical by nature, it is the whole of our Self that cares for the needs of our senses and of the organs which reckon in the evincement of love.
>
> It is the Eros of our amatory senses in heat, of our generative organs in erection, obedient to laws purely physiological and physical.
>
> Love is a psychic force, placed in us by the Creator, having its peculiar laws, its strength and its will; and just like each of our vital organs, by which life functions without the participation of our conscious will, love often forces upon us the

'I'

(5) *The same belief that man is polygamic and woman monogamic by nature is widespread in the West, and in some generally respectable quarters enjoys an acceptance quite in excess of what is warranted. Any such theory, so obviously lending support to an existing double standard of morality, deserves careful scrutiny. And even if the description of woman's "nature" seemed an accurate one, we still would have to wonder whether her monogamic disposition was not a superimposition, a creation of the male in a society where such feminine inclination is desirable, rather than any fundamental trait of the female. Studies of primitive societies, needless to say, often lend small support to the theory of the natural monogamy of woman.*

unhappy realization that we are all of us, most of the time, laughable and helpless beneath its despotic sway.

When our human and inherent need of loving and being loved manifests itself in all its organic might, such power is enquickened, stimulated, and lured by a twin force abiding in an organism other than our own and representing opposite physiological characteristics but answering, in a peculiar sort of harmony, to our temptational needs.

It is then the attraction of two organisms without the co-operation of the will, but often against the same, forming through this human frailty of mutual sympathy and natural attraction of like to unlike what we have called *sensual love*.

Without this, strange and illogical as it may seem, all creatures would be alike both physically and mentally!

The blood is, like human sperm but to a degree less, a liquid embracing a multitude of tiny worlds highly impressionable and greatly swayed by *light* or the vital principle and possessing, like the magnet and amber, properties both attractive and repulsive. It is they which grant a share of their strength to our nerves and our sensibility. But if they give unto us organic and fluidic force, they receive from our nerves the myriad impressions which flow from our brain or our imagination, that wayward and fanciful sultana of our very being.

It is this force, still more fluidic than organic, a force all-knowing as past and futurity, which has caused us to cry in moments of clairvoyance: "The blood speaks! Blood moves between us!" The name of this force is *muhhabbet el-gheri-zīyeh*, nature's mutual affection or blood speaking to blood.

Having therefore an element both vital and intelligent, the blood is apt to grasp and recognize exterior influences and the emanations of a strong will, or that which is at least sympathetic.

When the blood has been influenced by this will, it acts upon all the organs of our body, and by the intermediary or

19

go-between of the nerves, suggests to them the desires or the divers needs of our senses.

The desire of copulating with someone to whom we are attracted, someone who has acted upon our blood as we have so acted upon his or hers, is one of these suggestions.

Now when the imagination of a woman is strongly aroused or superexcited, it produces in her sexual organs such an irritation which, in the long run, becomes the master of her mind, her body and her logic, causing her to do whatever it wills. And among all the vital organs of her body, the uterus is the most impressionable and the one that holds the most sway over her brain, bringing about in fits of blind passion the fall of the female into the arms of the male.

It may have been Plato who first scientifically compared the womb to a wild beast. Solomon in any case had a comparable view (*Proverbs* 30:15–16):

> Three things are never satisfied; four say not, "Enough!"
> The grave and the open womb [Heb. *'ōtzr rehhm*, mouth of the uterus], the thirsty desert and the fire.

Much as the ancients believed the uterus to be the seat of hysteria and nervous disorders in the female (for "hysteria" is derived from *hystera*, the Greek word for "womb"), so in Arabic and Hebrew the usual term for uterus, *rehhm*, stems from a root ranging in meaning from "compassion" or "sympathy" to "uterine consanguinity" or "the attraction of like to unlike."

As far as our Khojeh is concerned, there is no other way of explaining why women of reason suddenly become "weak and wanton." It is the workings of their wombs, the sacrifice of their seat of sympathy! Thus Shaykh 'Omar en-Nefzawi declares that a woman's religion is in her vulva, that her god is the penis, and that neither reason nor reliance can keep her chaste once her womb sounds the call to coition.(6)

·‖·
_____

(6) *The hunger of the uterus is for seed (with copulation implied), while the hunger of the vulva (and vagina) is for the penis. It was a belief widely held in the past that the uterus craved semen (in the interest of impregnation), and that female sexual desire was awakened by, and in the interest of, the need for procreation—analogous to the phenomenon of rut in other female animals.*

An archaic term for nymphomania is uteromania, and doubtless the term is at least indirectly derived from this belief that sexual desire and pleasure are in the service of procreation and that lust radiates outward from the uterus.

The function of the uterus is of course misunderstood by anyone clinging to a belief in its role as the initiator of desire. Neither is it proper any longer to think of sexual desire and pleasure as being in the service of propagation. That is to say, human sexual psychology is by now so developed that neither morally nor otherwise is it fruitful to regard sexual intercourse as being primarily a means of perpetuating the race.

Obviously, there is a great difference between a desire regarded as emanating from the uterus and a desire regarded as emanating from the vagina and vulva. The moralist will conclude that in the one case the pleasure is a means, while in the other case the pleasure is an end. And it is precisely the refusal to regard sexual pleasure as an (legitimate) end that has so often corrupted our thinking about sexual relationships and has played a large part in our adoption of an antisexual morality.

Even though we no longer think of the womb as hungering after semen, we continue in many cases to insist that sexual intercourse must be in the service of procreation. Wilhelm Reich, for one, has shown how ridiculous is this view as a guide to sexual conduct, since the healthy human organism calls for several thousands of sexual acts during the course of a typical erotically active lifespan while

Man is deemed so constructed, by virtue of the pride he takes in his penis, that like some sort of phallic symbol he roams the face of the earth systematically impregnating every woman he can lay his hands on. Hence El-Halebi is of the same opinion as Hendrik de Leeuw, who observes that "the aim of Moorish and Arabian males seems to be to impregnate as many females as possible." (7) *Māshā'llāh*: it is the will of

---

the number of offspring the female is capable of bearing totals only a tiny fraction of that number.

(7) Whether the "pride he takes in his penis" suffices to explain the near-compulsion of the Arab to impregnate an abundance of females seems open to question. Neither should we make too much of the alleged universality of the craving. These are matters requiring more exhaustive study than we have given them, and apart from recommending suspension of judgment we will refrain from pronouncing any evaluation.

It is, however, possible to speak of the common motives for such conduct in the West. In general, the desire to impregnate a great number of women is no more than a variation of Don Juanism. The Don Juan strives for one seduction, or sexual conquest, after another. He is usually seen as driven by a fear of impotence, which in turn may derive from a latent inversion. By means of each conquest he seeks to prove to himself that he is potent, and that he is fully masculine. However, he is never sufficiently reassured and so must endlessly pursue and subdue the female.

The craving (or compulsion) to impregnate a great many women may be no more than a variation in this pattern of behavior. The pregnancy provides still further proof of the masculinity and sexual capacity of the seducer. Some regard the Don Juan as a sadist, who subjects the woman he has seduced to humiliating or brutal treatment, or who regards her as humiliated or defiled by the very fact of the intercourse—testimony to his guilt feelings about sex, to his

22

Allah! And what Allah wills will be done. For "man, unless he is tamed by woman, forever remains like a wild beast on the prowl."

Our Khojeh now wishes it to be clearly understood just what the word *nayk* (futtering) means, for it is certainly not the same as *jimā'* (coition):

> *Futtering* is the act of mutual flesh-fusion in all its brutal materiality, performed upon no matter who and no matter what. It is sexual intercourse without sentiment; it is a mere physical experience and an animalistic sensation. In a word, it is the putting of the peg in the hole!
>
> *Coition* is an act of fleshly union emanating from the direct will of Allah; in other words, an expression of love and mutual affection. It is not the wanton and cynical exploitation of a woman's open thighs. It becomes *futtering* only when it is practiced, without discrimination, with all kinds of males and

---

low self-esteem, or to both. Certainly, to impregnate a female may, in many circumstances, be an act of the greatest cruelty.

There are also a number of other motives to be encountered among the histories of Westerners who promiscuously impregnate their female victims—the word victim, in this case, requiring no quotation marks. However, to inquire into these more rare deviations would be inappropriate here. The Don Juan motivation is the common one, and it is possible that the same may be true of the Arab.

Yet to assert that the Arab is motivated by a fear of impotence would ill accord with the notion that he acts on the basis of the pride that he takes in his penis, unless penis pride, too, is to be understood as symptomatic of underlying anxieties about potency. And in fact there is reason to believe—on the basis, for example, that the Arab's homosexual tendencies are seldom latent or repressed—that the explanation for his "insemination mania" may lie elsewhere than in Don Juanism.

23

females. The passional or spiritual element is then missing, and the physical or bestial urge gains sway.

Thus, when we love we *copulate*; but when we lust we *fornicate*.(8)

·I·

(8) In the area of moral sexual values, as well as in that of sexual psychology, there could scarcely be a more important distinction than that one between futtering and coition, or loving and loveless copulation, with acceptance of the legitimacy of both. If the masses of Americans could but make this distinction, and mean it, it is not unlikely that many of our psychosexual problems would vanish within the space of a generation.

We may disregard, for our own (Western) purposes, that aspect of the definition of futtering which insists upon total lack of discrimination and upon "brutal materiality." Sexual intercourse without love or pretense of love need be neither indiscriminate nor psychologically brutal. A great number of sexual acts occur every day which are not at all indiscriminate or brutal, but which are not loving either. They are simply acts of coition between persons responding to the desires natural to the human organism and who find one another attractive on a (usually) transient basis, and between whom no other bond exists or is wished to exist.

The existence of such relationships is of course well known. Everyone is aware that there is sex with love and sex without love. The great problems arise out of our official condemnation of the latter: the conflict of our theory with what necessarily is our practice. Sexual intercourse without love is branded "brutish," "corrupt," "sinful," etc.; while the sexual intercourse of lovers is exalted as "romantic love" and uneasily eulogized in terms ordinarily reserved for philistinic appreciation of works of art and sunsets (however bad). Of course, this is when the intercourse of lovers is not held to be almost equally as despicable as that of non-lovers.

Americans generally say "No!" in thunder to the idea that the admittedly natural biological appetites of men and women should

He adds, however:

> Most certainly (and Allah is All-Knowing!) acts and ideas exist not as good or evil, right or wrong, natural or unnatural, but by reason of the nature of the prism through which our imagination considers and studies them. Judgment, then, comes from our reasoning; action from our will, the dynamic motor-force of our brain. Our blood and nerves, as well as our senses, bear the sensations; but our flesh and bones are mere slaves to the power of our will.
>
> Thus all things bear not of value save when we come into the human habit of bestowing peculiar worth upon them, and often merely according to the degree of physical pleasure or psychic satisfaction that they freely accord to us.

---

be gratified where no romantic affection exists. And yet it is plain that we fly in the face of all common sense when we try to pretend that the desires of persons who are not in love are less urgent than the desires of persons who are in love. To some extent our contemporary belief that erotic passion is made acceptable by love is a replacement for the belief that carnal cravings and indulgence are made less unpalatable by marriage. Those who have sexual intercourse with persons for whom they have no great affection are made by "modernists" to feel antisocial somewhat as those who engaged in extra- or premarital adventures used to be made to feel sinful (and still are made to feel sinful by fundamentalists).

The ability to allow for both futtering and coition, loving and loveless sexual intercourse, and to participate in either or both without guilt or anxiety, may well be an important factor in what seems to be the less problem-ridden sex life of the Muslim. In this respect we might do well to take him for our model (as we would not wish to do in some other areas of his erotic life). In so doing it is our ideology and then our most profound attitudes that would require revising; our everyday practice includes an abundance of futtering already.

25

Futtering may therefore be pleasurable to one person, while *coition* may therefore be pleasing to another, or such might be so for someone in both cases together. Most of us at one time or another have wanted to mount a woman like some sort of an animal, this being the manifestation of our bestial or primordial impulses, while at other moments we wish to have bodily communion with a woman, such being the manifestation of our refined or civilized instincts. And we all know that there is a great number of women who cannot experience an orgasm unless they are raped by their lovers, for these females respond rapidly to the most forceful thrusting and the most violent assaults. Allah accord them their desires! (9)

‘I’

(9) *A famous Western prima donna is credited with declaring that every woman wants to be raped. It is probably true, as some psychologists have held, that rape phantasies are universal among Western women (although the phantasies may be masked). However, it is also true that American women traditionally complain about the "brutality" of American males. Some even justify their experiments with homosexuality on the basis that the lesbian provides a tenderness (one of the magic words in U.S. sex mythology) not to be found in intercourse with a man. But there is not necessarily any contradiction here.*

What the woman means when she complains of brutality, is usually not brutality at all, but rather clumsiness. Similarly, what she refers to as the lesbian's tenderness is more likely to be skill. And when she phantasies rape, it is a skillful rape that she phantasies!

It is also true that women who are expected to be virginal before marriage and monogamous within it are much more likely to entertain rape wishes than are females not so bound. It is well recognized that rape affords a woman an opportunity to engage in prohibited intercourse without moral blame, and so without guilt.

True rape (coercive intercourse) apart, the desire for brutal penetration and violation is more common among Eastern than among Western females. Certainly this is the case when it comes to a

Finally, it is the inherent desire and drive of the male to impregnate, and it is the destiny and desire of the female to become impregnated; and no matter how much they think otherwise, the inevitable is the will of Allah. Men want to give women their sperm, even by violence if needs be; and women, unconsciously, thirst for the sperm of men. It is the calling of their wombs, and without it the human race would cease to exist!

Allah made the penis and the cunnus for no other reason than that they should be joined together, and He made the male for no other reason than that he should penetrate and ejaculate into the female.

In view of these truths, for which there is no valid refutation, I cannot say that there is such a thing as sin or immorality save the willful and criminal frustration of the law of nature. As for what is *right* or *wrong*, Allah made woman for man and man for woman. It is right that the male organ should enter into the female organ, and it is right that the female organ should welcome the male organ. Anyone who thinks otherwise is wrong.(10)

---

desire for the actual experience (as distinguished from phantasy desires which never really contemplate fulfillment). That the craving for such brutality is a fact will be made plain later on in this book. We have also suggested some of the probable reasons why it is a fact.

(10) This realistic view, no more than a statement of the glaringly obvious, is so abhorrent to traditional Western thinking, and so alien to traditional Western utterances, that one must turn to De Sade and a few other "extremists" to find it clearly expressed. We have endlessly pursued, or pretended to pursue, the "natural" in the area of sexual behavior. Our justification for this pursuit, which we seldom extend today to any other field of human affairs, is that we want to do God's will and behave in accordance with His

Hence we find Ibn Hezm declaring:

> There is no woman who, if invited by man, will not sur-
> render to him in the end. It is the absolute law and inescap-
> able decree of destiny.*

And hence we read in the *Arabian Nights:*

> Women and girls were created by Allah for no other pur-
> pose than to unite their delicate organs with man. The
> Prophet (upon whom be prayer and peace!) has said: "No
> woman of Islam shall grow old in virginity." †

There is a characteristically Arab proverb which proclaims
that "Complete subjugation of the passions is found only
among men and not among women." A Talmudic *mishnāh* or
oral law states: "A woman prefers one measure of luxury and
sexual indulgence to nine measures of luxury (11) and continence." ‡

---

*intentions. However, our attempts to define what is "natural" and
"intended" in sex have simply led us to that "willful and criminal
frustration of the law of nature" that El-Halebi brands immoral.*

*Nature knows nothing of marriage vows, arbitrary age of consent,
permissible portals of entry, etc. Nature gives appetites, erogenous
zones, and a wealth of erotic possibilities. Between male and female,
penis and cunnus, there exists a most natural attraction which man
frustrates at his peril.*

*(11) That woman's craving for luxury is intimately related to her
sexuality has been believed since the earliest civilized times. The
Talmud here raises the question of the extent of her craving for
luxury, and asserts that she craves sexual indulgence far more avidly.*

* *The Ring of the Dove,* translated by Dr. A. J. Arberry. London: Luzac, 1953.
† Mardrus & Mathers, *op. cit.*
‡ *The Babylonian Talmud.* 35 vols. London: Soncino Press.

But in the Western tradition it has often been the other way 'round.

Thus, some Christian thinkers, whose views were influential throughout the Middle Ages and for some time beyond, thought it a characteristic of the female to exploit her sexual talents in the interest of her craving for luxury. Even in the nineteenth century (and to some extent presently), it was believed that prostitutes are mainly motivated by their appetite for luxury. Those who declared that prostitutes found no pleasure in their sexual contacts thus bolstered their argument (and probably helped with the production of prostitutes who take no pleasure in their professional sexual contacts).

Later, after woman was denied all sex desires, her reasons for yielding to man under any circumstances could be (coercion apart) only two: greed—vicious; and duty—virtuous.

The belief that woman was mainly motivated by her luxurious tastes was always at odds with the belief in her ravening carnality. Especially this was true during the Middle Ages and up through the seventeenth century. The strange view—strange in the light of the "nature of woman"—that the prostitute was an oversexed female was in conflict with the theory of her motivating luxuriousness.

The idea that woman's desires derive from her impulsion to maternity raises still other problems. Man is conceived in sin and born in corruption; yet motherhood is a noble state. The hunger of the womb makes motherhood possible, but it also results in the bottomless lustfulness of woman. Woman is to be honored for giving birth, and for caring for her children, but is to be detested for what she has done to conceive them. It is small wonder that Catholics should so adore the Virgin Mary who has managed to become a mother without copulating!

But we should not single out for censure only antique and medieval Christian ideologists. In sexual matters, conflicting theories always exist side by side, and with a minimum of discomfort to the theorists.

29

Pandit Kalyanamalla, Indian author of the *Anangaranga* (Code of Cupid), thinks that a woman's sexual desire is ten times stronger than a man's. "A man can never keep a woman under control; women are always unbridled in their passion." (12)

'I'

(12) *One would expect the belief in such an extreme disproportion between male and female desires (and capacities) to have a castrating effect upon the male. So it has, in the West, given rise to neurotic potency disturbances. The Eastern male has not escaped altogether, but he seems to have got off more lightly.*

Early Christian pundits based their misogynistic doctrine not only upon such Hebrew opinions as Solomon's (given above), but also upon the antisexual doctrines of Saint Paul, and later Saint Jerome and others. Saint John Chrysostom expanded the equation of vulva with ravening beast to include the whole woman—though for him the whole woman was doubtless no more than a vulva; or "tout est cunnus dans une femme," as one pederastically inclined priest put it—declaring: "Among all the wild beasts there is none more harmful than woman." Commonplace were such statements about women as the one Jean-Paul Sartre puts into the mouth of a character in his Erostratus: "Women . . . they gobble you up with their big hairy mouths."

Christians of the period of the witch mania believed that the lustfulness of woman explained why there were so many more female than male witches. "All witchcraft," said the inquisitor-authors of the Malleus Maleficarum, expressing the view of the Roman Catholic Church, "comes from carnal lust, which is in women insatiable. . . . Wherefore for the sake of fulfilling their lusts they consort even with devils."

The idea that women are insatiably lustful is largely a product of male fear of the female; and the more profoundly and widely the idea is accepted, the greater the fear becomes: once more, the vicious circle. The question, again, is why the belief was more damaging in

30

According to Shaykh 'Omar en-Nefzawi, "the female does not love the male but for coition." One of the most famous classics of Hemmam bin Ghalib el-Ferezdek, a notorious poet-playboy at the court of the Caliph Harun er-Reshid, is a *qesīdeh* or long-poem entitled "To the Rescue," which aptly illustrates En-Nefzawi's assumption:

> Quoth she (and verily desire
>   Ran riot in her side,
> While the dusky veil of night
>   Let down the darkness like a tide):
> "O Night, in all your blackness
>   Is there none to come to me?
> Is there no sworder for this sheath
>   Of all men, far and wide?"
> Then with her palm she rubbed her parts
>   And said, the while she sighed
> The sighing of the sorrowful,
>   The sad, the weeping-eyed:
> "As by the toothstick's use appears
>   The beauty of the teeth,
> So like a toothstick is the prickle
>   Unto the coynte applied!
> O Muslims, stand your tools not up
>   On end and is there none

the West than in the East; and the answer doubtless resides in the over-all condemnation of sexual intercourse, the equation of sexuality with evil, to be found throughout Christendom but which never was accepted by the masses of Orientals. Neither, perhaps, was woman's lustfulness taken quite so seriously. Thus, the Easterner was able to regard it as somewhat of a challenge; while the guilt-ridden Christian, by contrast, was confronted with a hurdle that often proved insurmountable.

31

'Mongst you who'll save her who from you
    Doth beg relief?" she cried.
Therewith my rod thrust out, erect,
    From underneath my clothes,
And said to her: "Here! here's for thee!"
    And I the while untied
The laces of her drawers.
She made a show of fear and said:
    "O Allah! who are you?"
And I, "A youth who answers to
    Your beck and call!" replied,
And forthwith fell to thrusting in
    Her slit with wrist-thick yard—
A lusty stroke that well-nigh left
    Her buttocks mortified—
Till when, three courses run, I rose;
    "Fair fall thee of the swive!"
Quoth she, and I: "May solacement
    Yourself therefrom betide!"

Mardrus and Mathers offer us the following version of these verses:

I saw her gleaming in the night;
"O night," I cried in agitation,
"What is this phantom of delight?
Is it a tender ghost which haunts me,
Or a heated virgin wants me
For the joys of copulation?"
As in answer to this riddle,
She put down her hands and sighed,
Clasped the blossom of her middle
With her fingers, and replied:
"Fairest teeth need daily scraping
With an aromatic twig;
Chastest parts will sigh for raping

With a something bold and big.
Mussulmans, has this not wrung you?
Is there not a prick among you?"
Here I felt him crack his joint,
While the vehemence which swelled him
Lifted up the clothes which held him
To a noticeable point.
So I let him out, but she
Started back in terror:
"I said twig, and here's a tree;
Is there not some error?"

The following poem, a triumph of "penis pride," (13) was

'I'

(13) *"Penis pride," still to be encountered in Islam, and taken in its narrower sense, is seldom to be found among adults in the contemporary West. The literature of our more bawdy periods of the past affords examples, but present-day instances are confined to pornographic writings and, occasionally, to serious representations of the conduct of children and the "lower classes."*

The notion of taking pride in one's penis seems to the Western mind childish. Certainly it is behavior to be found almost universally among children and early adolescents. Comparisons of penile proportions, strength of erection (by lifting objects with the penis, etc.), and ability to ejaculate vigorously and swiftly in masturbation, may also be encountered sometimes among servicemen and in other situations where males are separated from females and undergo regression. Then, the activity is usually in some degree homosexual and exhibitionistic. The invert author Jean Genet is one of the few serious contemporary writers to give examples of conduct of this sort, including, interestingly, the case of a man who signs a letter to his girlfriend by tracing an outline of his erect penis at the bottom of the letter.

But however childish the "penis pride" of the Arab may strike us as being, there seems little question that it testifies to a sexual ex-

33

composed by the versatile Abu Nowas, one of the greatest poets of El-Islam:

> Allah knows, none has
>   A member of the size
> Of mine; so measure it—come,
>   Take my prize!
> Test it—hold it in your hands—
>   It's my noblesse;
> Whoever tastes of it
>   Feels tenderness
> And violent love for me!
>   It is a fact
> Its length is like a pillar
>   (It won't retract!)
> As seen from afar.
> If it raises and erects itself,
>   It lays me bare;
> Come, seize it! clasp it in
>   Your hands, if you dare!
> And put it in your tent,
>   'Tween where the mountains stand;
> Install it there yourself—
>   Pray take it in your hand!
> See how it holds its head up
>   Like a lofty banner;
> You'll never feel it let up—
>   It's a hardy spanner!
> It never will relax
>   Or slacken like a sail;
> As long as it's therein
>   It stays set like a nail!

---

uberance and self-confidence. Any suggestion that the behavior is mainly exhibitionistic, or that it stems primarily from potency anxieties, is typically implausible.

> Let it be the handle
>   Of the vase
> Between your legs, now empty
>   From its spout to base!
> Come, examine it!
>   Appreciate with promptitude
> How it is so exciting
>   In all its magnitude!
> See how in strong erection
>   It's enormous—
> Like a column, long and hard,
>   And so vigorous!
> If you desire a proper handle,
>   I advise,
> A rugged stirrer for to put
>   Between your thighs!
> Take this one—pray set it
>   In the very center
> Of your caldron, wherein all
>   Good shafts should enter!
> My dear, 'twill be a blessing;
>   You'll be stimulated,
> E'en though your pot were tinned
>   Or even silver-plated!

The Arabs say of a man who has a desensitized glans penis, thus making it difficult for him to achieve orgasm without a lot of frustrating exertion, that he is *muqasder* (tin-plated). Likewise, a woman having a nonsensitive vagina, thus making her hard to satisfy, is dubbed in the feminine *muqasdreh* (tinned). Abu Nowas comments:

> Though no one man can quench a woman's fires,
> Two armies she'll exhaust ere she retires!

Burton notes that many readers of the *Arabian Nights* remarked to him with much astonishment that they found the female characters more remarkable for decision, action, and manliness than the male, and were wonderstruck at their masterful attitude and by the supreme influence they exerted upon public and private life.

The modern Afghan poet, Ashref Khan, touched upon this subject with the following quatrain:

> Since I, the parted one, have come
> The secrets of the world to ken,
> Women in hosts therein I find,
> But few (and very few) of men.

In the same vein, a popular Turkish proverb proclaims that "Of ten men, nine are women!" (14)

In the Apocrypha (*I Esdras* 4:22) we find the following revelation: "Women have dominion over you. Do you not labor and toil, and give and bring all to the woman?"

A certain wise man in the *Mahābhārata*, that great Sanskritic

---

(14) *This is an age-old lament, to be found in most all times and places, and does not necessarily imply any true effemination or subjugation of the male.*

In West as well as East, sometimes with truth and sometimes not, the statement that "men are not men any more" is always being heard. We should recognize that the belief that such is the case has often resulted from a false view of what constitutes masculinity. Maleness has too often been identified with coarseness and brutality, so that an improvement in manners, a refinement in dress, etc., may be falsely regarded as effemination.

On the other hand, the complaint is being heard very often today on the sexual performance level—women lamenting that male potency is declining. It may well be true that we have entered into a period of comparative masculine inadequacy. (See the first note to this chapter.)

36

epic, states: "Led on by the unquenchable thirst for love, miserable man is ever ensnared by woman who is the weaver of the web of life." Isaiah (3:12) laments: "As for my people, children are their oppressors and women rule over them." The cynic wonders how our modern tyranny of teenagers and matriarchal monopoly compares with the ancient condition.

The Turkish historian Shemseddin Ahmed bin Sulayman Ibn Kemal Pasha, in his celebrated *El-Kitāb Rujū' esh-Shaykh ila Sebāhh fī Qūwet el-Bāh* (Book of Male Rejuvenescence in the Power of Concupiscence), tells the tale of a wise man who, returning home after twenty years' absence, suddenly runs away again into the mountains. "Where are you going?" a stranger asks.

"I'm fleeing from a place of misfortunes!" he replies.

"Why? What have you seen?"

"I have seen that all those who live there are the slaves of women!"

Kemal Pasha adds:

> It appears that the majority of men are not only the slaves of their passions but also the slaves of women; for if we will observe, the intelligent eye will see that all men struggle and strive, and wear and tear out their minds and bodies, and carry all they have won and acquired to their wife or their mistress.

Ibn Hezm quotes an old Islamic tradition: "The first blood shed upon the earth was the blood of one of Adam's sons, all on account of rivalry for the possession of women." * The Talmudic and Midrashic rabbis state that Cain killed Abel for the possession of one of their sisters.

To all this the Arabs add: "Whosoever says the *World* means *Woman*, ruler of men and regent of minds!" and

* A. J. Arberry, *op. cit.*

37

"What woman wants, Allah wills!" Nonetheless, cautions 'Ali bin Abu Talib, "be on your guard against the tricks of women and never take their advice; but do not oppress them, for that will only make them worse."

All of which seems to prove that woman has never been man's total slave in the East, harems and veils notwithstanding. Her periods of subjugation were in large part symbolic and superficial, social rather than sexual, for she often continued to dominate and regulate man from the most famous and influential throne of all: the copulatory couch.

2. GENITALIA

In our world, nothing is so esteemed in a man as a good weighty zabb [prickle], just as a jutting backside is the most excellent thing in women.

ARABIAN NIGHTS

Bernhard Stern observes that "the Oriental love physiologists measure the degree of pleasure during coitus almost entirely by the dimensions of the sex organs of the persons involved.(1) A small vulva is almost always desirable among

---

(1) That the dimensions of the sexual parts may be decisive in determining the amount of pleasure to be had from the sexual act is a conclusion stoutly resisted by many present-day sexologists and psychologists of the West. However, the people generally have another idea.

If we look a little more closely into the pronunciamentos of some of our contemporary marriage and sexual affairs counselors, speaking of those who disparage the significance of size, we will find something curious: almost always it is only the penis they are talking about.

Any penis not deficient to the point of deformity is fully adequate to the task of thoroughly satisfying the female, it is said. On the

39

women, and a powerful penis particularly embellishes a man." *
He adds:

> The Arab distinguishes himself through the display of a
> powerful glans penis. I have been told that from childhood
> on they rub the penis long and energetically to increase its
> size and strengthen it.
>
> Even though a large penis is desirable and makes a woman
> happy, it is not the *sine qua non*. In Islamic Bosnia they sing
> a song: "Whether a long one or a thick one it matters not, as

---

other hand, the possibility of an over-large vagina is not infrequently
noted. That something may readily be done about the (entry to the)
vagina while nothing may be done to increase the proportions of
the penis may underlie what is strange counsel: that the penis is
almost never too small while the vagina may often be too large. In
other words, any disabling disparity is always the fault of the woman.

As noted, the "folk" have their own notions about what is anatomically desirable. They are in accord with the Oriental love physiologists that "a powerful penis particularly embellishes a man"—
that is, makes him a particularly desirable husband or lover on the
sex gratification level.

It is true that one often hears the popular saying, "It's not what
you have, it's how you use it"—which emphasizes technique over
physique. But even those who take this statement altogether literally would probably not be inclined to dispute the view that where
technique is equal, size may be the basis for choice.

Largely absent from popular sayings and witticisms about (male)
sexual capacities and prowess is the matter of endurance, or "staying
power," which is likely to be most crucial of all. That is because
males invent most of such sayings, and it is in the matter of staying
power that the male feels most inferior to the female.

* Dr. Bernhard Stern, *Medizin, Aberglaube und Geschlechtsleben in der Türkei*.
2 vols. Berlin: 1933.

long as it satisfies in abundance!" The small penis is ridiculed.

Since the men wish their women to have a narrow vulva, it is generally customary for the women to spread alum in the opening in order to draw together the sex organ if it is wide.

The use of alum (*shebb*) to tighten and contract the vagina has been widespread throughout the Middle East for many centuries, and its popularity may be attributed to its effectiveness.(2) The powdered astringent is usually mixed with water and smeared in the vaginal orifice; then, in a thoroughly dissolved form, it is often injected into the canal. Colonel Dickson observed that "after the birth of a child Bedawin women, and more especially Arab townswomen, resort to various drugs, etc., to reduce the size of the vagina to normal or less than normal. This 'pleases the husband,' they say. Alum is the basic principal of the drugs employed."

According to Stern, "In the entire Orient, the Arabs are famous for the enormousness of their sexual organs, which are said to make it possible for them, while sitting on the ground, to have intercourse with a woman who is sitting backwards before them."

Stern concludes that both the Muslims and the Hindus be-

᛭

---

(2) *The use of the astringent alum to tighten up the sexual parts of women is universal (although it is difficult or impossible to separate fiction from fact). Both Europe and the United States offer a great store of tales and allegedly factual reports of much-fathomed females who, with the aid of alum, have successfully passed themselves off as virgins or as comparative novices.*

Houses of prostitution, during times of defloration mania and rampant nymphetry, have grown rich on the sale of "virgins" and "inexperienced girls," or so it has been written. There are accounts of some such innocents (alum be praised!) who have been deflowered as many as a dozen times in a single night.

41

lieve that carnal copulation between a "stallion man" (he who has a big thick penis) and a "gazelle woman" (she who has a narrow little cunnus) affords the greatest pleasure to both by way of extreme friction and intense pressure, "for it is a union of the largest penis with the smallest vulva."

When an Arab child asks one of his elders, "Are all people created equal?" the elder is apt to reply: "Not all women are alike to the eyes, and not all men are of similar size!" When the young and curious inquire about the hidden truths of life, the old and knowing show them their open hand and draw their attention to the varied sizes and shapes of their fingers. Thus, physiologically and sexually speaking, all men are not created equal. Nor are women for that matter!

In "The Tale of the Vizier's Son and the Bathkeeper's Wife," a masseur laments when he sees that the plump and hairless son of the prime minister has a penis no bigger than a peanut. Not wishing to apply the friction necessary for its development, the bathkeeper summons his wife and says to her: "I was rubbing a handsome boy when all of a sudden I saw that his prickle wasn't like that of other males, for its size did not exceed that of a peanut and it was well-nigh hidden between his thick thighs. So come, O wife, and see if you can rub it and revive it and start it growing again." This the woman did:

> Whereupon the boy's prickle stirred and swelled, for its smallness was in appearance only, since it was one of those which retire almost entirely into the belly when at rest. Suddenly it sprang erect, rising up on end as huge as that of an elephant or a jackass, a powerful sight to see. Then he mounted her with his magnificent member and thrust its greatness between her thighs; and for three hours he rode her and futtered her ten full times, while she sobbed and sighed and writhed and wriggled under him.

The obvious moral of this tale is that a wise man does not

judge by appearances. The size that a penis or clitoris assumes in erection depends upon the *corpora cavernosa,* a network of erectile tissue and blood vessels which produce expansion and distention of the penile and clitoral bodies at the onset of sexual stimulation. One type of penis appears quite small in quiescence, but when with tumescence its cavernous bodies become congested with blood and its muscular fibers are in fullest tension and extension it can greatly exceed its quiescent size. Another type of penis, often called "semi-erect" or "semi-hard," appears quite large in quiescence; but it is generally so constructed that it rarely increases more than a couple of inches during erection, also gaining very little in girth.

This remarkable erectility of the more flaccid type of penis is comparable to the remarkable elasticity of the vagina. Dr. Van de Velde (*Ideal Marriage*) observes that "this flexibility varies very much as between one woman and another, but is generally quite considerable." He adds:

> It is an interesting and well-established fact that it is hardly possible to draw any correct inference from the general bodily build and stature of man or woman as to the size of either phallos or vagina.
>
> But it is also noticeable that women of short stature and small bones can often meet all requirements in the flexibility and capacity of their vaginas.

En-Nefzawi writes that "the vagina of a small female distinguishes itself by virtue of its superior elasticity in that it is able to receive and accommodate the longest and thickest member on the face of the earth without the slightest discomfort; and the greater the tension at which it is stretched, the greater the pleasure and the sooner the woman experiences her orgastic enjoyment."

El-Ferezdek composed a clever set of verses concerning genital accommodation:

When I pulled down her pants and discovered her kaze,
I found it as tight as my worldly ways;
So I thrust it but halfway in, and she sighed.
"Too much?" said I. "Too little!" she cried.

Mardrus and Mathers present a variation:

She was a child, lifting her robe in the garden,
There was no sin a lover of love could not pardon;
It was as narrow as virtue, as easy as flying,
Yet I was halfway in when her petulant sighing
Stopped me. I asked: "Why, why?" And she said with a
laugh:
"Moon of my eyes, I sigh for the other half."

The Chinese do not seem to agree with the Arabs on the scale of feminine variation, for instead they say: "All the coins in the world are made with the same sort of hole." However, the Japanese are more cautious when it comes to generalizing about the masculine sex. Theirs is the following proverb: "A faithful wife has no knowledge of big and little penises." (3)

---

(3) *There was a story told in Europe during the Middle Ages about a gentleman with a very small penis. He (correctly) suspected his betrothed of having had many lovers, and on their wedding night (as some husbands have always been wont to do) he sought to trap her.*

"Do you think," he inquired of his bride when he had disrobed, "that you can endure such a big one?"

But the lady was not to be trapped, and concealing both her experience and her bitter disappointment, she demurely looked down at the floor.

"My dearest husband," she said, "how should I know whether it is a big one, or whether I will be able to contain it?"

The story delights in the quick-wittedness of the wife as well as

GENITALIA

Sir Richard Burton, after extensive erotic observations and investigations in the Middle East, was convinced of the anatomical difference between the "pure" (Semitic) and the "naturalized" (Hamitic) Arab:

> There is a great distinction between Arabian and African Arabs, as proven by their penis. The Arabian Arab, being of pure blood, has a very small member. The African Arab, on the other hand, is long, thick, and flabby; however, he lengthens very little from a state of quiescence to that of erection. Valid proof concerning this distinction may be obtained by tracing Egyptian ancestry; hence the Nilotic race, although commonly called "Arabs," has the membrum virile of the African Negro.*

Dr. Jacobus, quoted previously, likewise noted that "among those people who have a Semitic origin the penis is less developed when in a flaccid condition, but the difference when in a state of erection is more considerable than in the black of pure race." In other words, the detumescent penis of the Hamite and Negro is large because it remains "semi-erect," hanging long and smooth; but at the onset of erection it simply stiffens and, because it is not contracted in a limp state, increases very little or not at all in thickness and length. The detumescent penis of the Semite and Aryan is short and small because it becomes more flaccid; but at the onset of erection it elongates and, becoming dilated, often exceeds its cousin in length and girth. Jacobus continues:

in the stupidity and subsequent credulity of the husband, suggesting perhaps that it is sufficient if a wife seems to have no knowledge of big and little penises.

* Translated from a Latin note in Burton's *Personal Narrative of a Pilgrimage to El-Medina & Mecca.* 2 vols. London: Bell, 1898.

45

The Hamitic Arab is provided with a genital organ which, for size and length, rivals that of the Negro.

The Arabs I examined, in the proportions of their genital members, considerably surpassed the fair average of the Negroes.

In its usual condition their penis, instead of being quite limp, still maintains a certain consistency and feels to the hand like hollow india-rubber or like the penis of the Negro. The glans is well-developed and of a dirty red-brown. The corona is, in proportion, smaller than the circumference of the shaft of the penis. The maximum diameter is found where the foreskin is cut off in circumcision. This part of the penis [the band of cicatrice or root of the prepuce] sometimes swells out, like a fleshy collar.

According to the measurements I made, the penis of the Arab has an average length, when in erection, of 7 to 7½ inches by 1½ or 2 inches in diameter; but I have often found a penis measuring 8 to 10 inches in length by 2 or 2½ in diameter.

The organ then becomes a kind of pole which only a Negress could accommodate, while a Hindu female of the class called "hare woman" [shashastrī, she whose dainty and delicate vulva is no bigger than a lotus bud] would shrink from it in terror, and it would produce serious mischief in the rectum of any poor wretch who consented to suffer its terrible attacks. With such a weapon does the Arab seek anal copulation. He is not particular in his choice, and age or sex makes no difference to him.(4)

᾿Ι᾿

---

(4) While firm data to challenge Dr. Jacobus' findings are lacking, it might be said that the measurements he offers seem exaggerated. It is most unfortunate that this question of comparative phallic proportions has not been laid to rest once and for all. Military physicians, who might have made the most exhaustive studies, have been prevented from so doing by the prudishness of commanders and politicians.

Jacobus accurately deduced that these polelike penises are welcomed only by those vaginas of equal proportion or capacity, offering as proof the following observations made in India:

> It is certain that the Hindu women, who have small and short vaginas, since the Hindu men have small and slender penises, find that a normally constituted European is a trouble to them and suffer martyrdom when they have to do with a Negro or an Arab, whose enormously large penis is for them an instrument of torture. Nevertheless, this same conformation causes pleasure to an Arab woman, whose vagina is of a caliber in proportion to the copulatory apparatus of a male of her race.

He adds:

> Hindu women having frequent connection with Muslims and Negroes have the entrance of the vagina greatly enlarged. The average depth of the vaginal passage does not exceed 3½ or 4 inches, corresponding in length to the 4 or 4½ inch erect penis of the Hindu man. It often happens that a penis of more than average length will cause inflammation of the womb, by the repeated shock of the glans against the neck and mouth of the uterus.
>
> The thickness of a Muslim or Negro organ is, however, in an Indian female's favor; for the erect penis of an average male of her race measures only 1¼ inches in diameter.

Probably one of the best estimates places the length of the average human penis at about six inches and the diameter at about one and three-eighths inches (both measurements being, of course, for the tumescent organ). While variations are great, it is difficult to imagine that Jacobus could have encountered with any frequency penises eight to ten inches in length and two to two and one-half inches in diameter.

The reader is advised to get out his measuring tape before passing judgment in favor of the likelihood of such outrageous instruments.

47

The unfortunate fact, as Jacobus found it, is that the Mussulman prefers the little vagina of the Hindu girl to the large sheath of a female of his own race. Every year dozens of Muslim males are charged with brutally raping Indian girls and boys in the cunnus and anus, while countless others are never apprehended in their pursuit of forbidden pleasure.

El-hhemāmeh (the dove) is the nickname bestowed upon the penis of the Semitic Arab and the Jew, which measures from three to four inches in quiescence and from five to six inches in erection. This clever comparison becomes apparent when we note that in the circumcised penis the root of the prepuce encircles the neck of the glans like a fleshy collar, thus giving the male organ, when it retracts to the level of the scrotum, the appearance of a ring-necked dove resting upon two eggs. *Baydz* (eggs) or *baydzetān* (two eggs) are colloquial for the testicles.

Tōq el-hhemāmeh (the ring of the dove) is figurative for the circular remnant of the foreskin. Ibn Hezm chose it as the title of his treatise on the art of love because the *tōq* or band of cicatrized skin surrounds the most sensitive part of the circumcised penis. In masturbation, copulation, and sodomy the *tōq* elicits acute sensations of titillation when it is clasped and agitated by the fingers or by the vulvar and anal sphincters.

Es-samek (the fish) is the penis of the Hamitic Arab and the Negro, measuring from five to six inches in quiescence and from six to eight inches in erection. The preputial root of the circumcised *samek* does not form a pouch or fold around the corona, but is retracted; and the virile member, long and smooth and bellied, appears somewhat like a fish to the imaginative African.(5)

------

(5) The detumescent penises of American and European Caucasian males may be of either the "semi-erect" or small and flaccid types. Both types are common, though probably the "semi-erect" type of

The Sudani Muslims have a saying: *Zirāb en-na'jeh wa-zembūr edz-dzeb' wa-zubb el-qird zay'l-'ōrāt insānīyeh* (The vagina of the ewe, the clitoris of the hyena, and the penis of the ape are just like those of human beings). The clitoris of the female hyena often projects and hangs down; it is therefore comparable to the *zembūr* (hornet) of the Hamitic girl, the little head of which protrudes from between her labia. The penis (*zubb*, prickle) of the ape is generally long and slender, being comparable to that of the Hamitic boy. The vagina (*zirāb*, sheath) of the female sheep and other large animals is similar to that of a woman, a physiological fact which makes bestiality extremely popular among pastoral peoples.

Morphologically speaking, Muslim erotologists make a definite distinction between *el-kus* (the crack) and *el-ferj* (the slit). Some females, according to their pelvic inclination and general contour, have *ferūj* (slits) while others have *kesās* (cracks). For example, the vulva of a Hamitic or Negro girl often appears as a plump cleft high on the pubis. This vulvar cleft is very long and deep, for the labia are large and thick, and sometimes it gapes to reveal a red vestibule. Because this type of vulva is bereft of a *mons veneris*, it is technically termed a "slit." Conversely, the vulva of a Semitic or Aryan girl often displays a large hump of a *mons pubis* and a small cleft well-nigh hidden between the thighs. Because this type of vulva is dominated by a domelike swelling or mount of Venus, and because the labia are posed low on the pubis, it is technically termed a "crack."

Thus do the Egyptians facetiously call their womenfolk *zewāt el-ferūj* (the slit ones), because their vulvas are situated high on the pubic arch, while the Arabians title their females

---

penis, which lends itself to many jokes in the shower-room, but with which the owner is likely to be rather pleased, is the more rare of the two.

49

zewāt el-kesās (the cracked ones), because their vulvas are placed low on the pelvic arch.

The Babylonian Talmud presents the following information on the "becoynted ones":

> Our Rabbis taught: "What are the marks of puberty [*bāgrūth*, ripening]?"
>
> Rabbi Simeon stated: "When the *mons veneris* grows lower."
>
> "What is meant by *mons veneris?*"
>
> Rabbi Huna replied: "There is a rounded eminence above that place [the vulva], and as the girl grows in age it steadily grows lower."

There is an old Chinese criterion that one of the characteristics of an ideal girl is "she whose turtle is plump and smooth and placed high rather than low upon the pubis." This Taoist desideratum arose from the fact that most Chinese females are "low-cut ones." The Hindus class such a damsel as *padminī* (lotus girl) or "she whose vulva is no bigger than a lotus bud." The *sankhinī* (shell girl), or "she whose vulva is as large as a sea shell," is akin to the Japanese *akagai* (shellfish, fat cunnus) or *awabi* (shell, vulva). The *hamaguri* or "clam" is the tight little cunnus of a Japanese girl. In Sanskrit, *hastinī* (elephant girl) or "she whose vulva is as big as that of a baby elephant" would be classed with the "high-cut ones."

Jacobus noticed that "the little Hindu girl has the vulva placed very high." This anatomical peculiarity is apparent in classical Indian temple sculpture; for nearly all the naked dancing girls and goddesses are depicted with a long, plump, high-placed vulvar cleft and protruding clitoris. This girlishness of form is also made manifest by an absence of pubic hair.

Umm tertūr (mother of pointed headpieces) is the clitoris, which in many Muslim girls projects from between the labia.

In others, *el-mekhshūm* (the snub-nosed one) shows as a mere swelling in the labia without actually revealing its glans between them.

The tremendous popularity of sitting and squatting postures of copulation in the East may be attributed not only to the pliability of legs but to the high position of the clitoris. Increased inclination of the pelvis causes the clitoris to press firmly and continuously against the upper surface of the penis during vaginal intercourse. Thus the Arabs commonly call this tiny homologue of the male organ *zembūr* or "hornet," because the fully-developed clitoris presses down upon and "stings" the back of the penis during penetration.

In Sanskrit, *gūdhamanī* (she who has a hidden clitoris) is a Hindu girl whose little *madanachhatrī* or "passion peak" is concealed within the folds of her *labia minora* and *majora*. *Gūdha* (kernel) is synonymous with the Arabic *betzr*, whence the word *betzrā* (she who has a big tickler). When the little Indian maiden begins to masturbate by rubbing and plucking her *gūdha*, it then becomes like a bamboo sprout and its tiny head peeks out from between the large and little lips or lotus petals of her *yōnī* (vulva). When she starts to have constant intercourse, her labia loosen and widen; and the clitoris sticks out even more, its glans fully exposed. Then she is a *padmini* or "lotus woman," because her clitoris is like unto the carpel of a lotus which has just burst forth in bloom.

Ez-zerzūr (the starling) is the vulva of a young Muslim or Jewish female. Its outer lips are dark brown and its inner labia are rose-colored. In many Negresses it is glossy black with a crimson center, whence it is dubbed *esh-shehhrūr* (the blackbird). The little light-brown and pink vulva of an Arab girl is also called *el-'osfūr* (the sparrow).(6)

─────────────

(6) *Such a charming, even poetic, approach to the genitals is generally quite absent from American and most other recent Western*

51

As noted at the beginning of this chapter, the size and capacity of the penis and vagina are of considerable interest to Asians and Africans. Dr. Van de Velde writes:

> If a small phallos is mated to a large vagina, the normal coital friction will hardly suffice to produce orgasm, and the sufferer here will be the woman rather than the active partner.
>
> Negroes are generally longer and more massive than white men; and they also number among them, proportionally to their own large average, more extreme "phallic giants" than the whites.

literature and speech. In our fiction and poetry, any description of the genitalia of either sex is considered to be pornographic and/or obscene.

Nor does our medical and sexological literature offer anything of the sort. And the physician who attempted to fill in the lacuna would surely soon find himself accused of taking a reprehensible degree of pleasure in his work. The prose devoted to descriptions of the female genitals is no different from that to be encountered in a treatise on the dissection of the cadavers of rodents, and authors take pains to arrive at exactly such spiritless and unesthetic aridity. Some will plead that this is for the protection of the students, so that they will not be distracted, and so that the development of properly scientific attitudes will be encouraged. However, we must look for the explanation elsewhere.

As for everyday language, our terms for the female (and male) genitals are almost exclusively ugly in sound and drab or worse in the imagery they evoke. Occasionally, there is a note of levity; but it would seem that we can go no further. Surely we should expect to find that people who liken the genitals of their women to flowers and birds are psychosexually more healthy than people (us) who speak crudely of "gashes" and "snatches" and who, whatever the term used, commonly consider they are speaking "dirty words."

52

On the whole, a phallos of unusual size must be more agreeable to women, on account of increased pressure and friction in coitus.

Burton, in his comments upon the erotic tastes of *Arabian Nights* heroines, notes:

Debauched women prefer Negroes on account of the size of their parts. I measured one man in Somaliland who, when quiescent, numbered nearly six inches. This is a characteristic of the Negro race and of African animals (e.g., the horse); whereas the pure Arab, man and beast, is below the average of Europe: one of the best proofs that the Egyptian is not an Asiatic but a Negro partially whitewashed. Moreover, these imposing parts do not increase proportionally during erection; consequently, the "deed of kind" takes a much longer time and adds greatly to the woman's enjoyment. In my time no honest Hindi Muslim would take his womenfolk to Zanzibar on account of the huge attractions and enormous temptations there and thereby offered to them. And I may add that the same cause has commended these "skunks of the human race" to debauched women in England.

Although many Muslim women are readily responsive to internal or vagino-uterine stimulation, depending upon their psychic conditioning or constitutional sensitivity, the majority find their greatest capacity for orgastic response centered exteriorly or just inside the lips of the vulva: in the clitoris, the *labia minora* and the vaginal vestibule.(7) Hence the impor-

T
---
(7) These are also the areas which Kinsey found to be most sensitive in the human (United States) female. However, Kinsey declared that "all the evidence indicates that the vaginal walls are quite insensitive in the great majority of females." This statement placed him at odds with many other authorities, who assert that the clitoris

tant factor for them is girth rather than length; and the penis of the Semitic Arab, which generally measures between four and five inches in erection, is of a thickness well-suited for feminine satisfaction.

It often happens that any man endowed with less than five or six inches (probably about the world average) is decidedly displeasing to an Arab or Negro woman who is vaginally oriented in her sexuality. In East Africa, for example, many Muslim females refuse to serve Hindus because their penises are too short and thin, which only goes to show that nature did not intend the "hare man" to mount the "elephant woman."

Burton found that "Nothing for nothing" is a fixed idea and philosophy with the Eastern female, not so much for greed as for a sexual *point d'honneur* when dealing with her imaginary adversary: man. The Indian merchant is rejected by the Arab prostitute because of the meager dimensions of his virile member, but the same little penis drives the Hindu female into the ecstasies of orgasm. Moreover, a Muslim woman usually thinks twice before serving an uncircumcised man.

---

is the principal source of sexual satisfaction in the young girl, but that in the sexually mature female the principal source of erotic gratification is the vagina. The failure of such a transference to occur is held by these authorities to be a major source of coital frigidity in the female.

Kinsey agreed that some women find great satisfaction in vaginal stimulation, but he thought the response mainly psychological. In any case, there is no doubt that many American women are vaginally insensitive in varying degrees, and that such insensitivity does nothing to further the attainment of coital satisfaction.

It is likely that many more Eastern than Western women are adequately responsive vaginally. Some evidence that this is true will be presented later on; and we will also have a good bit to say about why this should be the case.

54

Dr. Jacobus, who examined hundreds of male and female organs from Malaya to Africa as a surgeon in the French civil and military services, gives attention to the fact that:

> In no branch of the human race are the male organs more developed than in the African Negro. I am speaking of the penis only and not of the testicles, which are often smaller than those of the majority of Europeans.
>
> The genital organ of the male is in proper proportion as regards size, to the dimensions of the female organ. In fact, with the exception of the Arab, who runs him very close in this respect, the Sudanese Negro possesses the largest genital organ of all the races of mankind.
>
> The penis is almost as large when flabby as it is in a state of erection. It was among the Muslim Sudanese that I found the most developed phallus, and notably one of the maximum dimensions, being nearly 12 inches in length by a diameter of 2¼ inches. This was a terrific machine [a veritable freak of nature!], and except for a slight difference in length, was more like the penis of a donkey than that of a man. The unfortunate Negro who possessed this "spike" could not find a Negress large enough to receive him with pleasure, and he was an object of terror to all the feminine sex.

Perhaps this black bombardier answered all wisecrackers with "I have twelve inches, but I don't use them as a rule." Jacobus continues:

> The Negro is a real "stallion man," and nothing can give a better idea (both as to color and size) of the organ of the Negro, when erect, than the tool of a little African donkey. The absence of hair on the pubes, which the Negroes remove, makes the resemblance more complete. Nor is it confined merely to color and size; for the penis of the Negro, even when in complete erection, is still soft like that of the donkey and when pressed by the hand feels like a thick india-rubber

tube full of liquid. Even when flabby, the Negro's yard still retains a size and consistency that are greater than that of the European, whose organ shrivels up and becomes soft and limp.

The average size of the penis generally appeared to me to be about 7½ to 8 inches in length by 2 inches in diameter at the swelling produced by circumcision. Except with young lads just arrived at the age of puberty, the penis is rarely less than 6½ inches in length by 1¾ inches in diameter. I took these measurements from most of the races of the Sudan. I often came across a penis of 9½ to 10 inches by 2¼ inches and once, in a young black barely twenty years of age, found a monstrous organ 11¾ inches long by 2½ inches in diameter at the circular circumcision mark.

Jacobus observed that

The vulva of the African Negress is black at the entrance, but becomes a bright red in the vagina. It is the same with the lips and the mouth. The pubis is completely hairless. In the adult Negress the vulva is placed very low and descends almost vertically, as does also the vagina, which is much longer but more narrow than in the European woman. The small lips assume, at an early age, an immense development and considerably exceed the great. Is this caused by repeated pulling, or is it a peculiarity of the race? The clitoris of the young Negress is very much developed, often the length of the little finger of a child, for after the nubile age it increases greatly.

Upon examining the mutilated genitals of Sudani, Somali, Ethiopian and Swahili women, one finds that the *nymphae* or *labia minora* are rudimentary, having been amputated close to their root, and that the outer lips gape open to reveal the dark-red vestibule. When not so mutilated, the inner lips measure approximately two inches in length and fan out or hang down in projection, exposing the vaginal orifice. This excessive enlargement or elongation of the *nymphae* is commonly called "Hottentot apron." In adults the *labia minora* are of a slaty-blue, whereas in young girls they are dark red. The clitoris, unless excised, continually stands out; in many cases it is from 1 to 2½ inches long in the exposed part. "Clitorism" is the technical term for hypertrophy or overdevelopment of the clitoris, a common condition sometimes dealt with by clitoridectomy.(8)

Jacobus offers us this description of the genital parts of a young Sudani prostitute whom he examined:

> When she was standing up, the prominence of the depilated *mons veneris* was immediately observable, as also the absence of the entry to the vulvar slit. This form of the *mons veneris* is connected with the transversal contraction of the pelvis, and its development recalls the ancient statues of Venus and the Graces, or of eunuchs, except that in the latter the orifice of the urethra is seen on a level with the skin. On looking closer, a linear cicatrice is distinguishable in place of the vulvar slit, above which the finger could feel the clitoris in its place but not very movable, hidden beneath the cicatricial tissue. It was only after the legs have been stretched

---

(8) The West, too, has "dealt with" the clitoris by lopping it off. Clitoridectomy used to be performed on females who masturbated "excessively." Since a large clitoris was believed to cause a woman to become a lesbian, or alternatively a nymphomaniac, clitoridectomies were sometimes performed to prevent or remedy those conditions also. Needless to say, these moralistic mutilations had little or nothing medically to commend them.

It is worth noting in passing that the belief that a large clitoris made for hyperhedonia had its counterpart in the notion that a large penis betokened exceptional virility and might incline its possessor to satyriasis.

apart that the vaginal orifice becomes visible in the form of a slit near the perineum; its edges were constituted by the ridge of the *labia minora* almost welded together with the *labia majora*, and by the fork of the vulva. Directly after this ridge the black coloration ceased, and the rosy tint of the vaginal mucous membrane began. So that in this manner the upper commissure, the clitoris, the orifice of the urethra, and the anterior half of the *nymphae* were hidden by the adherence together of the *labia majora*.

Nymphotomy or amputation of the inner labia,(9) usually followed by infibulation or a stitching together of the *labia majora* to prevent sexual intercourse, is practiced extensively by Muslim and Negro Hamites.(10) Nymphotomy presents a

---

(9) *We have found that the term nymphotomy is sometimes used to indicate amputation or drastic trimming of the nymphae (labia minora) and sometimes to indicate excision of the clitoris. We will use the term clitoridectomy for excision of the clitoris, reserving nymphotomy for the various mutilations of the nymphae.*

(10) *Mantegazza (The Sexual Relations of Mankind) describes an alternate method of infibulation found in the Sudan. The labia majora are scraped on their internal surface, a little funnel or catheter is placed in the urethra to allow for urination, and then beginning with the big toes the feet and legs are bound together up to the middle of the thighs. The purpose of this is to hold the thighs together so that the labia will adhere. When adhesion is complete, there remains but a little orifice for the passage of urine and menstrual fluid.*

He adds that when the infibulated girl is ready for marriage, a midwife partially opens her up with a single knife slice. When the girl is ready to bear her first child, the midwife completes the reopening process in the same way, so that there will be no natural obstacle to the emergence of the infant.

58

singular appearance in the black or brown female. Unless excised, the *glans clitoris* is usually buried in ashy scar tissue. When the girl sits and spreads her thighs, the holelike vaginal orifice is bared and the ringlike sphincter causes it to protrude slightly. There is no trace of *labia minora*, which are cut off at their root. Jacobus describes the operation as performed by Hamitic peoples:

> I questioned a circumciser on the nymphotomy of little girls, which is quite common among the Nilotic and Sudanese tribes. The man made use of both his hands to make himself understood. He represented the *labia majora* with the forefinger and thumb of his left hand, and used the forefinger of his right hand to represent a knife. He excises the tip of the clitoris and the totality of the *nymphae*. There is no suture, but as soon as the operation is terminated and the wound anointed the upper part of the child's legs are bound together and she is made to lie with her thighs pressed tight

---

Sad to relate, the cruel practice of infibulation is historically no stranger to the West. The Romans infibulated singers of both sexes in the hope of preserving their voices, thought to be unfortunately affected by venery. They also practiced infibulation on members of both sexes to preserve chastity—and, lest sodomy be practiced, infibulated the anus as well.

Later, chastity belts offered a somewhat preferable alternative to European women. The precaution taken by the Romans was, however, ignored; and in Italy girls and women thwarted fore took to entertaining their lovers aft. Corresponding to the female chastity belt was the famous little padlock. The prepuce was pierced and the padlock inserted and locked, with the key being handed over to its appropriate keeper. This keeper might be some guardian of morals eager to prevent coitus, sodomy, fellatio, and self-abuse. On the other hand, it might be some greedy matron anxious that her slave and lover should not squander his energies elsewhere.

59

until cicatrization has taken place in about five days. The girl can walk at this time, but with difficulty, and pain prevents her from parting her thighs for at least another week. Girls are warned against taking long strides or opening their legs too far, so that their genital organs may not become enlarged by stretching before marriage. The young husband alone possesses the privilege of dilating his wife.

Felix Bryk found that the virile member of East African Negroes is "quite large."

> Every adult without exception is circumcised. The glans of the circumcised does not differ at all in color from the distal part of the organ; in the uncircumcised it is lighter, somewhat rose-violet. Morphologically it is characterized in being much smaller in proportion to the rest of the cylindriform penis than it is among Europeans. In adults the opening in the glans is open, while in the European it is closed, and it is not bounded off by circumcallation. I could not definitely determine a condition of semi-erection observed by other investigators and described as normal.*

The Sudani, Somali, Ethiopian, and Swahili penis, measuring five or six inches in quiescence, is smooth and cylindriform. It increases only an inch or two in erection, and it feels like soft but elastic rubber to the hands. Detumescently semi-erect, its cicatricial skin is retracted; and it is generally horizontal when in a state of stiffness.

Bryk continues his observations, noting that the vagina of the Negress "looks somewhat strange on account of its unusual color."

> Just as the lips of the mouth are not very much differentiated in color from the dark hue of the face and are lost in a

* Felix Bryk, *Voodoo-Eros*. New York: Ethnological Press, 1933.

monochrome against the deep brown, and only upon opening of the mouth does the red of the inside of the lips as well as of the gums stand out in full contrast, likewise the vagina and its lips are brown or black externally but rose-red within.

Two types of vagina are easily distinguished in adult women, that without clitoris and that with excessively long labia. Characteristic of both types is a narrowness not in proportion to the fair size of the masculine organ. The *anklei-toridica* [declitorized] formation is without any richness of folds, sometimes without a trace of clitoris and sometimes with a small scarlike protuberance. In contrast to this ascetic form the *hypertelica* [overlipped], better known by the name of *Hottentot apron*, seems grotesque. Its color ranges from brown to violet. In profile the labia hang down limply like brown, wrinkled india-rubber bands; when opened they resemble a labiate in form. The Negress can stretch this to some length, like a rubber band. The length is variable, but its minimum is the length of the little finger.

Many Arabs declare that the *mehbil* (steam place) is characterized by a peculiar roughness of surface which affords the penis an almost masturbationlike rubbing. In his investigations, Jacobus noticed "a marked dryness of the vaginal mucous surface" among Sudani women, which accorded the kind of masturbatory rubbing to which the menfolk had become accustomed since early boyhood. This natural dryness of the mucous membranes heightens and intensifies mutual sex sensation through friction, one of the reasons why Arab men love to lie with Negro women. Young and experienced Sudani males who have swived several varieties of females often describe the genitals of Arab and European women as "large and too moist." (11)

.T.

(11) *This dryness presumably testifies to a dysfunction of the lubricating apparatus. That vaginal dryness should be considered a desir-*

Clitoridectomy is intended to induce vaginal sexuality, and whether or not it does so is a matter of individual psychophysiology. Certainly, it seems likely that removal of the clitoris would necessitate the development of orgastic response in the vagina if such response were to be present at all. Tactile sensitivity is then augmented by psychical elements, especially if the girl has been mentally and physically conditioned to prefer internal to external stimulation. For the declitorized female, erotic sensation is said to be concentrated in the labia (*minora,* presumably), the vaginal vestibule, the vagina and the neck of the uterus. Those who are vaginally sensitive may undergo vulvotomy (excision of the external genitalia: *labia minora* and *majora,* and clitoris) without suffering any loss of sensation or capacity for response. Thus, there is no proof that such a woman is necessarily any more frigid than one whose external genitals are intact; nor has it ever been shown that a "vulvotomized" female experiences greater difficulty in arriving at orgasm during vaginal intercourse than one not so mutilated.

Excision of the *glans clitoris* is known in Arabic as *tebtzīr* (declitorization), from the root *betzr* or "kernel," while resection of the *labia minora* is called *khefdz* (planing). One or both operations are privately practiced throughout Muslim Africa, the Middle East and Southeast Asia. In Arabia, for example, they are performed on girl infants a few weeks old; while in the Sudan they are usually deferred until the child is three or four years old. *El-khutneh* (the cut) is a simple resec-

---

able feature in a woman will seem very strange to anyone who has attempted copulation under such a circumstance. It is true that the female genitals may sometimes be "too moist," especially if they are also rather lax, but less moisture and far from total dryness is the desired solution. Surely the dryness Jacobus mentions is comparative; and it is likely that some lubricant is required before penetration can be effected.

tion of the clitoral prepuce, which effects complete exposure of the glans and insures maximum development of this tiny organ, a common Arab complement of male circumcision.(12)

For clitoridectomy, the little child is seated with her thighs held wide apart by the surgeon's assistant. Then the surgeon, generally a skillful if formally uneducated woman, seizes hold of the protruding clitoris with her thumb and forefinger and pinches or pulls it until it stiffens; whereupon she slices it off with a single stroke of the razor. If the clitoris is concealed within the labial folds, the surgeon will make a shallow incision or cut away the prepuce to expose the glans. Removal of the clitoral foreskin is often accompanied by excision of the *nymphae*. While in Upper Egypt, Dr. Jacobus examined dozens of Muslim women and made the following report:

> There is no trace of the clitoral glans, of its prepuce, nor of the minor lips; all these parts have been entirely cut away. In a couple of cases I injected the cavernous bodies of the vulva from their root, and it then appeared that these parts were absent up to their point of junction; from there, the injected matter penetrated no further and the parts were lost in a cicatrized tissue. An injection of the *bulbi vestibuli*, specially known as communicating with the vascular system of the clitoral glans, did not succeed. Therefore, it may be taken for granted that in this operation the clitoral glans, together with its prepuce, had been seized, drawn forth, and rather deeply cut away.
>
> The operator never cuts off the *labia minora* in those cases where they are not abnormally developed. However, I found them absent in most of the women whom I examined. The

'l'

(12) *Females are circumcised in the United States when the clitoris is "hooded," resulting in an inability to reach sexual climax. This little operation has saved many a marriage, enabling "frigid" wives to enjoy sexual gratification.*

clitoris is often found badly cut, for it is less easy to draw forward than the labia, which are elastic. Hence a woman takes her place behind the girl and separates as wide as she can the outer lips, so as to make the clitoris protrude far out. One circumciser admitted that he seized at one and the same time both clitoris and *nymphae,* and that he cut off the whole with one stroke of the razor.

In nymphotomy the *labia minora* are seized at the level of the clitoris and cut off almost at their root, at the inner surface of the larger lips, of which the mucous folds are the lining which hides the organs of reproduction. What remains of the lesser lips forms, by the cicatrization of the smooth walls which indurate and retract, a gaping vulva which presents a singular appearance in young circumcised girls.

In general, the little girls remain for a week without walking; and during another seven days they walk only with their legs wide apart. External sensitivity is increased twofold by the operation, which lays bare many genital nerves. This extreme tenderness and hyperesthesia is aggravated by friction, which accounts for the girls' walking bowlegged for a few weeks.

Among the Sudanis, an artificial clitorism is induced to facilitate the act of amputation. The girl spreads her legs apart and separates the lips of her little vulva so that the clitoris sticks out, whereupon stinging nettles are touched to its tip by the surgeon. The tiny prickles inflame the clitoris and cause it to swell strongly, at which time its head is snipped off.

Captain Burton was intrigued by the gaping vulvas of Somali girls, whose *labia minora* and *glans clitoris* were amputated with three sweeps of a razor: "The Somali prostitutes who practiced at Aden always had the labia and clitoris excised and the skin showing the scars of coarse sewing." At the same time, he observed a savagery known as *es-selkh* (the flaying) in which the entire skin or sheath of the penis is severed and stripped off, practiced in Arabia by primitive Bedawin tribes.

After studies in India, Dr. Jacobus writes that

> By the side of the Negro, the Hindu cuts but a sorry figure.
> . . . The result of my personal observations is that the great
> bulk of the Hindus may be classed as "hare men" [*shashajī*,
> he who has a thin short penis and a long tapering prepuce],
> averaging 3½ inches in erection. Only a small number are
> "buck men" [*mrigajī*, he whose glans penis is only halfway
> uncovered by the foreskin in erection], averaging 4½ inches, or
> "bull men" [*vrishajī*, he whose glans penis emerges from the
> prepuce during erection], averaging 5½ inches; and still a
> smaller number are "stallion men" [*ashvajī*, he whose penis is
> so long and thick that the prepuce is perpetually retracted
> and the glans denuded], averaging 6½ or 7 inches.
>
> The dimensions of the depth of the *yōnī* (vagina) corre-
> spond with the *lingam* (penis) of the men. As a general prin-
> ciple, the vulva and vagina of the Hindu woman are much
> less widely open [at the vestibule and orifice] than those of
> the Negress.
>
> The penis of the Hindu is generally covered by the foreskin
> when in its normal condition, and when in erection in the
> boy not yet arrived at puberty. It does not become bared in
> erection until the lad has arrived at puberty and is of an aver-
> age age of sixteen to eighteen, and then that is probably due
> to masturbation. The skin of the penis is dark, while the glans
> is of a more or less darkened red which is almost bright in
> light-skinned Brahmans.
>
> In its usual condition the penis is extremely flaccid, but
> increases greatly when erect, being then almost triple the size
> and as hard as that of the European. The average size ap-
> peared to me to be about 5 inches long by 1¼ in diameter.
> Many are from 3½ to 4 inches by 1 inch. Few are from 5½
> to 6 inches, which is nearly the European average and which
> here appears to be the maximum. The testicles are oval and
> the size of a pigeon's egg.

Jacobus, after examining the genital organs of hundreds of Chinese, found that

> The glans penis is of a reddish hue toned down with a dash of ocher. As to the size and conformation of the genital organs, it appeared to me that the Chinese closely resembles the European. The prepuce is but small and imperfectly covers the glans when in a state of repose. The Chinese of Southeast Asia also present the same characteristic of the imperfectly developed foreskin; and the glans, which is only half covered when the organ is flaccid, slips out very easily and completely when it is in erection. The testicles of the Chinese appeared to me to be a little smaller than those of the Europeans, but the difference is not very marked.

Jacobus again notes that the Chinese prepuce "scarcely covers the corona and leaves the glans almost entirely exposed. On several occasions I saw it leaving the crown free and forming behind it a little circular cap which naturally disappeared at erection. A Chinese boy, fifteen years old, declared that it had always been like this; besides, the prepuce bore no trace of any operation."

Because of their naturally short or retracted foreskins, Chinese males are dubbed *mōlūd mekhtūn* (born circumcised) by the Arabs. Chinese females are also deemed "born circumcised" by the Sons of Islam. Not plump and protuberant like the large-lipped genital of the Arab woman, the small-lipped Chinese vulva looks flat and fleshless.

The full-bodied Muslim female bears little resemblance to the minikin creature whose willowy form suggests genital infantilism. The diminution or complete absence of the prepuce in the Chinese male is matched by the arrested development of the vulva and vagina in the female. The clitoris alone is generally well-developed, doubtless due to habitual masturbation, and like that of a small child is readily reactive to the slightest

66

excitation. In fact, the adult form is most like that of an infant: small breasts, buttocks, and vulva offset by a large and hyperactive clitoris.

Islamic folklore speaks of "the narrowness of China," alluding to the girlish size of the adult vagina,(13) and Jacobus adds that "the object of the compression of the Chinese woman's feet was to develop the constrictor muscles of the vulva and the vagina."

The penis of the Japanese is similar to that of the Chinese in that it has a very short prepuce. In boys the foreskin covers the glans only halfway, merely encircling the corona, while in men it freely retracts and leaves the head fully uncovered. The shaft is smooth and, like the Chinese lotus root, of the "semierect" variety. The blue veins stand out beneath the dark skin. The average Japanese penis measures approximately four inches in repose and five inches in erection, while the Chinese member is about an inch longer and slightly thicker than the slender rod of the Land of the Rising Sun. When stiff, and after having undergone a considerable amount of vigorous stimulation, the ochreous Chinese penis becomes dark reddish-brown or henna, the color of the Japanese glans.

Unlike the ladies of the Celestial Empire, who may boast of a big clitoris, the Japanese women are renowned for their vaginal contractile powers. Their *labia minora* are elongated, appearing like pink (bright red during sexual excitement) caruncles from between the outer lips, and sometimes the clitoris protrudes at least a quarter of an inch. Repeated masturbation by rubbing and plucking, as well as frequent coition, are in-

---

(13) *American folklore has the Chinese vagina "sideways." In the United States, Chinese-Americans remain for the most part self-segregated and their women will seldom have anything to do sexually with a non-Chinese male. Thus, by want of opportunity to put it to the test, the legend of the "sideways" vagina is maintained.*

67

strumental in producing these genital proportions. Although the Japanese female is traditionally very thin and frail, her vulva is surprisingly plump; whereas the Chinese female, traditionally full-bodied, is often flat and fleshless between the thighs.

Jacobus records these findings on the Far Eastern female:

> The general appearance of the Japanese body is like that of the Chinese woman, but the pubes is not always deprived of its hair, for all the hair of the pubes is carefully pulled out by Chinese. In that case it is scantily furnished with a little black curly hair. The mucous surfaces of the vulva and vagina are lighter than in the Chinese woman, which are a rather bright carmine toned down with a dash of ocher. The general hue, a yellow-red, is nearly like that of a Spanish woman. The genital parts are also much better developed than in the Chinese woman. The breast is also more rounded.
>
> The larger lips show little stoutness of development, and even among young people they lack firmness. The vulva stands out very prominently. The vagina is short. I never found it to exceed 2¾ inches in length. I was never able to perceive a hymen. The vagina did not in general appear to be particularly wide. Congestion and erection of the *portia vaginalis* [tip of the womb] took place during examination much more frequently than it does among European women.
>
> It is said indeed that the genital parts of Japanese women are actually so narrow that medical men are appointed to choose out of the prostitutes those whose vaginas permit coitus with the more powerful virile member of the European.
>
> Maruyama, one of the most celebrated of modern Japanese artists, painted an aquarelle representing a naked woman squatting on the ground, with the motto: "A woman who has sinned in lust." Her "shame-slit" is depicted wide agape; the clitoris, as well as the smaller lips, stands out prominently; the larger lips, on the contrary, appear small with but little stout development.

Among Chinese women, the larger lips are more largely developed; but the *nymphae* are small.

As Jacobus noted, the hymeneal membrane is either rudimentary or entirely missing in most Far Eastern females, which he took to correspond to the lack of a prepuce in the male. They are, as the Arabs put it, *mōlūd meftūhh* (born already opened). Frequent vaginal masturbation and/or childhood copulation eliminate, by stretching and wearing away, any trace of a hymen by the time a girl reaches puberty.

A significant peculiarity which characterizes Japanese erotic artwork is a robust stylization of genital exaggeration. The penis and cunnus are depicted in gigantic proportions, at least three times their normal size. The male member is generally of forearm's thickness and length, with foreskin fully retracted and glans huge and handsome. The female organ usually assumes the length and width of the folded sleeve opening of a kimono. The *labia minora* are outstanding and corrugated, and the great cleft is beautifully fringed with a full crescent of wispy hair.

In Japanese, *dokyo* (strength) is the name of a fabulous priest-profligate who apparently had the strongest penis in the world; (14) and erotic picture scrolls from Japan portray wres-

(14) *The temptation to portray priests and other ecclesiastics, especially those supposed to be celibate, as sexual athletes, is irresistible throughout the world. Probably, however, no nation has so delighted in recounting the erotic exploits of the clergy as the French. The literature on the subject ranges from the light and the mild to the dark and the extreme, from the good-naturedly humorous to the (intendedly) viciously defamatory. An anthology of some interest could be compiled, but here we will limit ourselves to a single example, of the humorous variety. The author is of course Rabelais,*

tlers and muscle men duelling and doing battle with no other weapons save their long, thick, huge-headed, and erect penises. Legend has it that the Hercules of China was wont to smash copper pots with a single blow of his enormous phallus; while a bunch of big-membered bruisers setting out to conquer the Isle of Amazons soon returned successful, having paid the price of victory, their weapons wrinkled and shriveled from violent jousting.

These fanciful representations serve as effective psychic aphrodisiacs for the small-penised and -cunnused Japanese male and female. They are also sometimes humorous. Since the dawn of time man has depicted his generative apparatus as being of dimensions not in proportion to the rest of his body,

---

the time is the early sixteenth century, and the topic is the sexual behavior of monks:

"Where are you from, poor man?" Friar John broke in resolutely.

"From St. Genou."

"And how," asked the monk, "is your abbot, Tranchelion Gulligut, that true toper? How are the dear monks faring? God's body, may I roast in hell if they're not ramming your wives' pleasure-vents while you gad about, pilgrimizing."

"Bah!" sighed Dogweary. "I'm not afraid for mine. No man seeing her by daylight would ever break his neck to spend the night with her."

"That's incompatible, it holds no water, the cap won't fit. (I refer to your words, not to the vents.) Were your wife uglier than Prosperine, by God, she'd find herself jerkthumped as long as there was a monk within a thousand miles. Good carpenters use every kind of timber. The pox riddle me if you don't all find your wives pregnant on your return. The very shadow of an abbey spire is fecund!"

thus emphasizing their importance and symbolizing his phallic awareness. Montaigne wrote:

> In the greatest part of the world, that member of our body was deified. The most sacred magistrate was reverenced and acknowledged by that member, and in several ceremonies the effigy of it was carried in pomp to the honor of various divinities. The Egyptian ladies, in their bacchanalia, each carried one finely carved of wood about their necks, as large and heavy as she could so carry it; besides which, the statue of their god presented one, which in greatness surpassed all the rest of his body.

3. GENITAL INTERCOURSE

The most blessed thing in life and the only thing worth living for is to put one's lips to a woman's lips, one's body on her body, and one's genitals in her genitals.

'ABDU'L-'AZIZ IBN SA'UD,
King of Sa'udi Arabia

Nothing in the science of sexual intercourse occupies the Oriental mind more than the art of *el-imsāk*. *Imsāk*, from the root *misik* (to hold or prolong), is an Arabic word meaning "the prolongation of pleasure in coition by protracted penetration and withholding of the ejaculation."

Men ignoring the technique of seminal retention are contemptuously compared to barnyard cocks by Muslim and Hindu women who cannot be satisfied with less than fifteen or twenty minutes of continuous vaginal intercourse.(1)

---

(1) *It has been estimated that the average American male typically ejaculates in from one to three minutes from the time penetration is effected. Kinsey declared that a sizable majority ejaculate in less than two minutes. Five minutes has been proposed as an amount of time sufficient to bring many or most women to climax, although Kinsey found that ten to twenty minutes were commonly required (as distinguished from the one or two minutes needed by the female*

73

Systematic *coitus prolongatus* involves hastening the female orgasm while delaying the male ejaculation. The penis is firmly planted full-length in the vagina, without movement but with pressure, and friction is applied to the clitoris by the man's or woman's fingers. This suspended motion and digital stimulation serve to arouse the woman's senses to the vibrant erotic pitch of the man. When occasional or continuous movement is desired, the man applies pressure to the woman's pubes and effects a slight circular rhythm. When both partners have neared the point of climax, the man takes decisive action with a rapid succession of vigorous thrusts until both he and the woman convulse in the ecstasies of simultaneous orgasm. The Arabs call this coital technique *es-sibāhheh* (the soaking or swimming) because the penis bathes itself in the vagina before diving and plunging.(2)

---

to reach orgasm by means of masturbation). The wonder would seem to be that more than the smallest fraction of females ever reach orgasm by way of copulation; but everyday experience indicates that the situation is not quite so bad as the above-mentioned figures would suggest. In any case, the only male who could be fairly compared to a barnyard cock would be one who ejaculated immediately upon entry (ejaculatio praecox). On the other hand, disappointed females may be of the opinion that a two-minute lover might as well be a ten-second one.

(2) Techniques of coitus requiring that the penis remain entirely or almost motionless in the vagina call for a very high degree of potency in the male, and probably also for considerable practice. With probably most males, the penis will soon detumesce without the stimulus of friction resulting from movement. In India, certain women have learned to prevent this by developing sphincter control to an extent enabling them to apply such pressure to the base of the penis that the blood is prevented from flowing back out.

74

In Arab literature we find mention made of "the muscular violence of an Upper Egyptian wench," the *jedhb* (grasping, seizing) or *qebdz* (clasping, squeezing) which Burton notes as "alluding to a peculiarity highly prized by Egyptians: the use of the constrictor vaginae muscles, the sphincter for which Abyssinian women are famous." The *qebbādzeh* or "holder woman," as she is called by the Arabs, "can sit astraddle upon a man and can provoke the venereal orgasm not by wriggling and moving but by tightening and loosing the male member with the muscles of her privities, milking it as it were. Consequently, the *casse-noisette* [nutcracker] costs treble the money of other concubines."

The *Kāmasūtra* (Laws of Love) of Pandit Vatsyayana states that those women who have developed strong orgastic feeling and sensitivity in their vaginas are called *saraotāstrīyan* or "nutcracker women," because their sphincter and constrictor muscles are powerful and vibratory. Vatsyayana adds:

> When a woman holds the *lingam* in her *yōnī*, draws it in, presses it and keeps it thus in her for a long time, it is called *chimtī* (the pair of tongs).

The *Anangaranga* (Code of Cupid) of Kalyanamalla mentions the *samdhāmsa* or "pincers" technique:

> A woman must ever strive to close and constrict her *yōnī* until it tightly holds the *lingam*, as the muscle of the anus

---

The prolongation of coitus within reasonable limits, though preferably with movement, is obviously desirable in view of the comparatively tardy female climax. In the United States the male gets an assist in his efforts from various mildly anesthetic ointments. These, bearing such trade names as Pro-long and Stay-mor, are rubbed onto the penis some time before intercourse and in some cases are helpful in delaying the climax.

clasps the finger when it is inserted, opening and shutting at her pleasure, and acting like the hand of the dairymaid who milks the cow. The *lingam* then becomes the teat; and the *yōnī*, which represents the hand, extracts the *rasa* or vital essence by squeezing and wrenching it. This can be learned only by long practice, and especially by throwing the entire will power into the part to be affected.

So lovely and pleasant to man is she who constricts and is capable of milking the *lingam* with the inner muscles of her *yōnī*! (3)

---

(3) Similar techniques and accomplishments are presently being strongly urged upon American housewives, along with reciprocal oral stimulation of the genitals and other methods once regarded as depraved and/or un-American. The main impetus comes from the soaring U.S. divorce rate, accompanied by a vast upsurge in the popularity of adultery, which is attributed in large part to sexual incompatibility.

This is indeed a change. We have finally come (or been forced) to acknowledge that there must be sexual satisfaction of both husband and wife in marriage. American husbands and wives formerly stayed together, in the face of frustration that frequently ripened into hatred, not so much because they had a greater respect for the marriage vows as because there were no jobs for women. Now that most women are able to live in economic independence of the male, either by working or by means of (frequently unjust) alimony, sexual incompatibility is much more likely to result in divorce.

It must be admitted that the introduction of new extracoital and coital techniques and practices has not yet had any effect (or any clearly discernible effect) on the divorce rate. However, that could be because the generations hitherto exposed to the new marital relations counseling have been unable, because of inhibitions grounded in antisexual teaching, to follow the advice given. It may be that less inhibited future generations will fare better.

The Indian art of *vādhavākha* (noose-mouth), the imprisonment of the penis by the sphincter cunni, is known as *el-imsāk* (the clasp) or *el-qebdz* (the clutch) among the Muslims. The Arabs use the exclamation *imsik lisānek* (hold your tongue) in its sexual sense, i.e., "hold your penis." To the Turks, *emsik* means "cunnus-penis" and *emsik lisānī* (hold my tongue) would be the same as saying "hold my penis in your cunnus."

Dynamic *coitus prolongatus* involves repeated and energetic acts of sexual intercourse. Its performance depends upon masculine potency, sensitivity, and will power. The movement is strenuous and continuous, and suspension of thrusting lasts but a few seconds during the act itself.

Islamic folklore is full of violent scenes of sexual encounter, of "fifteen forays" being served or of much "thrashing and slashing" and "poking and stroking" all night long. To be known as *abū zeqqzeqq* (father of thrusts), one capable of "great strokes of the prickle," is quite an honor.(4) Among the

---

As for the development of vaginal sphincter control, milking techniques, etc., women resist such valuable acquisitions not only on "moral" grounds, but because of the time and effort involved. Physicians have attempted to overcome such resistance based on laziness by easing the task with various exercising instruments designed for the purpose. But even so, some effort is called for, and often it is more than the woman is willing to make.

(4) And not only in the East, as our Flynns and Rubirosas attest. Or, more precisely, we envy while not honoring such "cocksmen"— this term deriving, one supposes, from the number of hens the cock serves and not from the brevity of the individual encounters. However, the term "cocksman," while suggesting a large number of conquests, probably also implies a superior capacity as a lover.

It is interesting to note, in this regard, that Americans probably admire (and/or envy) a large number of conquests rather more than

Hindus, he who is a *dhakēlū* (pusher) is a sworder to whom no woman worth her salt would deny herself. And *abū hhimlāt* (father of assaults) is a fitting name for one of those "hardy cocks" of Upper Egypt, who can "take on twenty hens one after the other."

In classical India, *coitus prolongatus* was called *vīshratī* or "twenty-times copulation." The *Anangaranga* says that many women are satisfied "only by the violent thrusting of a stiff and solid *lingam*." The *Kāmasūtra* states that "in the beginning of coition the passion of the woman is middling and she cannot bear the vigorous thrusts of her lover, but by degrees her passion increases until she ceases to think about her body."

Chinese and Japanese erotic literature are monuments of coital dynamism. We read how "the spear was hard and strong," how "they sported for a long time," and how "he thrust his sword continuously in and out of her scabbard over three thousand times."

A typical example of a classical Japanese best seller is a treatise entitled "How to Make a Nymphomaniac Faint in One Foray." A hot-blooded damsel says to her lover: "I want to climax five or six times in succession, but you must use your penis continuously." How is he to perform such a feat? Thusly: When the woman cries, "Quick! do it with big motions," the man should pump up and down with pounding violence. If the woman has her legs wide open, stretched upwards, and encircling the man's waist, thus fully exposing her vulva and pubes to the man's jarring blows, his glans penis will strike her uterus, causing "a voluptuous feeling and a rapid orgasm." After several minutes of continuous intercourse, if the thrusting is so

---

they admire coital prowess. *This, in its turn, might suggest that the* "cocksman" *is envied more for his triumphs over taboo than for the pleasure he gives and receives—exactly what one would expect from a sexually malcontent, inhibited and anxious male population.*

furious as to bruise her thighs and batter her womb, the nymphomaniac will faint from repeated paroxysms. In other words, such a female must be "raped" brutally and unmercifully in order for her to achieve orgasm.

Japanese women, who are vaginally oriented in their sexuality, respond rapidly to coital stimulation of the neck and mouth of the uterus.(5) In a treatise entitled "How to Make a Woman Love You," we read this recommendation:

---

(5) *The repeated insistence in Eastern writings on the art of love that the mouth of the uterus is sexually responsive, and that it is desirable for the penis to strike repeatedly against it, must seem very strange to readers of Western "marriage manuals."*

It is true that gynecologists are familiar with American women who assert that the cervix must be stimulated before they are able to reach climax. However, as Kinsey has remarked, this would often seem to be the consequence of a failure to properly localize sources of sexual arousal. He reported that many women "insist that they feel the clinician touching the cervix when, in reality, the stimulation had been applied to the upper (anterior) wall of the vestibule to the vagina near the clitoris." It may be that some or most of the Eastern reports result from similar errors. Kinsey adds:

> *All of the clinical and experimental data show that the surface of the cervix is the most completely insensitive part of the female genital anatomy. Some 95 per cent of the 879 women tested by the gynecologists for the present study were totally unaware that they had been touched when the cervix was stroked or even lightly pressed. . . . Less than 5 per cent were more or less conscious of such stimulation, and only 2 per cent of the group showed anything more than localized and vague responses.**

* Kinsey, *et al.*, *Sexual Behavior in the Human Female*, p. 584.

79

> Thrust your weapon all the way in, up to the very hilt, till the tip of your penis touches something deep in the vagina. Rub all around the uterus with rapid motions, and even the most lukewarm lady will soon come to climax like a bursting dam.

In "The Secrets of Love" we learn:

> If a man wishes to fire a woman to passionate fury, he should push his poker fully into her furnace and rub its head against the opening of her forge. She will become super-excited and experience an orgasm.

Coitus between little boys and girls is quite common in Japan as elsewhere throughout the Orient. It is the prime fac-

---

He goes on to say that histologic studies find "essentially no tactile nerve ends in the surfaces of the cervix." Those surfaces may even be cauterized and operated upon without anesthesia being required. Deep cuts into the tissue of the cervix "may lead an occasional patient to register pain, and the dilation of the cervical canal causes most patients to feel intense pain. In none of these instances, however, is there any evidence of erotic response."

Our own findings are that many American females report that "hitting the bottom of the vagina" is painful. We do not overlook the possibility that the very vigorous and even brutal thrusting demanded by many Oriental females may result in more frequent contacts with the cervix than occur in most Western copulations. It is conceivable that as a result of these repeated contacts, the cervix may acquire some capacity for erotic response, or seem to. If this in fact happens, it may be that what results is pain experienced as more pleasurable than painful, and that the contact is craved on that account. Other theories might be proposed, but the main intent here is to note the strangely differing views encountered in East and West as to the merits of cervical stimulation.

tor in the development of vaginal sexuality, for the vigorous thrusting of the boy produces acute sensations of pleasure and conditions the girl at a most early and impressionable age to react readily to internal or copulatory rather than external or masturbatory stimulation. Available evidence seems to prove that orgasm is achieved easily and rapidly at each contact, because the mind and senses of the child are not disciplined like those of the adult. Consequently, the electric current of titillation spreads from the vaginal orifice into the sheath and up to the mouth of the womb. The girl comes to identify sexual satisfaction and orgasm with vagino-uterine instead of clitoral excitation, and a man's penis is more important to her as a woman than his hands or mouth.

The sadomasochistic element also enters into this subject of vagino-uterine sexuality. Young girls, seduced or raped by older boys or men, experience a savage thrill. Burning, tickling sensations attend the forceful stretching and stroking of the infantile vagina, barely two inches long, by the five- or six-inch erect penis of the male. As the glans continuously batters away at the delicate and sensitive tip of the uterus, forcing it up into the vault with each fierce thrust, paralyzing feelings of pleasure are mingled with paralyzing feelings of pain. Intense pressure and friction are brought to bear upon the clitoris, the labia, and the walls of the vagina, once tight and narrow but now distended and extended to their utmost tension. One result of this traumatic experience is that libido is drawn into and concentrated upon the vagina and the uterus. Direct stimulation of these parts by the penis or fingers produces congestion, erection, and orgasm almost immediately, so strong is the masochistic reaction.

A violent buffeting motion satisfies the Japanese woman. She likes to feel the shocks of the glans penis against her uterus, then thrill to the impact of the seminal fluid. Japanese

81

sexologists instruct men to "pump with big motions, in and out and in and out." When copulating with an experienced female, a male should "push his penis forcefully many times, prodding the uterus and rotating continuously, and the woman will get a torrential orgasm."

In Chinese erotica we find that only a shocking impact of the two pubes and a furious thrusting of the penis in the vagina can satisfy the sadomasochism of the Oriental:

> She took off her clothes and got into bed with him. The woman lay upon her back. He spread her legs apart and pushed himself fiercely, while her tongue grew cold and her lotus bud ran with moisture like water from a fountain. She called him all the tender names she could think of. It was the middle of the night and so silent that the noise they made might have been heard far away. He put his arms around her and kissed her, then told her to squat upon the bed and suckle him. She did so, to his great satisfaction.*

"While her tongue grew cold" means that she had reached the acme of sexual stimulation and was about to faint. So intense is the masochism of the Oriental female, so exquisite her sensitivity and response, and so strong is her passion in her utter abandonment to her lover, that a few forceful thrusts may be sufficient to set off her venereal climax once she has been aroused; and as long as the male continues his stroking, she may continue to climax in rapid succession. These repeated orgasms will not end until the pulsating titillation becomes so severe as to bring pain, until her entire body trembles violently with the piercing spasmodic thrill, and until she finally loses her senses and falls into a swoon.

In classic times there was hardly a Far Eastern female who, wishing to please her mate and generously feed his ego, did not

* Clement Egerton, *op. cit.*

seek to attain this orgastic ideal. Characterized by from six to twenty or more successive paroxysms, it is said to send the female into a state of *nirvāna* (paradisaic oblivion), and there is no question but that it nourished the traditional serenity and reservation of the cultured Chinese and Japanese woman.(6)

Dr. Jacobus carried out scientific experiments with hundreds of Japanese, Chinese, and Indian women to determine, on the average, how long it takes for an Oriental female to attain orgasm in vaginal intercourse. In many cases, no matter what the coital posture employed by two copulators, rapid response depended upon contact of the clitoris with the dorsal surface of the penis.

Arab physicians, after measuring the sizable clitoris found in the female hyena and then noting its acute sensitivity and observing the degree of orgastic pleasure and receptivity during the caresses of the male, concluded that utmost development of the human clitoris is necessary for satisfactory sexual intercourse. Consequently, female circumcision or removal of the clitoral prepuce has become a standard procedure among many Muslims. By severing or cutting away the little hood or fold of flesh which often conceals and constrains the clitoris, circumcisers certify that the little glans will be free to enlarge and fully exposed for direct stimulation during vaginal coition.

·|·
___

(6) *The reverse side of this coin is that failure to achieve orgasmic release of tension results in the "bad nerves" so common among Western women (and which of course may be otherwise caused). Orgasm is a tranquilizer in the best sense, and regularly and sufficiently experienced does indeed contribute to serenity and "peace of mind." For this reason, as well as for many others, a reasonable society will strive to remove obstacles to orgasmic response—which necessarily implies abandoning irrational ideas which serve to frustrate rather than to facilitate sexual climax.*

83

Van de Velde writes:

> We are probably right in believing that the clitoris was meant to be stimulated in coitus together with the vagina. The fact that this superlatively sensitive and excitable organ protrudes downward in erection, and seems to urge and press towards the phallos, tends to prove it.
>
> Perfect and natural coitus would give the woman a blend of both types of stimulation. Such a blend would involve supreme pleasure and probably very rapid orgasm.

Jacobus discovered that in the majority of Chinese women, owing to the well-developed clitoris, "forty times in and out" was sufficient to produce orgasm after a short period of pre-coital excitation. The two most favored positions were squatting and kneeling. "Forty times" is also found in the *Arabian Nights:*

> She took my hand and led me to her bed, and I stayed with her there all night. I charged her forty times and forty times she charged me, calling at each assault: "*Yū!* My darling! *Yū!* My soul!" *

Other women, even more avidly adapted to vaginal stimulation, climaxed after "eight shallow thrusts and two deep ones." Penetration was not preceded by any mechanical excitation such as titillation of the clitoris with the glans penis or fingers; in all cases the female was psychically stimulated or self-aroused by handling and mouthing the male organ. Jacobus found that most Oriental females, especially the highly passionate variety, prefer to prepare themselves for penetration and, instead of being excited by the caresses of the male, are more heated when they assume an active role and play with the penis.

* Mardrus & Mathers, *op. cit.*

According to Jacobus, Japanese women were stirred to the depths by "ten times shallow and slow, ten times deep and quick" repeated two or three times. Violent thrusts caused the vagina to vibrate and the uterus to throb, and eventually many females fainted.

Hindu women went passionately wild over "nine times shallow and one time deep." This rhythm was rapidly repeated several times. In nearly all instances there was a feminine desire for oral excitation of the clitoris as a preliminary to the coition.

Alternate "deep and slow, deep and quick" motions were very popular among vaginally oriented women, especially the Japanese, while surface strokes and shallow thrusts were preferred by the clitorally oriented up to the point of crisis, when they would lift their loins to receive forceful full-length shocks. Circular rhythms were also in demand. The "corkscrewing" technique was a favorite of females when they assumed an active role by mounting the man. The movement was classified as "grinding," (7) the very opposite of "churning," and

·T·
_____

(7) This is one of the few examples we have found of the woman "grinding" the man, and obviously it is significant that in this case the woman has mounted the man and so assumed the traditional dominant role of the male in coitus. Ernest Jones interestingly writes:

> . . . To grind, from classical myths to modern slang, has always been a symbol for sexual intercourse, as may be illustrated from the following passages from Nork (Mythologie der Volksagen und Volksmaerchen). . . . "In symbolic language a mill signifies the female genital . . . and the husband is the miller, hence Petronius' use of molere mulierum (to grind a woman) to describe the sexual act. Samson when robbed of his strength by Delilah has to grind in the mill (a typical talion punishment) . . . on which passage the Talmud comments as follows: by the phrase 'grinding corn' one has always to

was invariably accompanied by vulvar and vaginal constrictions and contractions ("milking") on the part of skillful Japanese girls. Those Oriental women who can effectively control their genital muscles generally achieve orgasm by squeezing or contracting the sphincter as hard as possible, which sometimes causes discomfort to the man, who is strangled as it were.

In "The Fabulous Feats of the Futtering Freebooters," an Arab tale immortalizing the erotic exploits of four noble fornicators from classic Baghdad, the following verses are set forth concerning the virtues of hashish (*hheshīsh*, hemp) which, as the Chinese say, causes the jade-stick to "become as hard as iron and hot as fire, fit for intercourse with a hundred girls":

> The member of Abu'l-Haylukh remained
> In erection for thirty days, sustained
> > By smoking hashish.
> Abu'l-Hayjeh deflowered in one night
> Eighty virgins in a rigid rite,
> > After smoking hashish.
> Felah the Negro did jerk off his yard
> For all of a week; hashish kept it up hard.
> The Negro Maymun, with opiate,
> Without stopping to ejaculate,
> > Futtered for fifty consecutive days.
> Allah bepraise him for having fulfilled
> > Such a task!
> But then, fresh vigor instilled,

---

*understand the sin of carnal intercourse. This is why all the mills had to stand still in Rome at the festival of the chaste Vesta. . . . It is now clear that every husband is a miller and every wife a mill, from which it is intelligible that every marriage (Vermaehlung) is a making of meal (Vermehlung)." ***

* Ernest Jones, *On the Nightmare*, pp. 280–281.

Obliged to furnish ten days more—
Making sixty days of coition his score—
He fain went on and finished the chore.
During this ordeal Maymun, in bed,
Smoked what held up his penis head:
  Hashish!

These verses, which appear to be the epitome of Oriental exaggeration, are nonetheless very realistic in that they reflect the avid amatory appetites of the Arab and the Negro. (8)

---

(8) *They also reflect man's perennial dream of (and search for) an aphrodisiacal drug that will arouse raging lust in women and endow the male with a superhuman potency. Needless to say, hashish (better known in the United States as marijuana) is not such a drug.*

Studies made in the U.S. indicate that marijuana is a sex stimulant only for a small minority of persons. The great majority receive no such benefits (unless, sometimes, when the benefits are expected and the response is really to suggestion rather than to the chemical properties of the drug).

In the East, the case is less cut and dried. Chemical analysis of hashish discloses no reason why it should yield erotically stimulating effects, yet there is a vast lore, including many personal and eyewitness accounts, of the aphrodisiacal effects of hashish. All of this evidence, with ample allowance for the distortions of folklore and legend, is not to be casually dismissed.

The Arab user of hashish may experience erotic visions as well as arousal and increase of potency. There is an analogy here to the effects of opium upon the Chinese. Many Westerners, on the other hand, report no sexual effects consequent upon the smoking of opium (although the Westerner is more likely to report such effects with opium than with hashish).

For quite a full discussion of the sexual effects of hashish, opium and many other drugs, the reader is referred to R. E. L. Masters' Forbidden Sexual Behavior and Morality *(Julian Press, 1962).*

Dr. Jacobus declares that the African Negro "is the most powerful human male animal, if we take into consideration the time necessary for him to complete copulation, for he can work almost an entire night without exceeding half a dozen emissions." Jacobus adds:

In order to spend the black requires a very prolonged rubbing, and the receptacle is large and well lubricated. A Negro is therefore able to make the act of coition last a long time before he spends and can even, if he likes, keep back the supreme moment by modulating his thrusts. He can thus accomplish amorous exploits which would knock up a European.

In the circumcised, the mucous membrane of the glans is tanned and less sensitive. It needs a rougher friction, a more prolonged rubbing, and the coition is prolonged to the great pleasure of the woman.

The Negro takes a much longer time before he spends than the white man does. I should estimate that he is, on an average, quite three times as long in finishing a copulation as the white man is; and I am not at all exaggerating. The reasons for this are very natural. Firstly, the sensitiveness of the genital apparatus is much less in the black man than in the white, for the same reason that the generative parts of the Negress are endowed with a less acute sensitivity than those of the white woman. It would be abnormal and contrary to the laws of physiology for the black man to accomplish the venereal act as rapidly as a European, while the woman of his race is very slow in coming.

The Negress requires a "man stallion" to make her feel the proper physiological sensations, and she seldom finds him except in the male of her own race. Added to this, her nervous system is not so delicately organized as in the white woman. Her mucous membranes are drier, especially as regards the genital organs. To obtain the sensation of voluptuousness under these conditions, the Negress requires a slow copulation which only the black man, with his huge penis, can give her.

It is certain that a well-fed, circumcised Negro can perform on a woman nearly the whole night and only spend five or six times.

Felix Bryk observed that the African woman "makes great demands of her husband's capabilities; she is hardly ever satisfied. I was told about a case in which a woman slept with ten men one after the other. Naturally, masculine potency has a good deal to do with the strength of the love relationship. The wife is actually vexed if her husband does not sleep with her at night and at dawn." He continues:

> From her eighth year onward a girl is common property. Anyone who has any command of masculine eloquence can have her. Very small girls sleep with boys of their own age; the older ones, about twelve years and above, are never scorned by unmarried men. Virginity is not very highly prized; perhaps that is why promiscuity is rampant among the black girls.

Dr. Jacobus now considers the Muslim male:

> The circumcised Arab is slower to ejaculate than the European, and *a fortiori* the circumcised Negro is slower still, on account of his possessing a nervous system that is less easily excited.

It is difficult to determine how Jacobus came to this conclusion, for there is no comparing the phlegmatic Negro with the choleric Arab. Although appearances often deceive, the average Muslim male is extremely high-strung and impulsive; and his easily excitable or "neurotic" nature often causes him to complain of premature or rapid ejaculation. Circumcision has

89

little or no effect whatever on speed of orgastic response. Circumcised Easterners respond to genital stimulation just as rapidly or as slowly as the uncircumcised, depending upon the individual. The circumcised and comparatively insensitive Sudani Negro usually ejaculates within three to five minutes of continuous stimulation of his penis, while the circumcised Arab generally ejaculates within one to three minutes of genital friction. There are of course many exceptions to the rule—some being rapid firers, especially under certain conditions, and others slowpokes. Stimulative technique also determines individual response. For example, rubbing of the sensitive underside of the glans commonly causes a quicker climax than when the relatively insensitive shaft of the penis is gripped and agitated.

Among Oriental males of especially sensitive constitution the moderate but systematic use of narcotics may become customary. Opium, in mild doses, excites the imagination while it dulls the senses. Hemp is said to desensitize the penis, prolong the erection, and increase the pleasure.

The Arabic word *kayf* (ecstasy), synonymous with the Chinese *yen* (fantasia), is employed to describe the effects of hashish or the state of ecstatic tension produced when the drug intoxication is accompanied by sexual activity. It is said that the Malayan and Indonesian Muslims and Chinese, after smoking opium or hemp and achieving the nirvanic *yen* or *kayf*, can keep the penis in vigorous erection for twenty-four hours straight. During this time they abandon themselves to almost continuous vaginal and anal copulation and manual masturbation, abusing their penises in the most intense and violent manner but ejaculating only a half dozen to a dozen times.

Burton noted that the Islamic peoples of North Africa and the Middle East use hashish as an *imsāk* or a medicine taken to prolong pleasure in carnal coition. Hemp is eaten, drunk, or smoked in small quantities to effect the desired result: a voluptuous stupor.

Many Muslims, in describing the incredible effects of hashish, state that it stimulates the nervous system and prolongs erection of the penis for several hours. Under the influence of *kayf*, a man has no moral inhibitions and no self-restraint; he will indulge to frenzy in any sexual act which it is within his power to indulge. One of the first impulses of a *mekaiyif* or "ecstatic" is to strip stark naked, take his penis in hand, and masturbate as long and as hard as he possibly can. Inflamed by *bhang* (hashish), young Indian Mussulmans, marauding in small bands, will attack, rob, and rape men and women and boys and girls, taking turns in a continuous assault throughout the night.(9)

·ï·

(9) *Such behavior, actually attributable to the effects of marijuana, is rather rare in the West. This does not mean that there is no popular belief in marijuana-caused violence and crime. When a group of psychopaths and/or hoodlums go out on a spree, and if they happen to be smoking marijuana, the marijuana is likely to be blamed. In general, marijuana is probably less likely than alcohol to lead to antisocial acts.*

The analogous drug, in terms of (Western) effects, would seem to be cocaine. The individual under the influence of cocaine may not only become violent, but a male may behave like a satyr and a female like a nymphomaniac. Resistance to deviant sex behavior disappears and there are few acts if any in which the cocaine-intoxicated individual will not engage. It might be added, however, that we have no reports of marauding bands of cocaine addicts, and it may be that the paranoid delusions occurring in cocaine intoxication discourage such group enterprises.

Merely to speculate—since our reports are largely to the contrary —we wonder whether some of the more extreme behavior attributed to hashish consumption in the East is not in fact the result of

91

When hashish has enslaved its user, it has a peculiar demoralizing effect upon both mind and body. Psychic love is brutalized into physical lust; civilized man degenerates to a primeval state of promiscuity. The victim of sexual fatalism and degradation lives only for the immediate gratification of his senses. He is primitive and unrefined in his selfish craving for raw pleasure, and his warped and decayed spirit drives him into a vicious circle of extravagant behavior which in many cases ultimately leads to self-destruction.(10)

Narcotics may unnaturally retard the natural reactions of the genital apparatus. The penis sometimes remains erect for several hours, and orgasm and ejaculation may not occur until the effects of the drug begin to wear off. Unless one is a devout masochist, the effects of hemp, like those of opium, can be extremely frustrating. The brain is supercharged but genital sensation is greatly diminished. The erection is stiff and persistent, and neither the most forceful nor subtle friction will ease the tension and produce orgasm. There is little or insuffi-

---

blending the hashish with various solanaceae drugs, as Easterners are known sometimes to do. The violence of the reported reactions would then be considerably more intelligible.

(10) That demoralization does in fact attend the long-term use of hashish in the East is beyond question. However, for this to occur the consumption must not only be over a considerable period of time but must be flagrantly excessive. It is well known that Muslims often do consume hashish in amounts which seem incredible to the Western scientist. Not only demoralization but physical and mental collapse (with delirium, attacks of frenzy, etc.) are the end-results and a large proportion of the patients in Egyptian and Indian mental institutions are hashish addicts. The wholesale abuse of hashish by Muslims is, by the way, usually attributed to the fact that the Koran prohibits the use of alcoholic beverages.

92

cient feeling, rather, a prolonged engorgement which both demands and refuses relief. The hypersensitive imagination fires
the drugged individual to enact the most extravagant sexual
stimulation, but the generative system will not co-operate. The
physical aspects of *kayf* are more akin to priapism than to
satyriasis, for in the latter case there is likely to be intense titillation attending friction of the penis. It is the superexcitation
of the brain but anesthesia of the penis, aggravated by persistent tumescence, which provokes general demoralization. All
attention is focused upon the penis, narcissistic libido is magnified out of all common proportion, and every last ounce of the
voluptuary's effort is concentrated in masturbational rubbing.

For a certain kind of sadomasochist, *kayf* is a paradisiac
blessing. He can, as it were, stimulate his penis unto eternity
without having to succumb to the end pleasure and detumescence. He can brandish a never-ending erection; he can abandon himself indefinitely to all sexual acts; he can sensually
satisfy any female on the face of the earth; and he can go beyond that to make of his potency an instrument of torture. His
only enemy is the orgasm or end pleasure; he must defy it to
the very death. Ejaculation and the loss of erection, the realities of universal quiescence, are the foes of his phantasy of
everlasting animation. What he loses in physical sensitivity,
he twice over makes up for in mental hyperesthesia: the exhila-
rating knowledge that he can perform the most fabulous erotic
feats with his omnipotent penis.(11)

_____

(11) *Of the two types of individuals just discussed, one craves and
pursues orgasm with a demoniacal intensity; and his failure to
achieve it, because of the effects of the drug, results in great frustration. The second type of individual is in this respect the antith-
esis of the first. He dreads nothing more than the orgasm—which
will puncture his megalomaniacal and other phantasies and bring
him crashing back to earth.*

93

The approach of the end pleasure is uncanny. In the fever of psychic delight there is first a neutral feeling, then a faint, growing tingling, in the glans penis. After that the dull but increasingly acute tickling sensations slowly emerge through the general numbness. This uncertain pleasure is unbearably pro-

---

The first of these types is doubtless the more typical (where Muslims are concerned). The second type reveals neurotic conflicts both serious and comparatively uncommon. A third type of individual— and his reaction is more typical of the Western male (under the influence of other drugs) than either of the two just mentioned— may derive a less frenetic but still considerable pleasure from the prolonged erection and deferred ejaculation. The elements of frustration and dread will be missing or minimal, and the benefits will far outweigh any drawbacks.

This type is the male who is somewhat anxious sexually, and who is uncertain of his potency, particularly his staying power, under ordinary conditions. While almost all males will take pleasure in the increased potency provided by certain drugs, the anxious or somewhat impotent male will particularly delight in this aspect. Diminished sensation, possibly failure to ejaculate, these will be of far less importance than the assurance that the erection will be sustained. Males of this type, who find a solution to their potency problems in narcotics, are more than usually likely to become addicts. If the drug is not addicting in a physiological way, then the risk of psychological addiction is still present.

Opium eventually renders the user impotent. It is physiologically addicting, though less so than its derivatives morphine and heroin, and less so for some Orientals than for Westerners generally. Hashish does not seem to be physiologically addicting in the usual sense. The addiction more closely resembles that of the alcoholic than of, say, the heroin user. Withdrawal symptoms do not occur unless the use has been long-term and excessive. Like opium, hashish may finally render the user impotent—but by general debilitation.

94

longed. The glans penis swells and throbs; the titillation seems almost benumbing and on the verge of pain, but no ejaculation occurs. The tempo of friction is heightened, whereupon the frozen sensations start to thaw, and suddenly the orgasm arrives.

Let us now consider Dr. Jacobus' observations concerning "The Peculiar Effect of Opium on the Organs of Generation:"

> According to my personal experience, and from avowals made to me by many Asiatic women, the effects produced by opium in moderate doses—say from ten to twenty pipes—are as follows:
>
> Under the influence of erotic excitement, either direct or merely mental, an erection is quickly produced if you want to copulate. But—and this has never been remarked by any other author—although the penis is in a very stiff erection, its nerves, and more particularly those of the glans, are anesthetized by the effects of the opium; and though the erection is strong, the emission on the contrary is much retarded and only takes place after a prolonged copulation.
>
> This same anesthetic effect is also produced in the nerves of the clitoris, the vagina, and the rectum of the woman; and the orgasm arrives very slowly. The constrictor muscles of the vagina, and especially those of the anus, undergo a kind of relaxation. Sodomy can be practiced much more easily, and without pain, even when the penis is of a disproportionate size.
>
> The stimulating effects of opium cease if more than fifteen or twenty pipes are taken. When a total of twenty-five or thirty pipes is reached, the erections are not complete; and at from thirty to forty pipes they are entirely wanting, in spite of the most energetic rubbing. Old opium smokers generally become impotent.

The orgasm under such circumstances, depending upon how much opium has been consumed, is often vapid and not decisively satisfying. Ejaculation is weak, the semen oozing rather than spurting from the penis. Semierection if not erection may continue for some time after the emission. The road to additional rubbing is now wide open, for irritation remains attendant upon congestion. The impulse is to repeat excitation and realize a stronger and more decisively satisfying climax. If the organ is in semierection, a few seconds of vigorous manual manipulation may make it perfectly stiff. The cycle of sexual response begins all over again and may continue until the *mekaiyif* falls senseless into a sleep of nervous exhaustion.

In the female, both opium and hemp may produce vaginal titillation and uterine congestion. The clitoris is swollen and throbbing with irritation; the woman's whole generative system may seem to be turgid and palpitating, and she too may masturbate or continue copulation until she faints from fatigue. Because she is often able to stand from ten to thirty orgasms or more, a woman may outlast a man by many hours.(12)

In India and Pakistan, *bhāng* or hemp is chewed or smoked like tobacco and is also made into an aphrodisiac drink called *sherbeh* (sherbet) or a narcotic confection known as *ma'jūn* (majoon). Majoon, which also contains datura (*dhattūra*, thorn apple) and other stimulating ingredients, has the reputation of keeping the penis erect for at least twenty-four hours. The *maded* (prolonger) or opium pill of India, and the *fesūkh* (re-

---

(12) *In general, hashish is preferred by the Arab and opium by the Chinese, the respective drug appealing to the respective temperament. However, the Arab sometimes uses opium and the Chinese, though quite rarely, uses hashish. Heroin and morphine, the opium derivatives used in the United States, also (in some persons) may prolong erection in the male and produce engorgement and intensify excitation in the female genitals and, sometimes, anus-rectum. These effects are likely to occur, where they occur at all, early in the drug user's experience. Later, male and female heroin and morphine addicts become impotent and frigid, and often sterile as well.*

tainer) or hemp wad of North Africa, are smoked, swallowed, or chewed along with betel nut.(13)

·¶·
___

(13) *Betel is to the East what tobacco is to the West, and untold millions, for centuries, have been habituated to its use. A great many persons have attributed aphrodisiac effects to betel chewing, but most moderns who have investigated betel deny that it could have aphrodisiac properties of any significance. It does induce a certain amount of euphoria and mental tranquility, and if there are any sexual benefits they must somehow reside in those effects and in suggestion. As for the combination of betel with hashish or opium, trustworthy accounts of the effects would seem to be wanting; however, there is little reason to suppose that the addition of betel to either of those narcotics would work any drastic change in their effects.*

Dhattūra (Datura stramonium), although seldom ever used in the West today, has a long and exceedingly colorful history and for centuries was a well-known and popular intoxicant in Europe. Datura, or Thorn Apple, belongs to the class of Solanaceae drugs, other sources of which are the plants Belladonna, Mandragora and the Henbanes. They contain the alkaloids atropine, hyoscyamine and scopolamine, among others. There is no doubt as to their sometimes-aphrodisiac effects, or that they may be deadly poisons.

The principal objection to the Solanaceae drugs, and it is a most powerful one, is the mental confusion accompanying the intoxication and its aphrodisiacal results. There may be what seem to be symptoms of grave illness, leading to the belief that death is imminent. Moreover, amnesia for whatever has occurred customarily deprives the user of the pleasure of recalling his erotic exploits. Toxicologists have attributed the dancing and flagellation manias of the Middle Ages, as well as some of the orgiastic behavior of witches, to the inhalation of Black Henbane fumes and to the consumption of Thorn Apple and other Solanaceae mixed in with alcoholic beverages.

97

Vaginally sensitive women throughout Asia and Africa sometimes employ these drugs to neutralize their genital nerves, but more often than not the drugs have the effect of making them nymphomaniacal. Like cantharides,(14) an opium pill is used dishonestly by the Muslims and Chinese of the Far East. It is frequently given to a man or woman in the form of a Mickey Finn, as Jacobus discovered:

> The women give it to their husbands or lovers either in meat or drink, and presently the man is as though he were half out of his wits. In Java it is said to cause such lust that the woman is often obliged to flee from the too energetic embraces of her lover.

A female under the erotic influence of hashish is reputed to be able to withstand and even enjoy the violent vaginal and anal assaults of well over a hundred men in succession. Thus it is utilized by many prostitutes, dancing girls, and other loose ladies in the Sudan, Somalia, Zanzibar, and other East African areas as well as at Timbuktu, Marrakesh, and sundry cities relatively unaffected by the meddlesome morality of the West. A *mekaiyifeh* (drug-intoxicated female) demands the deepest,

---

(14) *Cantharides (Spanish Fly) probably has a more extensive modern folklore in the West than any other aphrodisiac. It is usually taken orally, the powder being mixed in with some beverage, and when the substance is voided by urination there occurs an irritation of the bladder and of the urethra which produces powerful erection (and, in the female, genital excitement). Cantharides is a dangerous poison, often fatal; and when a less than lethal dose is administered, horrible suffering is still likely to result. The lore of the drug, which lamentably minimizes the great risks, has led to countless deaths and severe poisonings. Such cases still occur regularly today, although happily Cantharides is less widely used than in the past.*

most vehement and continuous thrusting. She wants a very large and rigid penis to produce the most intense friction and pressure, for the prolonged tension is almost maddening.

It habitually happens that an Arab female and a Negro male will take a little hashish, intent on making love the entire night without a moment's rest. The girl's reaction to the narcotic is that she desires desperately and deliriously to have the boy's penis unceasingly stroke her vagina for five or six hours straight. The Arab's *qirāb* (sheath) is three inches long and very narrow; the Negro's *qedzīb* (rod) is six inches long and fairly thick. The girl has no qualms or considerations; she jackknifes her legs, opens her thighs as wide as possible, and parts her labia with her fingers. The boy pounces upon her and she receives his fierce thrust full length; then he batters away at her without her batting an eyelash. Unless he is exceptionally sensitive, the male ordinarily lasts for about a half hour before his first ejaculation. Because the drug gives him increased capacity for two or three ejaculations without loss of erection, the act is prolonged for at least an hour. As long as the erection persists, friction is necessary; the male cannot stop, nor does he wish to. It is virtually impossible for him to withdraw. If he did so, he would be compelled to masturbate. In an hour the female is frantic, kicking and clawing in her crisis, desiring literally to devour the male organ with her womb. The excitement is so overwhelming that she swoons, losing and regaining her senses again and again.

Young Muslims seeking their first sexual experience at a smoker or coffeehouse are often given hashish by mischievous men and girls. When the youth approaches a woman with the resulting erection, a harmless variety of the ancient and dishonorable badger game is staged. The *fille de joie* teases and torments the cocky apprentice to the point where he is pressed to leave amid the laughter and seek his solace in a dark doorway. Occasionally the novice is manhandled and raped by primed pederasts, who take him by turns. The use (or rather abuse) of aphrodisiacs is so widespread in the East that masturbators and sodomists as well as fornicators are wont to join the seemingly endless array of hashish eaters and hormone enthusiasts. Arab, Hindu, and Chinese boys, looking for "kicks" or consummate thrills, take these ancient and modern activators lightheartedly; but they commonly end up in dark doorways, alleys, and other veiled places, abandoned to frenzied bouts of solitary and mutual masturbation and anal intercourse. If the boy is not driven to passionate self-stimulation he is inclined to rape, both anal and vaginal.

The mildest dose of opium is reputed among Orientals to yield about one hour of continuous genital stimulation, assuring the desideratum of at least three thousand phallic thrusts. We find poetic mention made of the opium pill in *Chin P'ing Mei:*

> Take but a speck of this, set it upon you, then
> Rush like a whirlwind to the bridal chamber.
> The first engagement will leave you full of vigor;
> The second, even stronger than before.
> Though twelve exquisite beauties, all arrayed in scarlet, wait
> your onset,
> You may enjoy each one, according to your fancy;
> And, all night through, erect your spear will stand.
> Soon, new strength will be given to limbs and belly;
> It will refresh the testicles, invigorate the penis.
> Each time, take but a grain or so.
> Your weapon will be merciless,
> Your manhood stiffened. Then at the first planting
> The seed will germinate.
> Ten women in one night will be as one to you;
> You'll feel no slackening of vital power.
> The old woman will knit her brows,
> The young one's strength will hardly stay the course.

100

When you are sated, and would give up the fight,
Swallow a mouthful of cold water. Then withdraw your
   weapon;
You will not be harmed.*

The effect of such a pill is vividly described throughout this Chinese classic: "He had worked long and lustily, yet his weapon was harder than ever, as stiff as an iron rod. Hsi-men worked for one whole hour."

Hsi-men mounted her in a fierce and ferocious manner, pushed himself forward and, while he pressed her thighs with his arms, drove his lotus stalk in with a marvelous sound. The lamp was shining and he rejoiced at the sight. The woman, who was lying beneath him on the bed, rose up to meet his thrusts and kindled even greater desire in the man above her. He put some red powder upon his member and inserted it once again; and seizing her firmly by the legs, he attacked her two or three thousand times. Golden Lotus' eyes closed and she began to tremble. "Darling," she whispered, "don't thrust so roughly; you will make my hair untidy."

The following scene is one of the most famous in Far Eastern erotic literature:

Hsi-men Ch'ing took off Golden Lotus' ornate scarlet-colored slippers, loosened the ribbons which bound her feet and tied them to the trellis so that she seemed like a golden dragon showing its claws. The woman's portal was wide open, and her purple valley was clearly visible and exposed to the vigilant watchman.

Hsi-men Ch'ing, taking his weapon in his hands, prepared to storm the breach. He strove with all his strength. Golden Lotus beneath him never ceased to murmur: "Darling, my

* Clement Egerton, *op. cit.*

101

darling." Golden Lotus lay weakened to the very core, so that she felt as if she were melting away, from toil and torment. Her starry eyes were half closed, and her body fell back limply upon the mat. "You are indeed a roguish enemy," she murmured. "You will be the death of me." Her voice trembled.

Hsi-men took from a pocket in his gown a case of love instruments. First he put on the clasp, and tied a sulphur ring about the root of evil. Not wishing to lance her, he played for a long while around the opening so that the woman cried furiously: "My sweetheart, my darling, either be a man quickly or I'll go out of my mind."

With one blow he seemed to penetrate her to the very marrow. Then he withdrew, and searched his pockets till he found the powder which procures a woman's pleasure. Smearing his weapon therewith, he thrust it into the frog's mouth. He attacked again, and instantly the warrior appeared tall and proud, full of fiery ardor. While Hsi-men admired his assault, Golden Lotus, lying on the mat, murmured with half-closed eyes: "O my bearded delight! O most magnificent of members! My darling, you don't know what you're putting into me. Your thing arouses me to fury. Spare me, I pray." Thus she pleaded shamelessly; but Hsi-men, putting his hands upon the mat to brace himself, straightway attacked with all his strength, now pulling out and anon stabbing in, charging down a hundred times to the deepest point before again withdrawing. The woman wiped off her tender blossom with a napkin, but to no avail. Her spring continued to trickle; and the warrior, still hard and ferocious, did not wish to stop fighting. "It is time," exclaimed Hsi-men, "for the monk to strike the gong." With a sudden thrust he reached the inmost arch, where within the gateway of the feminine citadel there lies what is like unto the stamen of a flower which, when touched by the victor, is affected with a wonderful pleasure. Golden Lotus felt pain and drew herself back, but inside her body the sulphur ring had already rattled and broken.

102

She closed her eyes and her breath came faintly; only a faint murmur issued from her lips, the tip of her tongue became icy cold, and her body fell back lifeless upon the mat.

There is one aspect that characterizes nearly all Oriental descriptions of the act of love: the vigor and violence of its execution and its participants, particularly the male.

There are two possible reasons for this: (1) Oriental males, who have highly developed sadomasochistic tendencies, wish not only to satisfy their mates in the most dynamic manner but also to subjugate them by means of continuous sexual intercourse. Thus the Oriental male wants to swive the Oriental female to the point of utter exhaustion, till she faints from repeated orgasms, or even to the very death—the Japanese *gokuraku-ojo* or "sweet death." (15) According to the Prophet Muhammed, to die in the glorious battle abed with one's belly on top is to die a martyr of love. The Caliph Harun er-Reshid was considered a hero of heroes because he died of heart failure during sexual congress.(16)

Dr. Van de Velde mentions "the intentionally violent spe-

·T·

(15) *The French describe the orgasm as "the little death," but fainting is not implied. Their "sweet death" is reserved for actual coital fatalities.*

(16) *As might be expected, in Christian countries death in coitus has been held to constitute a kind of final infamy on the part of debauched scoundrels. To attribute such a death to a man was to stamp him as the vilest variety of debauchee. Thus, anti-Catholics declared that various of the popes died fornicating. The popes in question might well have done so, but it is no longer possible to speak with certainty on the facts of the individual demises.*

A notable non-pope alleged to have died fornicating (with a blonde) was Attila the Hun.

103

cific movement in coitus to which many men sometimes resort during the act, and which is even more appreciated by their partners than by themselves." He adds that "this savage thrusting movement does not proceed from the conscious wish to heighten sensation by friction, for the special stimulus of friction is often keenest when the pressure is slightest. What both man and woman, driven by obscure primitive urges, wish to feel in the sexual act is the essential force of *maleness* which expresses itself in a sort of violent and absolute possession of the woman." (17)

(2) Oriental females, sensing this active-sadistic need on the part of the male and acknowledging the passive-masochistic impulse in themselves, respond to it by a reciprocal aggressiveness and/or a subtle passivity that invites an even more energetic assault which, designed to make them answer with equal activity, gives them the greatest pleasure and a rapid climax. The mutual orgasms are generally far stronger and more satisfying when induced by vigorous thrusting motions in the vagina, which would explain why violent vaginal masturbation is preferred by those who are deprived of this stimulation.

Throughout Chinese erotic episodes we find the female pleading and sighing for mercy, as if she were in dire pain. This is a beautiful example of Oriental subtlety and sensuousness. For an Oriental man encountering a woman who actively urges

---

(17) *Descriptions of such coital encounters often liken the penis to a sword, a dagger or some similar instrument, and the vocabulary is like that of fencing. The idea of stabbing is often present in the language of coition, and belongs equally to the thinking of both male and female—a fact about which much might be said. One reads of cases from time to time of girls who have injured themselves masturbating with swords, bayonets and other such weapons; swords and knives were thrust into the vaginas of witches by inquisitorial torturers; etc., etc.*

him on may feel passive or demasculinized and not consciously inclined to mutual response, but an Oriental man encountering a woman who begs him to be sparing will discover in this sweet supplication the incentive to drive her mercilessly on to orgasm with a vigor and vitality which she secretly encourages and enjoys. This is one of the prime artifices of sexual love, cultivated and practiced by the most accomplished courtesans and concubines in the East and in the West. Observant old Brantôme once wrote:

> The more a woman showeth herself rebellious and recalcitrant, so much the more doth a man wax ardent and push home the attack; and so having forced the breach, he doth use his victory more fiercely and savagely, and thereby giveth more pleasure to the woman.(18)

Among the "love instruments" employed by Hsi-men Ch'ing, the silver clasp is perhaps the most famous. Clamped about the base of the penis, its purpose is to prolong erection by preventing the blood from leaving the engorged organ, for which a rubber band is commonly used in the Occident.(19) Similar

·|·
_____

(18) *Another type of male, of course, prefers a more aggressive (or less subtle) female. Great delicacy is often required here, since too much aggression on the part of the female may chill the male's ardor, while the female may accomplish the same kind of psychical castration if her resistance persuades the male that he is not desired.*

(19) *Physicians often warn against the practice of applying some sort of tourniquet to the base of the penis, stating that it will result in ulceration. Given the long history and considerable incidence of the practice, we are uncertain as to the extent to which such unqualified predictions of calamity may be morally rather than purely medically inspired. Obviously damaging abuses are possible, and it is probably best to take no chances.*

105

to the Chinese clasp is the Japanese "pleasure ring," which is clasped about the penis to prolong erection, increase phallic thickness, and heighten vaginal friction. Many of them are ribbed or studded, the better to stimulate the perfectly smooth walls of the typical Japanese vagina. The sheath of the typical Chinese woman, being crinkled or delicately corrugated, generally does not necessitate the use of a ribbed rubber "pleasure ring."

The sulphur ring, which is bound around the neck of the glans, shields the sensitive corona and the frenal area against direct rubbing and a rapid orgasm. The sulphur, like alum in Muslim use, is intended as an astringent to tighten and constrict the vaginal walls and as a resolvent to absorb excess preorgastic secretions. The red powder with which Hsi-men Ch'ing sprinkled his saliva-moistened penis served to excite the vagina. It is composed of cinnamon, mustard, pepper, ginger, and other irritating substances which reputedly produce an extreme swelling of the vaginal mucous membranes and, at the same time, cause a tight compression of the canal upon the penis, which procures an intense mutual pleasure.

Other aphrodisiac devices, known under such names as the "hedgehog," the "tickler," and the "hairy ring," are studded with soft bristles, fine feathers, or blunt points to create extreme excitement in the smooth and insensitive vagina. As advertised, when a man uses one of these on a woman "her feeling will go to heaven; she will be tickled to death." (20) In many females the pleasure ring increases vaginal tension to such an unbearable extent, attended by a violent titillation, that the numerous and rapidly repeated venereal spasms are

---

(20) Cf. the famed "French ticklers" and similar devices of the West. It is commonly necessary to purchase them "under the counter," as distinguished from the openness with which they are displayed and sold in the "sex stores" of Japan.

actually painful. As seen in the foregoing episode, the female shakes and murmurs in a delirious fit and finally faints. Even upon recovery she is weak and trembling; and her vagina throbs with a half-burning, half-itching sensation. The successive orgasms experienced are said to number from five to ten or from ten to thirty or more, depending upon the extent of stimulation and the woman's capacity to endure intolerable tickling and then gnawing pain before swooning in a spasmodic ecstasy.

Witness this wild and woolly scene, as well known as the last:

> In his sleeve he had a silken kerchief. He opened it. Inside were a silver clasp, a lover's cap, a sulphur ring, a white silk ribbon with medicinal properties, and all manner of things for increasing passion. Porphyry set her head upon the pillow.
>
> She lifted her ivory-white legs so that the chicken's tongue appeared. Hsi-men asked her to put the medicine inside her thighs; while he himself fastened the silver clasp to the base of his member, added the sulphur ring, and anointed his pubes with perfume. Then the woman took his treasure in her hand, guided it in, and enjoyed an almost unceasing embrace.
>
> "Don't be afraid to move violently," said Porphyry. "Wouldn't you like me to raise my legs higher?"
>
> Hsi-men tied the woman's legs back to the bedposts with a pair of ribbons, and bowing down upon her he pressed her body and served her. Unceasingly the fluid of love flowed from her, like the juice from a digesting snail.
>
> Then Hsi-men, ablaze with lust, turned the woman upside down and attacked her blossom at the back door. Hsi-men advanced slowly; and Porphyry, by feeling with her hand, found that he had finished only half the journey. With his manhood planted in her body, she turned her head and entertained him with her alluring expression. "My darling," said she, "please go in slowly. Your root is too big for me to bear." Hsi-men

107

raised her legs so as to see the motions of his advances and retreats. "Porphyry, my child," he said, "there is nothing I enjoy more than this."

Then Porphyry raised herself upon her hands and knees so as to receive the river of life. Hsi-men was in such a rapture of delight that the fluid seemed to flow like a torrent of water. Afterwards he withdrew himself, still wearing the ring; Porphyry milked him with her lips, and they lay down on the bed together.

The "lover's cap" mentioned in the foregoing episode is the silken Chinese equivalent of the Japanese "playing rubber" or condom. The "medicine" which Hsi-men Ch'ing asks the omnivorous Porphyry to put "inside her thighs" (between the lips of her vulva) is an irritant designed to excite and supersensitize her "chicken's tongue" (clitoris) and "frog's mouth" (vaginal orifice). Inserted into the "heart of the flower" (vagina), such ointment or readily dissoluble pills fire the feminine sexual system with the savage desire for constant and furious friction.

Decisive orgastic relief rarely follows the use of such aphrodisiacs; instead, there is a slow and often tormenting release from insufferable tension and a gradual diminution of painful pleasure. Mental and physical exhaustion, or even coma, may incapacitate the woman for from one to several days. Even a strong, highly passionate female, ready and able to endure and survive such venereal violence without suffering from the usual enervating effects, nonetheless experiences an incessant tingling and smarting sensation in her vagina, attended by a continual swelling and hyperesthesia of the clitoris, which becomes permanently enlarged in many Oriental females. Masturbation or additional coitus only aggravate the condition and delay the process of restoration. An examination of Far Eastern females of all social classes reveals numerous case histories of compulsive vaginal and clitoral masturbation, promiscuous vaginal and anal copulation, sapphism (cunnilingus or lip-tongue stimulation of the vulva) and tribadism (rubbing of the genitals against those of another female), and other lesbian activities resulting from the immoderate use of aphrodisiacs. A morbid enlargement, protrusion, and extreme excitability of the *glans clitoris* and *labia minora* commonly characterize the Oriental nymphomaniac, who frequently contracts uterine cancer or less dangerous disorders as a result of the almost unbelievable abuse to which she submits her body for the sake of "kicks" and having a "good time."

Jacobus observed that the Muslim women of Southeast Asia, many of whom are mutilated by clitoridectomy and nymphotomy, are wont to drink an aphrodisiac beverage containing powdered cantharides (Spanish fly) just before coition. The drug produces an intense irritation of the vaginal mucous membranes. This insufferable itching permits no immediate relief and eventually leads to sexual promiscuity. The same practice is followed in the Sudan as well as among the Swahili of Zanzibar, where the Negro menfolk connive at supersensitizing their nymphotomized and clitoridectomized females. East African Muslims (including the Egyptians) actively encourage the feminine use of aphrodisiacs in order to keep their womenfolk, otherwise unrestrained and independent, in a peculiar sort of sexual subjection. In other words, by making their females the slaves of self-indulgence and sensual luxury, Muslim males manage with some success to minimize the effects of the primarily matriarchal status quo.

The tendency to excess also characterizes the Oriental writer, who effectively employs exaggeration in order to get his point across to the reader. Even in works of fiction, such as *Chin P'ing Mei*, we must not mistake this deliberate magnification as pure ignorance or credulity on the part of the author. As Burton notes, "systematic exaggeration is held necessary to impressionize an Oriental audience." Why? Needless to say, by reason of the brutal reality of their existence and a traditional preoccupation with violence and venery, which realistically presented impresses virtually no one.

The classical Jews took a fancy to portraying their sacred heroes as victims of satyriasis. As for the man who is endowed with extraordinary *'ōn* (genital power), "water shall flow from his buckets" (Numbers 24:7, *yizzel mēm mi-dōlyāv*, semen shall pour out of his testicles); "his seed shall be in many waters" (*zera'ō be-mēm rebbīm*, his semen shall be in many vaginas). Exaggeration plays a prime role in Oriental life and literature as a sledge-hammer device to stir almost shock-proof people into erotic reaction and as a medicament for phallic inferiority fears and related potency and fertility anxieties. Exaggeration or extravagance, be it in fantasy or in reality, is also a clear reflection of Eastern hedonism and fatalism.

We read in the Babylonian Talmud:

> Rab Judah said in Rab's name: "Even during David's illness he fulfilled the conjugal rights [eighteen marital duties] of his eighteen wives, as it is written (Ps. 6:6), *I am weary with my groaning; all the night make I my bed to swim; I water my couch with my tears.*"

By so doing, King David was observing to the letter the law of Moses (Exodus 21:10): "Her food, her clothing, and her craving for copulation shall he not diminish." Even the Sabbath Song of the Hebrews tells how the groom embraces the bride "and does what is pleasing to her by continuous grinding." The Talmudists add:

> And we read (I Kings 1:15), *And Bathsheba went in unto the king into the chamber.* Rab Judah said in Rab's name: "On that occasion Bathsheba dried herself thirteen times."

When Rab Judah says that Bathsheba dried herself thirteen times, he alludes to the tradition that she and David had sexual intercourse thirteen times in succession; and after each orgasm, according to Mosaic law and custom, Bathsheba was obliged to wash and/or dry her vulva. The Talmud notes, referring to II Samuel 11:2 ("And it came to pass, in the early evening, that David arose from off his bed"), that "he copulated by day instead of night so that he might be free from desire by night." The number of times that King David discharged his vital essence into the bodies of his eighteen wives, in order that he might enjoy a good night's sleep after draining himself of desire during the day, is vividly revealed by his own words:

> I am tired of my moaning; every night I flood my bed with tears [Heb. *dim'āth*, prostatic and/or seminal fluid]; I soak my couch with my weeping.
>
> My strength is exhausted through my groaning all the day long; my moisture [semen] is dried up like the drought of summer.
>
> I am poured out like water; my moisture is evaporated as by the heat of the hot season; I am weary of my weeping [continual ejaculations].

The Talmud also tells us that Samson was blessed by Yahveh with "great potency." Rab Judah said in the name of Rab: "His manly strength [sexual virility] was like a fast-flowing stream [during sexual activity Samson never ceased to ejaculate]." In its commentary upon Judges 16:21, "And he did grind in the prison house," the Talmud reads:

> Rabbi Johanan said: "*Grind* means nothing else than sexual intercourse, for thus it is stated (Job 31:10), *Then let my wife grind unto another*. It teaches that everyone [of the Philistines] brought his wife to him [Samson] at the prison, that she might bear a child by him who would be as strong as he was."

111

Rabbi Papa adds: "That is what the proverb says, *Before the wine drinker set wine; before the plowman an untilled field.*" According to Talmudic tradition, the Philistines had a prime purpose as old as time in capturing Samson: to breed a nation of supermen. By blinding him, they obliterated the risk of his becoming psychologically impotent as a result of seeing those whom he was compelled to impregnate. Sustained erection and orgastic response depended purely upon friction of his penis, for blindness blotted out the psychic factors involved in tumescence and detumescence. Mention of this ancient practice of sexual slavery is made in Lamentations 5:13: "They took the young men to grind."

It is estimated by commentators that Samson swived some three thousand Philistinian females during his grinding sojourn at the prison in Gaza. The Talmud offers some illumination on the subject of sexual slavery:

> If it be suggested that idolaters compelled him to copulate, surely it may be pointed out that Raba stated: "There can be no compulsion in sexual intercourse, since erection depends entirely on the will!"

It is apparent that Raba was not familiar with the principle of "pleasure without responsibility." The *Lust-ohne-Schuld* or "gratification-without-guilt" theory implies that Samson satisfied his senses without contending with his conscience. Rabbi Hiyya hypothesized that the Philistines seized Samson, who was playing with Delilah, "while he was in the state of erection," thus explaining how they compelled him to copulate with the three thousand females. Others, however, contend that the Philistines rubbed Samson's penis erect with their hands after they blinded him. Loss of sight quickened his senses, making his penis respond rapidly to friction. In Judges 16:25–27 we read how the phallus-worshiping Philistines suffered the naked Hercules of Israel (21) to offer seminal sacrifice in appeasement of their fish (phallus) god Dagon. A cabalistic connotation is attached to the Hebrew verb *sāhheq* (to rub repeatedly), which in Arabic is *sehhq* (to rub or pound the genitals in masturbation). Thus all the lords and ladies of the Philistines looked on while Samson rubbed (or beat) his penis repeatedly with his hands.

So the ancient scribes, in creating the fabulous fables of the Old Testament, intimated that the superior might of the Philistines was attributable to their being the very seed of Samson.

The celebrated Arabian traditionist Jabir bin 'Abdallah, a disciple of Muhammed, sets forth the following tradition:

> When the Most Manifest Book *El-Qurān* was being revealed to our Apostle by the archangel Gabriel, Muhammed abstained, during sexual commerce with his wife, from the spermatic ejaculation into the genital organs of Lady Khedijeh.

Muhammed, rather than practicing *coitus interruptus* (*'āzil* or "withdrawal"), never ejaculated at all (*coitus reservatus, imsāk* or "withholding"), but purposed in saving his semen to

---

(21) *The Hercules of Western mythology was a sexual athlete of the most formidable prowess. On one occasion, for example, he deflowered all half a hundred daughters of Thespios in a single night. Sculptures of Hercules usually cover his genitals, which typically are of no more than human proportions, with a fig leaf or some garment; but the stout cudgel he carries is reputed to represent his penis. Such a Hercules with cudgel, high atop a monument, dominates the city of Kassel in Germany; and it is said that German maidens sometimes visit him surreptitiously, to ask that the males they have chosen for their lovers be endowed with Herculean virility.*

113

preserve his vital strength and have it flow into his bloodstream for aiding and invigorating mental power. Jabir adds that the Prophet practiced "keeping it in" or "holding back the sperm" for several hours. Feeling refreshed, he would then retire to his mountain retreat for inspiration.

Muhammed employed *coitus reservatus* to prepare his sensitive brain and nervous system for self-hypnosis and extrasensory perception.(22) Muhammed was an epileptic, of extremely delicate and galvanic constitution, and prolonged sexual tension supercharged his telepathic faculty until hallucinations marked the advent of detumescence. These visions, accelerating the release of tension without emission, produced a deceptive or delusive sensation of vitality offset by a weakening and anesthetization of the entire generative apparatus. The fact that none of the Prophet's other wives ever bore him any children suggests that Muhammed so conditioned his mind and inured his senses against the end-pleasure during his early years of protracted copulation with Khedijeh that in later life, when she lay in her grave and when he built his harem, Muhammed could no longer achieve orgasm and ejaculation except in his sleep or involuntarily during the day. Hence the Apostle of Allah ruled that "the emission of seed in wet dreams of dalliance or at the sight of a strange woman does not violate the Fast of Ramazan."

One of the ancient principles of Yoga and other ascetic systems of self-discipline is the renunciation of erotic pleasures and/or sublimation of sexual energy. Continence is encouraged, and sexual intercourse is recommended only for procrea-

---

(22) *Similarly the magicians of the West traditionally have abstained from sexual intercourse before the commencement of and during their magical operations. The production of hallucinations or visions by sustained erotic excitation without climax is also a method known to Western occultists, but its use is rare.*

114

tive purposes and as a means of achieving psychic union with the divine forces of nature. This union (*yōga*) is realized through the physical act of *coitus reservatus,* which is a denial of the negative factors of termination and death (ejaculation and detumescence) and an acceptance of the positive elements of commencement and life (erection and eternal tumescence). The denial of the end reality is akin to the concept of reincarnation or the transmigration of souls. It is also related to the almost universal belief in life after death. Moreover, the *lingam* of Lord Shiva is eternally erect. It is the symbol of everlasting vitality.

Dhāranaratī (prolonged copulation) is sometimes a refined form of masochism which seeks to retain the erotic tension and reject the terminating pleasure. This conscious retention of tumescence but rejection of crisis-provoking titillation has a narcotic effect on the senses, for sexual sensations are then replaced by nirvanic illusions. The erection slowly subsides without the knowledge and control of the conscious will, and neither orgasm nor ejaculation occurs.

In ancient and esoteric Taoist and Tantric doctrine, the utmost prolongation of the act of sexual intercourse is said to be spiritually, physically, mentally, and supernaturally beneficial to both male and female. If the man retains his semen for at least an hour, then if he ejaculates or does not ejaculate at all but allows his penis to soften in the woman's vagina "and his sperm to flow into his bloodstream to nourish his brain," it was taught that his entire system is strengthened, his wits are sharpened, his nerves are solidified, and his potency and virility increased immeasurably. By the retention of his own vital fluid, and by the absorption of the woman's essence, he is made a new man! (23)

ᛏ

(23) *It is possible to find many warnings against* coitus reservatus, *including predictions of eventual impotence as an inevitable con-*

According to the T'ang Dynasty "Classic of Medicine," sexual intercourse with young girls and retention of the sperm are conducive to long life and good health. Man is nourished and invigorated by the vaginal secretions of a plump nymphet, and a nubile female is strengthened and kindled by the spermatic fluid of a potent male. With Taoist know-how, male and female are said to be able to engage in and enjoy continuous genital congress for twenty days. The secret: prolonged erection, limited motion, and delayed ejaculation.

While it is recommended that the male retain his semen, the female is supposed to climax as many times as possible, and

---

sequence. However, the experience of the Oneida Community in New York, where coitus reservatus was systematically practiced, along with a wealth of other evidence, casts doubt upon these ominous forecasts—though it is always possible that there may be damage in individual cases.

Whatever the results for Westerners, practitioners of Yoga and similar disciplines quite possibly escape any ill effects. The practitioner of Yoga sometimes acquires a degree of control over his body and all of its processes that seems simply unbelievable to the Western observer, even when he sees the performances of the yogin with his own eyes and measures them with his own instruments. An accomplished yogin may cause his penis (by mental direction of the flow of blood) to repeatedly tumesce and detumesce; and he is able to induce ejaculation in the same way.

"Mental masturbators" are found in the West as well, though they are less common, and their usual technique is excitation and termination of excitation by means of mental imagery. (Sometimes, autohypnosis is employed with suggestions of tactile stimulation.) The practice of inducing orgasm by means of mental imagery is not without its perils, since involuntary ejaculations may occur when the individual encounters objects or situations resembling those utilized by his imagination to precipitate climax.

while the man must not suffer fatigue due to an "excess" of emissions, the woman may freely tax herself to exhaustion and eventually faint from "excessive" stimulation of her genital senses.

Multiple vaginal and clitoral orgasms are to be brought about by external friction and prolonged internal penetration. It is absolutely necessary that the female experience her venereal spasm, which is said to supply and replenish the vital essence emitted by the male. The extent of the male's enrichment depends upon how copious and powerful this feminine paroxysm is. He must masturbate her repeatedly and persistently, for direct rubbing of the clitoris sets off a strong and torrential climax. He must, while holding his penis in her vagina, masturbate her clitoris with his fingers until all of her essence is extracted and absorbed.

Girls between the ages of thirteen and nineteen are said to discharge an abundance of mucous membrane secretions, which energize and revitalize the male. They respond rapidly to clitoral manipulation and are able to endure continuous excitation without tiring. The longer the penis stays in the vagina, and the longer the girl can receive stimulation and achieve orgasms, the more vital essence is absorbed and exchanged. Moreover, the rule that the girl is to have as many orgasms as possible is backed by the belief that the female essence or *yin* is limitless in quantity and that a woman can climax continuously without suffering from any enervating loss. She therefore becomes even more vigorous and vital after each successive spasm. The male, however, suffers a devitalizing loss and so must retain or replenish his vital essence or *yang*. Ejaculation may be withheld in the case of girls because they are very fluid and do not necessarily need to absorb any seminal fluid, although they do "soak up and benefit by" the "unceasing stream" of prostatic and other glandular liquids

117

which flow out of the erect and hypertense penis. But in the case of women, who tend to "dry out" as the years go by, semen is insatiably absorbed and extremely beneficial to their well-being.

Thus, for the sake of psychophysical vitality, Taoists and Tantrists encourage continual copulation with fluid females— and the juicier the better, the more the merrier! Man's vital forces would become almost superhuman were he to serve a sufficient number of girls in succession.

One of the traditional qualities of an ideal Chinese girl for carnal intercourse is a "juicy vagina." Among the signs of pleasure in a girl is "vaginal flow," which is provoked in profusion by a "rapid movement of the jade stick." "Hardening of the breasts" indicates the approach of orgasm, for the pulsating tension in the genitals by reflex action causes the nipples to swell. When the girl raises her legs, she desires a "deeper penetration" and wants her vagina rubbed vigorously by the penis. "Squeezing the man's body with her legs" is an expression of supreme excitement and pleasure, indicating that the titillation has become so intense that she can scarcely bear it. "Moving the body from side to side" indicates her desire for a rotary or corkscrewing motion of the jade stick. When her loins begin to shake, and when there is "trembling between her anus and cunnus," the girl is about to have her orgasm. Lifting of the loins, or pressing up for full penetration, is the signal of ecstatic crisis and "complete happiness" followed by a violent throbbing of the vagina and a torrential burst of fluid; while "relaxation of arms and legs" marks the end of orgasm and the advent of inner peace.

During vaginal intercourse, the ideal Chinese girl has a copious surge of secretions. Her body shivers and shakes; she is quick to climax. The inner and outer slipperiness of her sexual organs testifies to her passionate receptivity. Legend has it that the fabulous Emperor Shih Huang-ti, Builder of the Great

Wall of China, had continuous coition with twelve hundred such girls, whereby he became a saint in paradise.

With as many as a dozen wives and several hundred concubines, the rulers of the Celestial Empire were avid adherents of the Taoist code. By conscious control of the mental faculties as well as the muscular and nervous systems, they slowly but surely trained and conditioned themselves to prolong vaginal coitus indefinitely. By delaying sexual sensation and emission, an emperor could serve several women in a single night without ejaculating more than once or twice. Even then, however, this orgastic response occurred voluntarily. Constitutionally sensitive officials were sometimes obliged to use narcotics, generally mild doses of opium, to aid them in maintaining stiffness and retaining semen. Emperor Yang Wang, a famous fornicator of the Sui Dynasty, had a very sensitive penis but would mount from twelve to twenty females every other night of the week. He lusted after little girls between the ages of six and ten. Although his penis often remained in erection for twelve hours straight, with the aid of opium Yang ejaculated only two or three times at the most—sometimes not at all. When he felt the spasms of orgasm arriving, the emperor would contract his anal and perineal muscles as tightly as possible and so delay the advent of ejaculation.

Sexual relations with prepubertal and pubescent girls became systematized throughout the Orient. The Taoist idealization of a high and hairless vulva reflects the Chinese predilection for a nymphet or even younger girl child. Erotic preoccupation with little girls, known technically as nymphophilia, is still commonplace and customary throughout Asia and Africa.(24) We find it institutionalized in some areas,

---

(24) The term nymphophilia, meaning the adult male's sexual attraction to and intercourse with female children, is proposed in Forbidden Sexual Behavior and Morality. While imperfect, it is to be

where the child bride (25) wedded and bedded between the

---

preferred over the more common pedophilia, which usually does not distinguish between the sexes, and which in any case should be applied only to homosexual desire for and intercourse with boys.

The term nympholepsia, defined as "nymph bewitchment," has occasionally been used. However, nympholepsy in everyday parlance is a kind of trance state induced by indulgence in erotic daydreaming. Another possibility might be parthenophilia; however, this term is rejected as laying too great a stress upon the aspect of virginity; and parthenophilia is best reserved for the sexual desire for virgins, which may be quite a different phenomenon from nymphophilia. Parthenophagy (very rare) has been used to denote a sexual appetite for young girls; but the term is correctly applied only to the cannibalistic cravings of psychotic homicides (lycanthropes, victims of other theriomorphic delusions, etc.).

(25) We in the West have conveniently all but forgotten that the Common Law age of consent was ten years, that the French penal code raised the limit from eleven to thirteen years just a century ago, that England only in 1929 abandoned the ancient Christian usage which placed the age for marriage (of the female) at twelve years, etc., etc.

Marriages of child brides were commonplace in the United States until quite recently, and still come to light occasionally, provoking great public outrage. However, such marriages were probably as successful as most others. The same is to be said of the child marriages traditional in the East, and which in many cases have been prohibited not because of the "enlightenment" of the peoples involved but only through the application of pressures by Western do-gooders.

What needs to be understood here is that marriage was often (and is often) the best alternative available to many young girls. The child bride ordinarily came from a home where poverty was severe, and she was seldom ever "deprived of a happy childhood" as senti-

ages of three and nine makes Lolita look like Whistler's mother.

Nymphophilia and child marriages are products of what the Arabs call *khebl-hhūrī* or "nymph madness," which is a peculiar passion involving an adult male's animal desire for an immature female. This powerful and prevalent manifestation of the masculine libido causes no end of controversy and confusion in the Western world, while in the East there are but a handful of females who do not have their vaginas penetrated at least once by the male penis before the age of puberty. If penetration is not effected through experimentation between children, who learn about and witness the act of copulation from their earliest years, it is the result of rape or some milder form of seduction. The sexuality of Oriental boys and girls is

---

mental and meddlesome matrons, egged on by pothersome parsons, were pleased to suppose. It is the old story: a minimum of concern for the well-being of the people involved; a maximum of concern for the delay and prevention of sexual intercourse.

In China, selling little girls to prospective husbands, or to brothel-keepers, was often the only alternative to infanticide or starvation. The American child bride frequently came from a scarcely less desperate background, and it was rare that her situation was not improved at least slightly by marriage.

This was true not only in an economic sense. Such girls were seldom sensitive types, and the marriage bed held for them few or none of the horrors depicted by imaginative (and sometimes wishful) reformers. Many girls today could improve their lot by marrying at twelve or thirteen (when in many cases they would be escaping, among other things, incest at home and neighborhood promiscuity). But at a time when sexual maturity is arriving earlier than ever before in this country, and is accompanied by an unparalleled sophistication, many of our states have responded to the challenge by raising the age of consent, to as high as twenty-one years in some cases.

121

aroused to a feverish pitch, and from the time they are able to walk their erotic impulses are constantly besieged and abused.

Little girls succeed where little boys fail to resurrect the drooping desires of the jaded lecher. Shaykh Sadiq bin Tebib el-Isfahani, Persian author of the *Bāh Nāmeh* (Book of Lust), offers us the following observations:

> The desire to deflower a virgin is an acquired taste, but it is nonetheless the acme of sensual delight.
>
> Is the prevalent desire of enjoying little girls an original dictate of natural lust, or is it a symptom of refined experience or impotent fastidiousness?
>
> This lust after the untouched morsel I take not to be of an original nature, but to result from much experience and dalliance with women. When satiety begins to set in, I esteem the tender child to be, with respect both to the mind and body of the voluptuary, the highest aggravation of sensual delight.
>
> I mean not only in the coyness and resistance which she makes to his efforts, but when he is on the point of accomplishing them and when, in pity to a tender virgin's sufferings, he is entreated not to break fiercely in. The resistance which the small and as yet unopened mouth of bliss makes to his eager endeavors serves only, and that on a physical principle, to strengthen the instrument of his attack, and concurs with the instigation of his ardent fancy to reinforce his efforts, to unite all the co-operative powers of enjoyment, and to produce an emission copious, rapid, and enrapturing.
>
> Fancy has been known repeatedly to heighten fruition. In this case, part of the delight arises from considering that the most precious part of your body is firmly fixed in the delicious center of her body, and that you feel the convulsive wrigglings of the little nymph.
>
> The time of enjoying immature beauty seems to be while yet no ringlets adorn the tender mount, when all is like her

lily hand, both bare and smooth, and while her bosom boasts only of a general swell rather than distinct orbs.(26)

In accordance with Arabian marriage customs, 'Ayisheh bint Abu Bekr, Muhammed's famous child bride, experienced the penetration of the Prophet's penis into her vagina when she was only six years old. Islamic erotologists theorize that the premature introduction of highly imaginative and easily excitable girls to repeated sexual stimulation is the principal cause of their becoming promiscuous and even nymphomaniacal. They support their theory by citing as prime examples those wives and daughters of the Prophet who were subjected to constant copulation in early childhood and who subsequently developed an indiscriminate or "excessive" craving for genital excitation. 'Ayisheh cuckolded her husband more than Mus-

<hr/>

(26) A common motive for rapes and seductions of small children encountered in the East—the craving for heightened sensation resulting from greater friction—is almost unknown in the contemporary West. In the West, rapes of little children are committed either by mental defectives, ignorant and brutal persons who care nothing for the age and condition of their victim, or by deviates whose psychopathological motives may vary.

A Western motive of the past, now rare, was the Satanist's desire to do evil by defiling or corrupting the (pure and innocent) child. This last-mentioned motive is as alien to the East as is the pursuit of greater friction by intercourse with infantile organs to the present-day West. The sexual use of children by jaded individuals seeking novel titillations, and by senile old men, is met with in all civilized countries. Some of the psychopathological motivations, particularly the more well-defined sadistic ones, are also universal among civilized (and some "primitive") peoples. Parthenophilia, or so-called defloration mania, may be sadistic or merely vicious. It has also, at times, been a fad.

123

lim historians dare to admit; while Umm Kulthum, Muhammed's youngest daughter, is one of the *imthāl* or "proverbial examples" of the Arabians for adultery and debauchery.

There is an old Arab tradition that a woman would prefer an additional inch of penis to anything this world or the next can offer her. The prophet Ezekiel cries out against the exaggerated lusts of luxurious Israel: "You have prostituted your beauty and spread your legs wide open to everyone who passes by, and have multiplied your whoredoms. You have played the whore with the Egyptians, your lustful neighbors, who are great of flesh [big of penis]."

The Egyptians were, as the Romans regarded them, *bene vasatos* (men with meaty members). This feminine fixation on a "fat" phallus first became noticeable among the Jews not when they were in Egypt, where such "fetishes" were readily obtainable yet where the need was not felt for them, but much later and upon the institution of a law stating that girls may be wedded and bedded at the age of three. This extraordinary *mishnāh* was enacted by none other than Moses after the venereal plague at Shittim, which rendered all postnubile females unfit for copulation.(27)

Consequently, the proportions of the adult penis as seen by the child were permanently fixed in the young and imaginative mind. Combine this psychic exaggeration with the physical pleasure and pain experienced during the initial act of intercourse, which usually involved only the insertion of the glans

---

(27) *As recently as the seventeenth century three-year-old girls and boys were being burned to death or severely punished in Europe for abominably copulating with demons, witches and sorcerers. Strong sexual passions (for intercourse) were attributed to the youngest children, and none other than the great Jean Bodin, one of the most eminent legal authorities of his time, declared that six years is the appropriate age of consent for the female.*

between the labia and the stretching or breaking of the hymen, and we may easily understand why the Hebrew woman was intensely masochistic and even in many respects erotomaniacal. Moreover, the constant extension, distention, and friction to which the infantile vagina of the little Israeli girl was subjected by the well-developed adult penis resulted in the fact that when the innocent child became a worldly woman she necessarily (even compulsively) sought and demanded a large penis for her psychophysical satisfaction. The subsequent slackness of the adult vagina, which had received all its wear and tear in early childhood, was instrumental in leading the Israeli male into anal intercourse and pederasty; whence the tremendous growth of public and religious prostitution to serve the new varieties of sexual taste.

In Ezekiel 23:32 we find allusion made to the spacious genitals of the promiscuous Israeli female: "You shall drink of your sister's cup [kōs, coynte], which is deep and large [wide]." Kōs is analogous to the Arabic kus (cunt, vulva).

In the twenty-third chapter of his chronicle Ezekiel examines the extravagant whoredoms of Aholah and Aholibah, personifications of the two great sister cities of Samaria and Jerusalem, notorious for the general promiscuity and prostitution of their feminine populations. He announces that "they played the whore in Egypt; they played the whore in their youth. There were their breasts pressed and squeezed, and there were the teats of their virginity handled and bruised. . . . They multiplied their whoredoms in calling to mind the days of their youth, when the Egyptians lay with them and battered their bosoms, and when they took as lovers those whose flesh [penises] is like the flesh of asses and whose fluid [ejaculations] is like the fluid of horses. Thus they longed for the lewdness of their youth, when the Egyptians pressed their paps and stroked the nipples of their nubility."

According to the account of Ezekiel, the women of Israel

125

increase their inordinate licentiousness when they see the long thick penises of handsome young Assyro-Babylonian warriors or *qō'āim* (rutting stallions). Since the Chaldeans, like the Egyptians, had large and well-proportioned penises, the lustful females of Israel abandoned themselves to those "whose genital members were like the genital members of asses and whose seminal emissions were like the seminal emissions of horses." We understand by this that while the penis of the Israeli male was relatively short and thin, the virile instrument of the Chaldean male hung down long and thick between his sinewy thighs; and that while the Israeli males ejaculated only modest amounts, the semen of Chaldean males poured out in thick milky torrents like the copious ejaculations of horses and mules (in Biblical Hebrew, *zerīmāh*, from *zārīm*; a cloudburst or violent gush of water). Jeremiah (5:8) mentions the genital delight of Jewish women as being *sūsīm mūzānīm* (fat stallions, well-fed lusty horses) or *meyuzzānīm* (*bene vasati*, men with weighty tools). *Māzōn* (meaty-membered) is a sworder of the first order, well-provided with a long thick instrument.

After the conquest of Midian and Moab, and the great venereal plague, Moses says to his people (Numbers 31:15–18):

> "Have you saved all the women alive? Behold, these caused the children of Israel . . . to commit evil against the Lord by way of Baal-Peor. . . . Now therefore . . . kill every woman who has known man by lying with him; but all the young girls, who have not known a man by lying with him, keep alive for yourselves."

All the pubescent and postpubertal females among the Midianites and Moabites had engaged in such extensive and promiscuous intercourse that they were branded as breeders of venereal disease. Since the only females left fit for marriage and wholesome relations were prepubescent virgins, the following law (which is found in the Babylonian Talmud) was instantly enacted:

> Rabbi Joseph said: "Come and hear! A maiden aged three years and a day may be acquired in marriage by coition."
>
> *Mishnāh:* A girl of the age of three years and one day may be betrothed, subject to her father's approval, by sexual intercourse. If one is younger than this age, intercourse with her is like putting a finger in the eye.
>
> *Gemārā:* Our Rabbis taught: "A girl of the age of three years may be betrothed by sexual intercourse." But the Sages say: "Only one who is three years and one day old."
>
> An objection was raised: "A girl of the age of three years and even one of the age of two years and one day may be betrothed by sexual intercourse."
>
> It is written (Num. 31:18), *But all the female children that have not known man by lying with him, keep alive for yourselves;* but do not spare them if they have known man by lying with him. Consequently, it must be said that Scripture speaks of one who is fit (one who has attained the age of three years and one day) for copulation, not one who had actually experienced it.

The Mosaic tradition concerning feminine eligibility for sexual intercourse is an indisputable exposition of the systematic nymphophilia of olden Israel. Today, in many parts of North Africa, Arabia, and India, girls are wedded and bedded between the ages of five and nine; and no self-respecting female remains unmarried beyond the time of puberty. Among African Jews, for example, girls are routinely mated with older boys between the tender ages of three and five; and no socially acceptable female remains unwed, whether she be prostitute or lesbian, after her first menstruation. The same attitudes and customs exist among certain classes of Hindus, who hold that sexual intercourse is permissible before the age of puberty because "even very young unmarried children often do something improper."

According to rabbinical rulings, the appearance of two pubic hairs is indicative of the capacity to conceive; while the ability to obtain pleasure from copulation is reckoned at from two to three years. Why? Because girls were observed to begin masturbation by digital friction of the clitoris at these early ages. A boy is said to assume the potency and responsibility of manhood at nine years and one day, because the majority of males were found to begin active masturbation at this age.

An anecdote is related in the Talmud upon this remarkable subject:

> Our Rabbis taught:
> A story is told of a certain woman who came before Rabbi Akiba and said to him: "Master, sexual intercourse was forced upon me when I was under three years of age."
> "I will give you a comparison," said he.
> "To what may the incident be compared?" said she.
> "To a babe whose finger was submerged in honey. The first time and the second time he cries about it, but the third time he sucks it. He ultimately enjoys the experience!"

The Hebrew word *'ālēm* (Arabic *ghelm*) denotes "lustful," and it is used of both sexes between the ages of three and thirteen. An *'elem* (Arabic *ghulām*, *ghulaym*) is a boy who has begun to masturbate or have sex relations, while an *'alemāh* (Arabic *ghulāmeh*, *ghaylem*) is a girl who masturbates or is lustful for coitus.

The *'alemāh*, generally between the ages of three and ten, plays an important role in the sex life of North African Jews. At least a dozen people, or from two to three families, live in the large two- or three-storied houses of Tangier, Fez, Marrakesh, Algiers, Oran, Constantine, Tlemcen, and other great Jewish centers. Wife swapping or communal marriage, as well

128

as boy-girl friend exchanges or premarital promiscuity, is a good deal more prevalent among the Jews than among the Muslims. Incest, though forbidden as no other erotic act is forbidden, is so common as to be considered customary. There is no personal privacy, and the children see all the sexual activities of their elders.

Like Arab children, Jewish urchins are thoroughly educated and sophisticated in sexual matters from their earliest years of understanding; and the very manner in which they speak of sex in the streets—openly, blatantly, and matter-of-factly—is in accord with their off-the-street exploits. Boys and girls (sisters and brothers, cousins, and other relatives) often sleep naked together in one room. There is no sense of shame or modesty, the cultivation of which is common among Muslim females, who both despise and envy the "brazen" Jewess. Genital play and vaginal and anal coitus are the natural consequences of this loose living. It is not at all unusual for Jewish boys, and even girls for that matter, to experience at least one orgasm per night owing to their free-for-all *modus vivendi*. Boys play with each other's penis before going to sleep and then upon awakening, the morning erection being an excitant, a pattern of conduct is established that becomes almost routine. Girls follow the same pattern of behavior, but to a lesser extent; unless stimulated by boys, their frequency is not as high. When boys receive a new bedmate, such as a visiting relative or friend, they initiate him *pro forma*. Each takes a turn at masturbating him; then a give-and-take orgy of penile manipulation, oral excitation or fellatio, and anal intercourse is enacted. A popular masturbatory technique, designed to prolong sensations, is vigorously to shake the penis until the titillation becomes acute, then stop for a moment—then resume, then stop—thus protracting the pleasure for as long as desired, perhaps a half hour or so.

Sleeping with older relatives sometimes awakens a child to

129

active sexuality. From the time a boy is able to walk, when he associates with older lads and leaves the cradle for the common bed, his genitals are subjected to a somewhat systematic stimulation. Little girls, sleeping with older females and males, have the clitoris manipulated and are introduced to cunnilingus. Although vaginal penetration is rather rare, a father will often rub his penis between the thighs or buttocks of his daughters and finger their genitals in an affectionate manner. Mutual fellatio is a spontaneous phenomenon in very young boys, perhaps a manifestation of the powerful lactation complex. They often lie contraposed, each with his penis in the other's mouth, and fall asleep in this position. Older boys teach them the technique of oral excitation, for these little ones merely hold the member in the mouth, which produces a pleasant sensation. Cunnilingus is rarely spontaneous in little girls, who are ordinarily attracted to the male organ for the satisfaction of any oral impulse. Brother-sister fellatio is widespread; to gratify her oral eroticism a small girl will hold a baby boy's penis in her hand and then put it into her mouth.

Two-, three-, and four-year-old children, imitating their elders, play games wherein they approximate or rub their genitals together; and partial as well as complete penetration is universal. The hymen, if present, is gradually stretched and worn away. Few Arab and Jewish females retain any trace of a hymen after a girlhood of frequent copulation and/or vaginal masturbation. This often causes some degree of contention with their grooms, who deem it their duty to draw blood on the bridal night as a token of their superior swordsmanship, but nature will have her own way nevertheless.

North African Jewish children are betrothed in early childhood, usually between the ages of three and five, and are traditionally married between the ages of twelve and thirteen. However, custom and rabbinical rules allow for exceptions to the common code. Many boys and girls are mated at the betrothal

130

age, while others begin to engage in marital relations at nine or ten.

The union of four- or five-year-olds is a kind of *mariage de convenance* for parents and other elders. Since the Talmud states that a maiden may be betrothed by sexual intercourse, the whole household takes due advantage of this declaration by invading the little child's genitals. The married or betrothed girl is brought into the abode of her groom or fiancé; and if the two small tots cannot be given a separate bed, much less a separate room, they are put in with the rest of the children. The *'alemāh* is then regarded as a new sex partner, and all the boys and men of the house have genital connection with her. Meanwhile, as a reward for his "generosity," the *'elem* is masturbated and fellated by all his bedfellows.

The orthodox Sephardic Jews, who are mated at puberty, are not so promiscuous in their social and sexual customs. While the "ordinary" Jew mingles boys and girls in the same room as well as the same bed, the orthodox and rabbinical families ordinarily separate males and females in sleeping quarters, which may mean that the upper classes are more homosexually inclined than the lower, numbering among them more masturbators, fellators, and analists. Whether or not this be so, the fact is that well-nigh all orthodox boys and young men are addicted to mutual masturbation and cultivate a passionate taste for fellatio.

In these child marriages, the father of the groom enjoys the privilege of the primitive *jus connubii* (right to copulation) or *jus primae noctis* (seignioral right of the first night). This *droit du seigneur* is also observed among many classes of Muslims and Hindus who marry their daughters off between the ages of nine or ten and twelve; the father-in-law relishes sexual relations with the girl, for his son customarily and legally waives the franchise of defloration and consummation. The North African Arabs lump all lawful varieties of marital license and exchange under *tezāwuj* (intermarriage) and *tebādul* (reciprocity).

In the evening of the betrothal or actual wedding, the little girl (ranging in age from three to nine) is led by her father-in-law into an empty bedroom, where he strips her naked. A sadistic man will be fired by the child's wide-eyed innocence, and thus seize her and serve her brutally. But most seigniors are gentle and careful. Seating her on their knees, they will kiss the child and fondle her body—especially her little vulva, until "it starts to tickle." The man will say to the girl: "Let me feel the little turtle you have inside your legs." The *'alemāh* is reassured and does not resist; only haste and cruelty cause the child to cry and struggle to get away. Freeing his erect organ from his clothes, the considerate seignior will then straddle the girl over his thighs, which he opens so that her own legs are forced or stretched as wide apart as possible. So doing, he slowly lowers her upon his glans penis, which he works between the labia and round and round the little orifice by holding the child by the waist and swaying her to and fro and from side to side. Gradually and mindfully he forces his glans penis all the way in, pressing through the tight vaginal orifice. The rotary movement titillates the vulva and produces acute pleasure in the little *'alemāh*, who often experiences an orgasm during the procedure, the result of both psychic and physical excitement.

The seignior will force his penis no further if he feels that it will cause pain; besides, by now most men have come to climax. If not, he continues the movements which frictionize his corona and her orifice, sometimes lifting the girl up and down so that her sphincter firmly clasps and "jerks" the circumcisional cicatrice as in masturbation, until he finally ejaculates. Depending upon their desires, other men merely rub their penis between the girl's thighs or buttocks, or attempt to penetrate the anus, spurred on by the child's struggles. With tenderness and graduation, even a frightened *'alemāh* rarely sheds a tear. But when encountering a three-year-old, many seigniors dare not consummate the contract but induce the little lass to handle and/or mouth their genital member.

One Jewish man described the nymphophiliac experience with unusual emotion, especially since it is habitually considered a most salacious and ultraexciting activity:

> It was so little and smooth. I turned around and around at the tight opening, slowly pushing my way in. The head was so big she could hardly hold it, but it tickled the lips and gave her extreme pleasure. She wriggled and giggled all the while. I came in a moment and took it out, but the dear girl's soft little hands clutched the object of her desire and tried to put it in again.

The father-in-law is not supposed to touch his new daughter after this, but nearly all abuse their seignioral authority by using the girl whenever they please. The young couple sleep together, and genital play as well as coitus occur, but often imperfectly depending upon their age and experience. Now that she is an *'alemāh* and "fit for free pickings," all the older boys take turns mounting her; they belabor her little body constantly, while her husband is handled in ways befitting his new status.

Nymphophiliac cults, sects, and secret societies are found throughout Africa and Asia. Among the most famous are the Druses and Nusairiyeh of Syria, the Yezdi of Turkey and Armenia, the Sabaeans or Mandaeans of Iraq and Iran, the Kurds and Kazaks of Central Asia, the 'Ali Ilahi of Afghanistan, the Ismailiyeh of India and Pakistan, and the Taoists of the Far East.

Dr. Jacobus observed:

> The little Hindu girls are deflowered by the little boys with whom they play, and repeat together the erotic lessons which

133

their parents have unwittingly taught them on account of the general promiscuity of family life throughout India. In all the little girls of less than ten years of age the complete hymen is wanting. There is an Indian proverb of brutal cynicism: "For a girl to be still a virgin at ten years old, she must have neither brothers nor cousins nor father." (28)

Incest is often the rule rather than the exception. Girls and boys mingle promiscuously—with the result that might be expected—girls and boys going partially or completely naked until the age of twelve years, which condition facilitates and indeed encourages the girls' constantly handling the boys' genitals, resulting in continual erections and repeated coition. That is why it is rare to find an Indian girl of more than ten years of age a virgin.

Eastern children as well as adults generally sleep in the nude, and nudity in children naturally arouses curiosity and leads to mutual exploration. As Jacobus noted, by the age of ten the hymeneal membrane of the Hindu girl is widened, stretched back, or worn away by repeated coital and/or masturbatory contact. All her brothers, cousins, and other young male relatives and playmates try her out *per cunnus* and *per anus*—nor are many adults denied access to her little chambers.

The same situation is true among the Indians of East Africa, who supply a high percentage of prostitutes. The vagina, natu-

---

(28) *In the American Ozarks: A virgin is a five-year-old girl who can outrun her daddy and her brothers. The same saying, only slightly varied, is found in the Kentucky mountains and in various other sparsely settled areas where suitable sex partners are at a premium and incest consequently is frequent. Such activity is becoming increasingly rare today, owing to population increases, improved transportation and other factors, but it has been only a few decades since some of the mountain people made the saying given above no more than a slight exaggeration.*

134

rally narrow and shallow, through daily penetration all during childhood becomes widened and stretched and readied for copulation with Arabs and Negroes in adulthood. That is why the African Hindu male, having (like his Asian brother) the shortest and most slender penis on earth, is an avid masturbator and active pederast; for his wife's vaginal orifice is too wide and loose and does not provide the maximum amount of friction afforded by the anal sphincter or a gripping hand. Moreover, most Indian boys get into the habit of vigorously shaking their little penises like masturbating monkeys. Self-stimulation is practiced from their earliest years, and it is not easy for them to shake off this habit after adolescence. Besides, there is much talk in East Africa of monkeys masturbating, which gives an impetus to their inclinations, although many Muslims facetiously compare the masturbating monkey and his little genitals to the masturbating Hindu with his small apparatus. Unfortunately, no matter how long and how hard they manipulate, their meager members, though as stiff as bone, do not increase in length or thickness. The only visible change is a retraction of the foreskin, which ceases to cover the glans and forms a cap around the corona.

North African Jewish children, many of whom (as mentioned) are mated between the ages of four and five, present similar peculiarities. Through constant intercourse with the well-developed penises of adults, the vagina of the little girl loses some of its elasticity and the orifice becomes strikingly wide. The penis of the little boy is often no match for it, and he therefore prefers to masturbate or attack his companion from the rear.

Jacobus examined about a dozen Algerian and Tunisian prostitutes, only eight or nine years old, who entertained vaginal coitus with men at least twenty times a day and whose sexual organs were "hypertrophied from excessive use." These little girls of the Ulad Nayil and other Berber or Kabyle tribes

135

specializing in prostitution are noted for the size of their vaginas, which are stretched by older boys and men back home in the hills before their exodus to the great cities. Jacobus also reports from Alexandria and Port Sa'id:

> Little girls are deflowered very early. I have seen, during the feast of the Ramazan, a little girl of six years of age and a boy of five acting coition in the street; they were merely imitating what they had witnessed. Sometimes little Arabs of from three to four years old are summoned by a little girl of their own age to enact coition in the open street.
>
> Little girls, who begin to have connection with men from the age of eight to nine years, have the vagina very large. It is all distended, stretched, and has lost its elasticity. I had an opportunity of observing this in Cairo on a little girl. Her vagina was monstrous in width.

Burton noted that "familiarity of Negro boys with white girls and of girls with black slave boys is common in Egypt; Egyptian blood is sufficiently mixed with Negro to breed inclination for miscegenation." In Muslim Africa, for a white or brown Arab female to have sexual intercourse with a brown or black Negro male is quite common and even customary. The same attitude assumed with regard to homosexuality is assumed with regard to miscegenation: what a person does to achieve sexual satisfaction is his or her own business, and who can account for personal taste?

The Hamitic ethnological group evolved from a union of Caucasians and Negroes, thus forming the ancient Egyptian and Ethiopian races. When the Arabs and other Islamic peoples entered the continent of Africa, they soon assimilated themselves with the Negroid civilizations or converted the primitive tribes to Islam by means of intermarriage and interracial copulation. With the exception of a few Bedawin tribes in remote desert areas, all Muslims of pure Semitic origin interbred with Hamites and Negroes, thus forming the Semito-Hamitic and Semito-Negroid stocks. The so-called Hamito-Negro nations, being a blend of white-black with black, were in existence since the diffusion of ancient Egyptian culture.

Muhammed encouraged miscegenation in order to improve the social and spiritual estate of humanity. If Islam were to have any positive influence on non-Islamic nations, its followers and missionaries had to identify themselves with the people they planned to proselytize. Consequently, the Prophet of Allah set an example in Arabia by taking several Ethiopian females into his harem—to say nothing of Greeks, Persians, Jews, and other "infidel" women. Arab men sought Negro women for sexual intercourse, and Negro men sought Arab women for sexual intercourse, and vice versa both ways. Arabs and Negroes also became and still are passionate companions in homosexual pleasures, the Muslim having introduced fellatio and cunnilingus among the primitive tribes. Today, the Islamized Negro is as bisexual as his Arab brother.

Colonel Dickson writes that "there is a curious and widely accepted belief, among Arab townsmen especially, that to have connection with a Negress makes a man sexually strong once more if he happens to be suffering from debility." Many Arabs expressed the same belief to Jacobus, giving as their reason the fact that the Negro female is more sensuous and receptive than the Arab woman, who is often taught greater modesty and self-possession. But as a rule the Negro woman puts on an act of orgastic ecstasy when in bed with an Arab, writhing and wriggling and sobbing and sighing, the better to win his favor. When in bed with a male of her own race, the Negress expresses her affection with less affectation.(29)

‘I’
_____

(29) The reader may be struck by the resemblance to the practices of Negro prostitutes of Harlem, who find it economically advantageous to preserve the white customer's belief in the greater ardor

Owing to early conditioning, a great many Muslim women admire a large penis and are relatively unresponsive in vaginal coitus unless they are served by a long and/or thick sexual organ. African and Arabian Semites, both Jewish and Muslim, seek Hamitic males to satisfy their sadomasochistic impulses. They love to fondle the large phallus of the Hamite, to feel it entering between their thighs, provoking swift orgasm. Indian girls commonly run after Negroes, a manifestation of their masochism.

In the cities of Muslim Africa and Arabia, Arab and Negro boys and girls play together in a sexually promiscuous manner. Jacobus treated *vaginitis* (inflammation of the vagina) in several little Arab girls between the ages of two and ten, since there is no secretion of lubricating fluids in prepubescent chil-

---

of Negroes. However, some Negro prostitutes have reported that so great is the white man's expectation of unrivaled sensuality, that even if the black female lies like the proverbial log, the white male still persuades himself that he is enjoying a raging response.

The grass always looks greener on the other side of the fence, and most peoples attribute to other tribes, nations, and races a sexual responsiveness (often described as depravity) greater than their own. Especially there is a world-wide lore among whites of the sexual "animalism" of blacks, and sometimes this is reflected in superstitions such as the Arab one mentioned by Colonel Dickson and the American one that intercourse with a Negress may bring a change of luck.

The fact is that, as Kinsey once put it, it is impossible to generalize with accuracy about the sexual behavior of an entire race. Negroes are susceptible, like other men and women, to the values and other conditioning factors of the societies in which they live (although the degree of susceptibility may be less when the values are non-Negro ones). And just as with other peoples, there are great differences between individuals.

dren. These liquids lubricate the genitals of adults and protect them against rough and abrasive friction, but rigorous and repeated coitus among small children often inflames the tender and delicate tissues of the vagina. Jacobus found that some boys (for their own comfort no doubt) would smear a sufficient amount of saliva over their penises, particularly the glans, or would have the girls hold them in their mouths and suck for a short while—unless rape was to be enacted, in which case the most forceful rubbing is sadistically desired.

Vulvitis (inflammation of the vulva) was observed in young Arab girls raped by older Negro boys. Unless the boy lubricates his glans penis with saliva, the violent and continuous friction of intrafemoral copulation irritates and abrases the girl's labia and clitoris, inflaming the external parts of her vulva. Girls anticipating such contact will spit on their fingers and smear their genital lips with saliva, a general preparation for masturbation. Anal irritation is also prevalent in young boys and girls, the result of forcible experiments.

Arab literature is loaded with tales, some factual and some fictional, concerning the sexual relations of Semites and Negroes. One of the most popular of these tales contains an erotic incident which occurred between a ten-year-old Egyptian girl and a twelve-year-old Sudanese boy:

> She ran up to me and began to sport with me, and I with her, and we played a thousand little games together. She bit me and I pinched her; and we tickled each other so wantonly that soon my little rod swelled and rose up on end like a big bolt, sticking out under my breeches as stiff as can be. The little girl laughed; and pulling me down on my back, then mounting astraddle my belly, she began to wriggle and to rub herself along me until she had uncovered my prickle. When she saw it standing so straight with its head held high, she seized it in her hand and began to tickle it by rubbing it

139

against the lips of her little slit, through the thin fabric of her panties. During this game, hot lust stirred in me and I threw my arms around her while she hugged me with all her might until, in a sudden second, my prickle (which had become as hard as iron) pierced her panties, penetrated between the lips, thrust through her maidenhead, and entered her slit all the way with one stroke.(30)

This "little game of genitals," as it is called, is commonly played by Arab, Jewish, and Negro boys and girls of all classes. In its most innocuous form they merely touch or rub their organs together, but the play often ends as in the foregoing episode. In a distorted imitation of adult intercourse, a young girl will pull down a little boy's pants, lift her dress, set his stiff penis between her thighs, squeeze as tight as she can, and lurch her little bottom back and forth. If she knows what to expect, she usually pulls down her own panties also. Pressing and rubbing the penis between her legs produces pleasant sensations

---

(30) One encounters in the literature of the East, far more than in the literature of the West, a preoccupation with the sexual activities of children among themselves. In part this reflects the Eastern reality, where such activities are in fact often common and not subject to being banished from consciousness as in the West. But the sexual relations of children also engage adult phantasies in the East to a degree not found in the West.

While this subject demands lengthy analysis, impossible here, it is worth noting that in Western pornography, where most accounts of childish sex activity are to be found, that activity is almost always conducted in participation with or under the auspices of one or more adults. The adult is seen as corrupting the children, and it is precisely this aspect that is titillating to Western erotic sensibilities. If the adult were excluded from the action, the scene would be much less exciting.

in her clitoris, while boys sometimes find the "trick" rather frustrating.

In the *Arabian Nights* we read about a sultan's daughter in Cairo who fell furiously in love with a black slave boy who subsequently ravaged her virginity, "and she became so passionately addicted to futtering that she could not do without it a single hour." The moral of the tale? "Nothing pokes and strokes more strenuously and abundantly than a black man and a baboon!"

Arab women frequently marry Negroes, especially if they satisfy them in bed, and the black eunuchs of Mecca and Medina ordinarily have white wives.

Systematic castration, once a profitable aspect of the African slave trade, is now well-nigh extinct. Arabia is one of the last outposts of the eunuch. Perhaps the most celebrated of these are the distinguished *Āghāwāt* (Masters) or black eunuchs who guard and attend to the great sanctuaries and harems at the forbidden cities of Mecca and Medina. While in Arabia, Sir Richard Burton had occasion to converse with several of these huge castrated Negroes and discovered, much to his surprise, that most of them entertained three or four wives "with whom they practice the manifold pleasures (masturbation, irrumation, soixante-neuf, cunnilingus, etc.) till they induce the venereal orgasm." Burton reports finding their circumcised penises "long, thick, and flabby in quiescence, yet when erect not much more distended." Even the most vigorous masturbatory manipulation will not stiffen the shaft of the Negro eunuch, which (as Jacobus discovered) feels like a strong rubber tube when held and squeezed in the hand.

The bruising or excision of their testicles in boyhood, although it causes sterility, does not produce impotence. The psychological and physiological reactions to the operation include an intensification of psychic libido which often leads to physical satyriasis. This general erotomania or *taym* (rut), as the

141

Arabs call it, makes the eunuch who retains his penis extremely popular with vaginally oriented women for at least two important reasons: (1) he cannot ejaculate impregnating sperm, and (2) he can perform the act of vaginal coition almost indefinitely.(31)

As long as his heart and circulation keep sound, the eunuch's erections are frequent. In fact, by virtue of his hyperactive and uncontrollable genital nervous system, the castrato's penis will become congested in an instant at the slightest provocation; and often nothing short of friction will soften it. The eunuch requires and desires the most energetic and prolonged stimulation of his penis in order to alleviate his extravagant lust, which explains why these dark giants are active pederasts and passionate masturbators.

Sudani, Somali, and Swahili Negroes, as well as those brought from Timbuktu, are celebrated in Arabia for the size

---

(31) Other investigators have reported different findings. It has often been said that the eunuch is potent following castration only if he was sexually active previous to the operation. The famed castrati, or choir boys castrated in order to keep their voices from changing, apparently were impotent in many cases for the reason that no pattern of sexual response had been established previous to emasculation.

It is also more usually reported that the eunuch who is sexually potent subsequent to castration typically becomes impotent after a few years. There is said to occur a gradual feminizing of body contours, accompanied by a diminishment of libido and a creeping impotence that at last becomes total. However, many of these declarations seem to have been based upon observation of American and European castrates, who have either been accidentally emasculated or who have suffered the same fate in other ways. Our data indicate that it does not follow that the Eastern eunuch, often leading a very active sex life, will react in just the same way.

142

of their penises. However, the (by Arab standards) handsome Ethiopian with his relatively small phallus is preferred as a eunuch because he is less a danger to feminine morals than his "mule-membered" cousin from Timbuktu. The Ethiopian eunuch's penis generally remains the same size as at the time of his emasculation, and his erections are perfectly rigid like those of a prepubescent boy.

A few of the eunuchs, owing to some imperfection in the operation, experience azoospermic ejaculations. The discharge, either weak and watery or thick and copious, is very much like normal spermatic fluid save that it lacks the characteristic seminal odor and contains no spermatozoa. It consists principally of the secretions of the seminal vesicles, the accessory glands of the urethra, the prostate, and Cowper's glands, and the discharge from the secretory glands of the urethral mucous membrane.

In obtaining this ejaculate, one discovers that many of these eunuchs are habitual and even compulsive masturbators, being capable of repeated orgasm from six to ten times. They are fond of fellatio, but almost invariably desire that the shaft of the penis be manipulated by hand at the same time the glans is sucked in the mouth. Copulating castratos, who indulge in anal and vaginal intercourse, are held capable of great erotic feats and reputedly can achieve orgasm from fourteen to eighteen times a day. They thrust in the most violent manner until they are exhausted, continuing for several hours without withdrawing, which makes them extremely popular with highly passionate women. A eunuch's wife once reported that her husband climaxed between twenty and thirty times over a twelve-hour period of continuous penetration, leaving her afaint from repeated paroxysms.

Islamic law forbids castration but does not prohibit the use of eunuchs, so Muslims generally employ circumcised Christians to manufacture the black *tewāshī* or *khessī* (detesticled

143

one), who is said to symbolize the purity and neutrality of the Holy Places. In Lower Egypt and the Sudan, Coptic monks supply agents of Arabian officials with at least a dozen castrated boys per annum. Circumcised Sudani Negro orphans and bastards, preferably five to six years of age, are delivered into Coptic castrators' hands by Arab *fuqehā* (schoolmasters). The boys are operated on scientifically by the Copts; a horse-hair is tied around the scrotum, which is made loose and insensitive in a hot bath, and tightened until circulation is cut off. Then the little pouch is amputated with a scalpel and the wound stitched. Death rate is virtually nil due to modern antiseptic conditions. Eunuchs and slave boys are also supplied by Timbuktu, where the operation is in the old tradition: slipshod. Negro barbers and circumcisers cut off the testicles of other Negroes and sell their human merchandise to the highest bidders, slavers and harem owners. All purchasers are guaranteed proof of sterility. The postpubertal eunuch is led into a private room at the place of sale, where either the dealer or the buyer handles and rubs his penis to determine erectility. If erection results, proving potency, the eunuch's penis is masturbationally manipulated until he has an orgasm. If any fluid is emitted, it must not contain spermatozoa; otherwise the deal is off. Every castrated male who passes from one employer to another must submit himself to this potency-sterility test. Arab dealers and buyers not wishing to perform the masturbatory test themselves usually employ Negro boys for the manual labor, which they thoroughly enjoy.

Rape, as a primitive form of sexual outlet, has for centuries been systematized in the fatalistic East. In many areas, a man is not considered a man until he has successfully raped a woman, and done so in such a manner as to turn her fear or pain into fervor and pleasure. Among Sudani tribesmen, rape reckons in many puberty rites and initiation ceremonies. A circumcised boy does not become a man, is not considered a warrior, until he has ravished a virgin girl from a rival society. Among many others, Margaret Mead discovered that despite civilization and the attempted refinement of promiscuous instincts and primeval impulses, rape (like incest) is still the secret erotic ideal, especially in those societies which forbid it.

Rape, and other crimes of passion, are on the increase throughout the civilized world. According to recent reports from Africa and the Orient, the rate of sexual disorder is rapidly growing. Bands of boys rape girls; homosexuals torture one another; married couples mingle promiscuously. Sex continues to be wielded as an effective weapon against the tyranny of the gods.

The Egyptians have a proverb: "The girl did not cry for help until after the boys had raped her ten times running." This is an oft-repeated Oriental sentiment: that women are their own seducers. For example, in "The Tale of Nureddin 'Ali and the Damsel Enis el-Jelis," when the vizier's son rapes the sultan's new virgin concubine, the chief matron of the harem cries: "You say he came in and kissed and embraced you? Allah forbid, did he do anything else?" To which the wide-eyed girl makes ready reply: "Indeed he did! But he did it only three times." Although the hermetically sealed mind cannot conceive of such an "obscenity," open-minded observation both East and West has revealed that well over half of all cases of sexual seduction and assault are induced by the "victim," either innocently or otherwise. The extremely prevalent but inscrutable urge to rape and to be raped doubtless originates in sadomasochistic impulses common to all creatures.(32)

·I·
_____

(32) The idea that the "victim" usually or often provokes the "rape" is a very old one. Western law enforcement officials and courts are cognizant of the fact that many rape accusations are blatantly false, and that in many other cases the so-called rapist had abundant provocation.

145

One of the principal reasons why there is such a prevalence of sexual aggressiveness in the Orient is that children, from their earliest years, are wont to see their elders in genital union.

The large penis in erection, the alternating active and passive coital positions of the woman, the vigorous thrusting action, the agitation of limbs and the tossing of two conjoined bodies, the sighing and groaning—all these elements of copulation, and many more, convey to the acutely impressionable mind of the young child the idea of violence and brutality. The sadomasochistic elements of the infantile libido feed upon this adult demonstration and are magnified in proportion to the over-all effect. The man's lusty lunges and the woman's passionate cries rudely awaken the little boy or girl to the realities of life, hence coitus among children is a common if not customary phenomenon throughout the East. Parents set the example, and children naturally imitate. Moreover, the widespread Eastern preoccupation with a large penis is due in part to the small boy's comparison of his own little genitals with the well-proportioned implements of his elders. African and Asian children of both sexes regularly see their parents and

---

French studies have shown that from 60 to 80 per cent of all rape accusations are without foundation in fact. The English estimate that there are twelve false rape accusations for every true one. False accusations undoubtedly outnumber valid ones to a similar extent in the United States.

Even so, policemen, juries and not infrequently judges have been regularly taken in by the horrifying tales told by wide-eyed and innocent looking "rape victims"; and a rape trial often generates so much emotion that reason goes out the window and it is difficult for a defendant to win acquittal even when the evidence is very largely in his favor. (Emotion also works to bring to trial in the first place many individuals who would never have been charged with the offense had an objective examination of the case been carried out.)

146

other adult relatives naked, and attention invariably focuses upon the male organs. To the young boy or girl, the fully-developed adult penis, whether in erection or repose, appears absolutely enormous; and sisters commonly tease their brothers about genital size, especially since the jealous girls have no "tassels" of their own.

The Arab woman's overt or latent desire for a big penis and for savage thrusting in sexual congress may in many cases be traced to an early girlhood experience. Many Muslim girls encounter complete copulation between the ages of six and eight, some even earlier and others a few years later, be it with boys or with men. It is quite common for a young girl to accost a couple of boys, saying: "Come, pierce me violently with your prickles!" (*Te'āleh, zeqqzeqq-nī bi'l-ghesb bi-zebāb-kum*). She wants it "long, hard, and dry." Pulling up their dresses, little females will entice little males by thrusting one or two fingers in the vagina. If she wears panties, the child will move her middle finger up and down and then point between her legs. A few even poke their fingers in their posteriors, while others push their thumbs in and out of their mouths to simulate fellatio.

In the instance of a pubescent boy or an adult male exposing himself before a five-year-old girl, the latter sees (perhaps for the first time) a full-sized penis in erection. It appears huge to her, for she has known only the little member of a boy her own age. It may frighten her, but more commonly it excites her imagination. With daring curiosity she takes hold of it, wondering how it could be so enormous and if, since it is much bigger, it is any different from the small ones to which she has become accustomed. When it is thrust in between her thighs, a strong sensation of pleasure accompanies the pain produced by the great disparity between the large penis and the infantile vagina. At least half of the male organ plunges in and out, stretching the little sheath to extreme tension and

147

evoking a fierce thrill which nearly paralyzes the child. The glans penis batters her sensitive uterus; the effect is ineffable. Orgasm may be instantaneous; spasmodic titillation is sustained or rapidly repeated as long as coital stimulation continues.

The outcome of this traumatic experience is likely to be a magnification of the masochistic impulse. There develops in the girl a taste, often morbid, for vaginal violence. The memory of the big phallus seen and felt in childhood remains embedded in the woman's libido. While it naturally looked large and out of proportion to the child, this impression of exaggeration is nonetheless carried into adulthood, consciously or unconsciously affecting the woman's judgment. She may be disappointed in the size and function of many virile members, which seem relatively small to her and unable to execute vaginal intercourse with continuous vigor. Some leave her anesthetic, for she has associated orgasm with the pleasure produced by a painfully large penis. She does not always realize the cause of this erotic anesthesia, which may be traced to the masochistic need for a bigger and stronger—indeed pleasurably painful—penis in vaginal penetration, and so relies upon extracoital contact or excitation of the clitoris to achieve orgasm. When such a female finds a male whose phallus is as thick as her wrist and nearly as long as her forearm, she abandons her body to him no matter what his over-all appearance may be. That is why many Muslim, Jewish, and Indian women chase after Hamites and Negroes, who are admired for their phallic length and girth.

Dr. Jacobus, who made exhaustive inquiries among African and Asian Muslims upon the subject of rape, presents the following report:

> The Arab has retained some instincts of the animal, and also some of its habits. He throws his victim to the ground,

goes on his knees in front of her, seizes in his brawny arms the thighs of the unfortunate, and seeks to hasten by well-studied movements the instant when his lubricity will be satisfied. At other times he is still more brutal. Always on his knees, he raises the legs of his victim onto his shoulders, the posterior part of her thighs being then in juxtaposition with his belly, and then rushes his performance to its completion. Lastly, he sometimes takes a child by surprise—having led her into a corner—her clothes are thrown over her head, and in a trice the poor thing is cruelly outraged.

Nothing stops the Arab, neither the narrowness of the vestibule nor the tears or the cries of his victim. He is before the door; it resists; he breaks it open. Thanks to the attitude he has chosen, he is not obliged to lose either time or strength in turning round about the, pubis; he goes straight ahead, carving out a sanguinary passage.

Such brutal rapes are not limited to the Arabs. There are many examples among the Mussulmans of India, Turkey, Iran, Southeast Asia, and other Muslim areas.

In some cases the child, her back turned to the violator, is placed upon his knees; the virile member is introduced between the upper part of the thighs, being rubbed against these and the perineum by movements imparted to the child's body. This is *coitus intrafemoris* or intercourse between the thighs, without intromission. But more generally the child is placed upon the edge of a bed or some other raised object; and the criminal, on his knees in front of the child, pushes his virile member between the upper parts of her thighs: these being raised up and sometimes crossed so as to form, together with the perineum, an enclosed space. In this case again, the violator imparts certain movements to the body of his victim, always passive and inconscient.

It is very seldom that there is any attempt at intromission of the virile member into the genital organs. This would necessarily be almost impossible, either by the disproportion between the parts or by the relative positions of the criminal and of his victim. External or perineal copulation with little girls is therefore quite common and popular.

The brutal instincts of the Arab, seconded by a hot temperament, will lead to excesses of frenetic lechery. In Algeria, a young shepherd woman came to me for treatment. She had suffered a brutal raping by two young men. The inner and outer lips of her vulva were abrased and inflamed, the orifice irritated and dilated, and the vagina stretched to the point of laceration, there being also a slight inflammation of the cervix uteri.

It was evening, and she was walking alone on the road. They seized hold of her, laid her down under a tree, and while she was held down by one of the two, the other violated her. His companion then took his place, and so they continued alternately relieving each other during two hours. The unfortunate woman calculated that she had been outraged about fifteen times.

The infamous vice is so deeply rooted among the Arabs that it is almost hopeless to find any efficacious means of repression.

Intrafemoral intercourse is a peculiar form of masturbation. The thighs of the female, pressed firmly against the penis, are a substitute for the male hand. When the man imparts movement to the girl's pelvis, the skin of his tightly squeezed penis is jerked up and down and the corona is rubbed against the inner thighs and vulva. Many Muslims and Jews prefer coitus intrafemoris to vaginal intercourse because, as in anal coition and manual manipulation, there is more vigorous friction of the penis. The velvety surface of the vagina, its slipperiness and often slackness, cannot offer the rough rubbing to which the masturbator is attuned. Besides, a sensitive Easterner quick to ejaculate prefers having the shaft of his penis agitated, thus prolonging sensation, to having his glans frictionized for a rapid emission.

Tekhfīdz (planing or polishing) is the legal as well as general term for intrafemoral intercourse, alluded to in the law books of El-Islam as a kind of rape most commonly carried out on little girls, the Latin *penem fricatum inter femorum* (rubbing the penis between the thighs). The Jewish lawgivers of Talmudic times were also familiar with this refined form of sexual savagery, mentioning "those who play [sexually] with children, those who practice pederasty, and those who practice onanism through external contact (by way of limbs)." According to Talmudists, Jews who entice children to masturbate them and who manipulate the genitals of children, who sodomitically abuse the anus of boy or girl, and who rub their genital member between the thighs of children and adults are said to "delay the advent of the Messiah." Manustuprative friction of the penis in any form is forbidden by the rabbis. Jews attempting to disguise their predilection for masturbation by employing a child's thighs instead of their own hands are Talmudically exposed. Nevertheless, *tekhfīdz* is traditional among the nymphophiliac Jews of North Africa, whose girls become habituated to masturbation even in infancy as a result of having their little vulvas rubbed by the male organ.

Colloquially, intrafemoral intercourse or rape is known by many names among the Arabs; e.g., *el-muqammet* (the lifting and lashing of legs), *rīsheh ne'-āmeh* (the ostrich tail), and *el-hedūlī* (the hanging). *Tirād el-kebsh* (the ram's attack) is the most ancient technique of rape practiced in the Orient. The Mongols were notorious for it, and there are many Chinese and Rajput prints depicting Moghul warriors raping women and girls in this attitude. The female being thrown upon her side, the assailant lifts her upper leg and sits at squat in the interval of her two thighs. Bernhard Stern, who observed this method among the Turks and Bosnian Muslims, writes that the rapist sometimes shifts position by lifting the girl's legs upon his shoulders "like a yoke"; whereupon he holds her

151

thighs tight in his arms with all his might and, kneeling, "drives his sex organ into her, throwing himself upon her with all his weight, untroubled by her sighs and groans." Stern also notes a variation wherein "the boy raises the girl's legs in front of him and then, thrusting his member between them, moves back and forth," a technique favored in folk songs: "He raises her feet towards the ceiling and thrusts his big one between her thighs!"

Jacobus, examining a young Indian woman who had been ravished exteriorly in this manner by three lusty Mussulman youths, found that "inflammation often results from a brutal and rapid friction, performed not only on the clitoris but on the whole vulva itself." Sufficient lubrication lacking, the continuous violent rubbing by the penis of each of these boys between the girl's thighs irritated and inflamed the labia; while the clitoris was red and swollen, its glans protruding between the lips, as if she had indulged in frenzied masturbation.(33)

In many instances the Muslim rapist will lift a little girl upside down, securing her knees in the crooks of his arms, and slide his penis in between her thighs. One Arab vividly described these heels-over-head besiegements launched on little

---

(33) *While intrafemoral coitus is occasionally practiced in the West as a method of preventing pregnancy, such rapes are unknown or of the last rarity. The kind of rubbing desired by some Easterners does not appeal to Western senses as does the moist friction of coitus. Obviously, the rapist, risking severe punishment, will engage in the kind of activity he most desires, whether on sensual, symbolic or other grounds. Thus, in the West the only kind of rapist likely to commit an intrafemoral rape would be one whose deviate desires were directed to such a means of gratification. In the case of the rape of a little child, copulation between the thighs may take place, as a substitute method of gratification, when penetration of the vagina proves impossible.*

152

females as "just like strapping up and stripping a slaughtered sheep." Unless genital penetration is effected, the child is more frightened than harmed by such a shocking experience. The Arabs have a proverb, "The slaughtered sheep does not worry about being skinned," meaning that most young females, having experienced actual intromission, do not fear being raped by mere surface strokes.

Close-fitting panties facilitate rape by serving as shackles for the ankles. In North Africa, for example, Muslim boys often run up to Jewish girls in the back streets and alleyways, pull down their tight panties, push them to the ground, pry open their knees as wide as possible, and then pounce upon them. An eight-year-old Algerian Jewish girl, raped by an Arab boy in a dark doorway, described her experience to Dr. Jacobus in the following words:

> He seized me and pressed me against the wall. Without pulling down my underpants, he pushed it between my legs and rubbed back and forth. The rubbing excited my senses, and I all but ceased my struggles. Then, still holding up my dress, he ripped down my underpants. He thrust it deep into me, fiercely in and out, then he suddenly withdrew and forced it between my legs again. When he finally let me go, my underpants were about my ankles and there was a sharp tickling inside my thighs.

In many North African alleys, Jacobus saw little girls pull down the pants of young boys who thereafter chased them into some secluded spot for a "good going over." If followed into her house, a little girl loves to run into her bedroom, feign exhaustion by falling back on the edge of her couch, and allow the boy (or boys) to stand between her parted legs, pull up her dress, and fall to furiously. If the girl is wearing panties, the boy will yank them down to the level of her knees, lift her legs till her thighs press against her belly, and start sporting.

153

Burton, having questioned many Muslim rapists as to female reaction, came to the conclusion that "Easterns do not often notice this feminine venereal paroxysm which takes the place of seminal emission in the male. It often happens that the woman, unless she has a loathing for her violator, becomes infected with the amorous storge, relaxes her defense, feels pleasure in the outer contact of the parts, and almost insensibly allows penetration and emission. I have seen it happen to many a girl." Masochistic females welcome venereal violence for the most intense orgastic satisfaction. Many Eastern and African women seek rape or a rapelike relationship, for they thrill to the pounding drive of a man's pubes. Japanese girls are said to delight in subtle endearments soon followed by brutal embraces which excite almost instant orgasm.

The fact that the common Arabic word for "rape" is *kebs* (ramming) bears witness to the vehemence of Islamic passion, for a virile male is encouraged (like a battering-ram) to impale a female with the deepest and most vigorous thrusts.

To be seduced or debauched, in the Turkish language, means "to be standardized" (*'ayārtilmek*) or set in sexual harmony with the rest of devirginized womankind. *'Ayār* (standard) is that set by the Prophet Muhammed; namely, no female shall remain a virgin in El-Islam. In other words, she must be "standardized"—no matter how or by whom, and no matter what her age. Thus the Turks, among other Muslims, have become adept at *mu'-āyireh* or "standardization."

A "non-virgin" fad, which has been called a neurosis, is as epidemic in modern Turkey as it is in the state of Israel, where to lay claim to a hymen is just as disgraceful as to lay claim to a foreskin. Girls born without hymens are "blessed from the womb," and even the most rudimentary membrane must be obliterated by the age of puberty. Anxious to relieve herself of what she deems an insulting burden and a sexual stigmatism, and not wishing to appear socially heretical, the Turkish and

Israeli female unloads her maidenhead at the first opportunity, usually by the time she is ten or twelve. The old saying still holds true: "No grass shall grow on any soil whereon the Turk has trod!"

In the Westernized East, virginity has been stripped of its sacred veil where it wore one, and a premarital intercourse mania prevails. The teenage Jewish girl whose vagina has not been penetrated by her boy friend's penis is considered rather odd and old-fashioned by her ultrasophisticated companions, who borrow and trade lovers according to a free-and-easy system of exchange.

4. PROMISCUITY

Woman is like a washerman's tyke,
Not of the house nor Ganges dyke!

HINDU PROVERB

In "The Philosophy of Physical Love" section of the Turko-Persian *Bāh Nāmeh* (Book of Lust) we read the following revelation:

> A woman may be enjoyed by two men at the same time. The performance would doubtless require an extension of parts; but whoever reflects on their proverbial extensive quality will not doubt of their admitting with ease two guests, after a trial or two and with sufficiency of natural or artificial lubrication, provided themselves could accommodate their entrance to the convenience of each other.
>
> And in the way above alluded to, I am confident that this might be effected. The woman must lie straight, on either side, and the man who attacks her in front must, after entering her, lift her uppermost leg on his buttock. The antagonist in the rear must then accommodate himself to her posture, and glide in likewise.
>
> The men may knock her as hard as they will; so long as the

157

woman is careful to keep herself exactly straight, and not to withdraw from one or the other, their violent shocks will only serve to make her more fixed and steady.

Such activity is common in Oriental harems and houses of prostitution, and Muslim dancers and dancing girls are wont to entertain well-paying guests with erotic exhibitions in which two or more males will serve one female and vice versa.

Dr. Jacobus, who examined dozens of slender North African Arab girls between the ages of ten and fifteen, found their vulvas quite large and plump, the vagina long and ample, and the orifice rather wide, sometimes loose and gaping from "excessive" intercourse with men and repeated penetration by very thick penises. Most girls admitted having engaged in vaginal coition with two boys simultaneously in a standing position, one introducing his long slender penis from behind while the other penetrated in front, facilitating the dual intromission by lifting up one or both of her thighs as high as possible.(1)

---

(1) Many Western psychologists are accustomed to assert that any sharing of a female by males is "homosexual" activity. That may be true, but the point is of negligible importance in many cases. The male who "shares" a female with another male may never engage in any other sexual act with a person of the same sex, may be capable of vigorously and with satisfaction executing the heterosexual coition he consciously desires, and may never have any of the problems likely to result from a latent inversion.

Since Arabs and many other Africans and Middle and Far Easterners are so often "bisexual," and remain so throughout their sexually active lives, it may be that the intercourse of a female with two males affords the latter homosexual as well as heterosexual excitement and pleasure; while the contact of penis with penis would certainly encourage such response. But if so, one might expect the homosexual component to be as conscious as the heterosexual. Yet

Every *ghāzīyeh* (professional dancing girl and prostitute) examined by Jacobus in Egypt had large genitals and a wide vaginal orifice, for these females engaged in bilateral sex acts at private parties. Because their opening was so ample, the doctor discovered that men preferred to serve them per anus; hence the *ghāzīyeh*, "apt for two tricks," won fame and fortune through anal intercourse.

Jacobus reported that the average introitus vaginae, when fully dilated, measured between 2 and 2½ inches in diameter—extensive enough to receive two penises at once. From their earliest years, the girls had been addicted to vaginal masturbation with bananas, candles, and other large objects, which eventually stretched their organs. Forceful penetration by the penis of an older boy produced the masturbation habit in little girls. On examining their anuses, however, Jacobus found strong sphincters and perfect muscle tone despite the fact that these girls entertained "excessive anal abuse."

The *ghāzīyeh* is usually declitorized, and all her sensitivity is centered in the vaginal orifice and the anus. These gypsy women are famous and skillful *mubetzrāt* (declitorizers), and are much sought after by Muslims to perform the operation on their infant or young girls. Dickson, after inquiring as to the surgical skill of these gypsies, found that the mode of operation is for a needle and thread to be passed through the *glans clitoris*, which is pulled outwards to its full length by means of the thread. When so extended it is cut off close to the body.

---

this does not seem to be the case, and the activity is usually understood by the participants as heterosexual.

It seems more than a little possible that those Western theorists who describe as invariably homosexual all males who share females, as well as or including all pimps (said to have their inverted intercourse vicariously, by way of the prostitute), are on somewhat unsteady ground.

The *ghāzīyeh* frequently masturbates by rapidly pulling a piece of cloth back and forth between her thighs and buttocks. This is a part of her dancing act, which she performs in the nude. Because she has no clitoris, it requires a prolonged rubbing of her labia to produce orgasm; thus all during the dance she artistically flings her shawl around and repeatedly flicks it between her legs, exercising the fiercest friction and emitting animal cries of ecstasy, finally finishing her *danse du ventre* at the advent of orgasm. The *ghāzīyeh* is also a famed fellatrice, oral stimulation of the male organ being her supreme specialty. While fellating a man, she will rub her vulva against his thigh or lower leg, which she squeezes between her own.

In his rare and curious *A Night in a Moorish Harem*, Lord George Herbert records a multiple copulation which occurred between three Muslim males and a Circassian girl in a Turkish seraglio at Erzurum. Such incidents as he describes are common throughout Asia and Africa:

> We stripped entirely naked and amused ourselves by imitating the attitudes usually given by art to the most celebrated heathen deities. It was not enough for me to compare the forms of the young men by observation; I freely caressed and handled their genitals with my hands until they lost all restraint and gathered so closely about me that I was squeezed in their joint embrace.
>
> I flung my arms around Qasim and bade him lie down on his back with me on top of him; his loins were elevated higher than his head by the pile of cushions on which he lay. I worked backward while he guided his shaft completely into me. My buttocks presented a fair mark for Selim, who mounted me behind and slowly worked his shaft into the same orifice that Qasim had already entered. It was the tightest kind of fit. The first entrance had stirred my desire to a flame, and made me welcome the second with great greediness. Qasim's position was such that he could hardly stir, but Selim plunged

160

his long and slender shaft into me again and again with thrusts that required all his strength. My sheath was stretched to its utmost tension by the two shafts, but all its distended nerves quivered with lust.

Rashid now knelt close in front of me, with his knees on either side of my head. I lay for a moment with my flushed cheeks on his genitals, then I grasped his shaft in my hand and played rapidly up and down on it. Qasim, with his arms wrapped around my waist, was sucking my bosoms. Selim squeezed my thighs in his grasp at every thrust he gave. I felt my crisis coming, overwhelming threefold intensity, inspired by the contact of three such vigorous men at once. In my very wild abandonment I sucked Rashid's crest in my mouth, then I thrilled and melted with a groan which resounded through all the room.

All three of the young men followed me to the realms of bliss to which I soared. My sheath overflowed with the double tribute which gushed into it; my mouth was filled with Rashid's sperm. Both pairs of my lips were dripping; my whole frame seemed saturated with the exquisite fecund moisture. When the mingled sighs of the young men, which echoed to my prolonged groans of rapture, had died away, I sank into a semi-unconscious state from which I did not rise that evening. It was a deep, dreamy, voluptuous repose which an occasional smarting sensation in my strained sheath did not disturb.

In the same book, a work elevated by its literary quality far above the status of pornography, is to be found an account of an Arab girl's intercourse with a stallion:

Mohammed was my favorite stallion. He was more fleet than the wind, and so gentle that he obeyed my slightest word. He was of a bright wine color and his shape was perfect. His head was small and gracefully set on his arching back. His brown eyes had almost human intelligence. His

161

limbs were slender, and he walked so proud that he seemed to spurn the ground.

He came up to me, and after I had fed him from my hand, I spent some time braiding his mane. Then, for want of something else to do, I thought I would take a bath. A pool where the water gathered from a spring which fed the oasis made a fine bath. It was shaded by palm trees from the sultry heat which glowed on the surrounding sands. After bathing I threw myself at length on the short grass which bordered the pool. I was in no hurry to dress and stretched myself lazily on my back at full length.

Mohammed came and stood over me as if for company in our loneliness. I amused myself by making him stand with his forefeet on either side of my chest. Nothing could have induced him to step on me, not even if a gun had been suddenly fired. But there was nothing to startle him. We were entirely alone.

Pretty soon—as stallions will when standing in perfect repose—his shaft hung dangling out. In a spirit of mischief I put up both my feet and took it between them and began rubbing it gently. It gradually stiffened, and its crest hung down between my thighs and pressed against the lips there. He put his head down and touched my bosoms with his velvety nostrils. I still continued to rub up and down his shaft with my feet, till its presence between my thighs awakened a pleasant sensation. In fact, I became wanton with desire and worked my feet more rapidly up and down his shaft. It suddenly shot out, and, stretching my sheath to its greatest tension, penetrated me to my loins.

I was ravished with the fierce thrill and the stallion's gushing sperm. It found no room in my distended orifice and spurted out of it again like a fountain descending over my belly and thighs. Luckily for me, the distance between his loins and mine was sufficient to prevent anything but the end of his shaft from entering. Otherwise I know not but that it would have been driven through the length of my body and come out of my mouth.

As it was I scrambled out from under him with my lust completely quenched. From my waist to my knees I was dripping with the stallion's thick milky sperm. I hastened to wash it off and to bathe and cool my smarting sheath in the pool. For a long time I had to keep Mohammed away from me with a switch, but I did not strike him hard. I could not bear to hurt him for the consequences of my own folly.

Jacobus notes that Dr. Paul de Régla, who spent several years in Turkey, examined hundreds of Turkish girls and, like Jacobus with Japanese and Hindu females, found very little or no trace of a hymen in any of them. A predatory character in the *Arabian Nights* extols "the bottom of a blind alley, which is the very place for assaulting and giving in assault." De Régla questioned several girls who were well acquainted with what goes on in dark alleyways. Each of them had invited the amorous assaults of older boys and men, and a couple got more than they bargained for. Three boys, attacking one girl, forced her into dual penetration and fellatio. The violence of their embrace provoked immediate orgasm, which was somewhat painful in its intensity.

The erotic dance ritual of Somalis and Sudanis is a sanctification of promiscuity. If this secret but nonetheless customary ceremony is to be described it should be depicted in detail; otherwise the intensity of its mounting fervor, from flirtation to foreplay to the dynamic finish, is lost as symbolic of the eternal ebb and flow, the calm and violence, of universal nature.

The modern sex dance, once a sacred fertility rite, is now enacted purely for entertainment and sometimes as a sex club initiation. Hamito-Negroid East African "secret societies" or promiscuity coteries require of their new members a potency test in which the male or female is subjected to the consecutive embraces of the already initiated. A girl is often obliged to

163

bear up under a hundred successive assaults,(2) while a boy must keep up his resources for at least three orgastic rounds.

The dance is generally performed by the youngest males and females of the group, both married and unmarried, between the ages of ten and twenty. Every dancer (and clique member for that matter) must be circumcised, the males having their foreskins and the females their inner *labia* and/or *glans clitoris* amputated, and thus fit to sacrifice their vital secretions for club membership or for the viewing pleasure of well-paying sex party guests. Somali and Sudani circumcision is traditionally practiced on boys between the ages of three and five, while clitoridectomy and nymphotomy are performed on girls at the same age. The same is true of the Swahilis, who are also ardent

---

(2) *"A hundred successive assaults": This is a nice round number, and it occurs with some ubiquity in the sex lore and testimony of many times and places. The girl who "took on a hundred men in a single night" is met with repeatedly. One such girl, by some accounts, was Cleopatra, the Serpent of the Nile; the same feat was attributed by the Romans to both Messalina and Julia. However, sober mathematical analysis raises some doubts.*

Simple calculation reveals that if a woman were successively assailed by a hundred men, each of them attacking, accomplishing his mission, withdrawing, and making room for the next within the space of five minutes, almost eight and one-half hours would be required for the completion of the parade. Common sense would suggest that the assembly-line precision demanded for the accomplishment of a hundred acts of coition in a single night alone makes the total unlikely. Neither is it likely that the most ravening nymphomaniac could take pleasure in so formidable and mechanical an operation. And groups of precisely one hundred males are probably rare on such occasions. It might be added that one searches the literature almost in vain for "eighty-seven successive assaults," or one hundred and eleven.

participants in promiscuity parties, while the Ethiopians perform circumcision in infancy after the Israeli fashion.

Several naked youths, hot with anticipation, kneel and beat their drums with a cadenced rhythm. Then from an enclosure adjoining the area of performance there step the dancers, two separate troupes of boys and girls with nothing about their nude bodies but the traditional *fūteh* or narrow blue breechclout, which hangs to the level of their knees, just barely concealing their private parts. The spectators now notice that the boys' loincloths are beginning to lift; their sexual organs are starting to swell at the very expectation of erotic activity, further aroused by the effects of alcohol or hashish. But they control themselves admirably, and none experiences an actual erection.

The girls, covering their pear-shaped breasts with their hands, move to the right side of the drummers, their little round buttocks shining in the light. As the drummers increase their hollow pulsation, the boys begin to move by way of signaling to the girls with their eyes and hands; but the females, turning away with stylistic modesty, seem not to entertain their amorous advances. Then the males start to pound their feet and slowly, lustingly dance with a measured beat toward the young women who, becoming alarmed at their bold approach, draw back with bashful movements and coy expressions. The boys increase their alluring gestures as they come closer; but the girls turn their backs to them, hiding their faces in their hands. The light glows upon the girlish contours, beautiful bottoms which excite the ardor of the youths considerably; for the spectators observe that several begin to experience full-sized erections underneath their scant covering.

But seeing that the girls will have nothing to do with them, the boys glance at one another, make a few flamboyant gesticulations and grimaces of indifference and disgust, and slowly start to retreat. The females, becoming aware of this with-

165

drawal, peek about rather coyly; seeing that the males are ignoring them, nonchalantly enjoying whiffs from their hashish pipes, the girls take their hands away from their faces, turn around once again, and sway their shapely bodies to an erotic rhythm—the better to attract the boys.

Pretending not to see this, the young men, after a time of smoking and daydreaming, suddenly answer their call and come forward with the same sort of movement, thumping their feet and wagging their buttocks and shaking their shoulders. The girls, seeing them coming, fall back in maidenly terror, again turning their bottoms to the advancing boys, who also withdraw when they find the females uninterested. This ritual of tantalizing temptation is enacted several times more, the boys and girls alternately alluring and evading, drawing nigh to and withdrawing from each other, when finally the males, growing impatient and somewhat angered, retreat into the enclosure. There they smoke their pipes in earnest.

Now the lovely females, becoming uncommonly bold, strut forward and dance in tempo with the monotonous beat of the drums. They perform the classic *reqs es-surreh* (belly dance or nautch of the navel) by writhing and wriggling and shimmying and shaking their lithe young bodies, proudly thrusting their ripe rounded breasts and buttocks out, undulating and gyrating their smooth bellies and hips, and teasingly uncovering, then covering again, their secret parts by a quick sideward flick of the *fūteh* with their nimble fingers. When the boys do not emerge from their covert, the girls, in a white heat of amorous agitation, rip off their loincloths and reveal themselves stark naked.

With a wild cry of triumph the boys, pulling off their own breechclouts, leap out of hiding, revealing their virile members in violent erection. They approach the girls in a frenzy of measured movement, their handsome black bodies glistening with perspiration, their every muscle rippling and aquiver,

166

their long slim penises vibrating in the palpitant heat of excitement. The dance now reaches its climax.

The boys pair off and approach each girl, dancing around her and making as if to seize her in their embraces. She pretends to resist, shifting her shoulders from one side to another, covering her eyes, her breasts, then her sexual parts. Now one of the boys comes up behind her while the other frisks about in front. In order to ward off the latter, she bends slightly forward and so prevents him from touching her between the thighs. Also, to hinder him from entering, she puts forth her slim hands and greedily grasps his penis, rubbing it in her palms and stroking it up and down while he struggles to take her hands away by grabbing her forearms and clutching her breasts.

Suddenly the youth in the rear darts forward and thrusts his organ between her buttocks, which are presented to him in perfect form. The young woman releases an ecstatic cry, her face taut, and lurches her loins forward as the lad in back begins to force her. Then the young man in front, seizing his opportunity, yanks away her hands, snares her in his embrace, and pushes his penis completely into her vagina. It is sometimes difficult to determine whether the boy in back has his organ in the girl's anus or in her cunnus; but nymphotomy facilitates dual intromission by removing the labial barriers and leaving a gaping orifice for easy and instantaneous entry.

Then both of the boys hug her tightly and, still prancing about, thrust in and out rhythmically until she begins to tire, her legs trembling and sagging. The girl now stands perfectly still, her thighs slightly apart, while the two boys, grinning and shouting and pressing her body with legs spread on either side, joust rapidly in time to the throbbing of the drums until she moans and sighs and is nigh to swooning. The perspiration pours from their bodies; and the semen oozes out from between the girl's thighs, trickling down her legs. Suddenly they

167

withdraw; and the girl sinks limply to her knees, jerking her shoulders and rolling her head in a cadenced delirium, her eyes closed, her mouth open.

The two youths attack another female, whose partners leave her and take the one who has fallen. They lift her and the dance begins again. Meekly she grips the genitals of the male in front, but she is too weak to resist. He is dynamized, inflamed to frenzy by hashish; but she is languid, spent with motion and repeated orgasms. His penis is hot and hard and slippery. Her hands cannot hold it; it slides into her vagina. He pulls her loins forward with a shocking jolt, while the boy in back squeezes and fondles her breasts, then takes aim and enters, also with a jerk.

The orgy seems unending. The girls writhe in pleasurable torment, their faces twisted and twitching in orgastic convulsions; while the boys, spurred to pulsatory violence by the beat of the drums, continue to torture them with continuous thrusting. The youths lurch their buttocks furiously; they attack and retreat unmercifully. They rotate by turns, abandoning themselves to frenetic spasms of lust, alternately assailing front and rear until they well-nigh lose their senses and faint from overexertion. When they can stand no more they sink to the floor, male and female together, pawing and clawing each other. The girls squirm and groan; they hotly and hungrily handle their delirious partners. The drummers, afire with desire, rapidly masturbate with a free hand.

A few dancers, in a final burst of vigor, feverishly mount their trembling damsels, then roll over in a swoon. The drumbeats slow and cease *a tempo* to the syncopation of detumescence. A quivering and sighing prevails. The young females lie with their legs splayed wide and their tremoring hands pressed between them; they have endured the most vigorous ordeal of womanhood. The young males also lie with their limbs spread apart, hands trembling between; they have stood the tremendous test of virile manhood.

Erotic dances are also performed by naked Negroes in North African and Middle Eastern coffeehouses and hashish parlors, as well as at private orgies. Many of these celebrated *reqqāsīn* and *reqqāsāt es-surrāt* (bobbers of the belly) are "bull men" with big penises and "elephant women" with bulging breasts and buttocks, the better to excite the enraptured audience.

A *daiyūth* (man of ease) (3) is one who winks at and/or profits by the fornication of his wife, sister, daughter, and other female relatives. He is both pimp and cuckold de luxe! A *sāyibeh* (loose woman) is a wife who lets herself go a-whoring; she is the free lance, the amateur prostitute and adulteress de luxe. It is no exaggeration to say that in this day and age, well over half of all Muslim husbands and wives are *daiyūthīn* and *sāyibāt*.

After his exhaustive observations in the Arab world, Dr. Jacobus calculated that at least 80 percent of all married couples were actively involved in adultery; i.e., they were enter-

---

(3) *This is one of the world's more charitable terms for a pimp. The closest (American) English comes to it is "kept man," a designation more commonly applied to the male lovers of wealthy women. Needless to say, the pimp whose earnings are derived from the prostitution of his wife and daughters is even less beneficently regarded in the West than is the pimp who is not related to the prostitute(s) who works for him.*

The psychopathology of the pimp, as seen by psychoanalysts, is an interesting subject and sometimes a complex one. Western psychologists and analysts seem scarcely to allow for the possibility that a pimp may be without neurosis or psychosis. It would appear that, by contrast, the "man of ease" is thought of in his own society as more to be envied than censured while almost no one suggests that his conduct implies emotional problems, etc.

169

taining and apparently enjoying from one to three or more extramarital coital contacts a week. Jacobus adds that many Muslims offered him similar estimates, listing self-interest as the prime factor determining such a high incidence of both secret and flagrant infidelity. No discerning student of Eastern sexual behavior can estimate less than 75 percent, for in certain countries and many areas the figure is at least 95 percent.

While traveling in North Africa, Hendrik de Leeuw was surprised to discover what a fabulous fairground of fornication is the Muslim world. He writes that "there seems to be no line of demarcation between a good and a bad woman," noting how married females "whose husbands' incomes are often insufficient for the luxurious tastes of their households" freely fare forth on the loose in search of charitable lovers. "They sell their bodies with, and sometimes without, the consent of their husbands. This is not looked upon as infidelity by the defenders of the system, who have indeed a flexible conscience." * And if a wife is not polyandrous or promiscuous by nature or inclination, she will exploit her daughter or urge her husband to become a kept man, a gigolo or *telīq* (licensed libertine), the masculine of *telīqeh* (a free-living female).

A young Arab university graduate and romanticist in Damascus told reporter John Roy Carlson: "Our women adore money. . . . I am sorry we have no ideals of love." † Among many others, Colonel Dickson discovered that most Muslim girls are avidly inveterate gold diggers and thrill seekers: "The desire for money, love of adventure, curiosity and instability of character, which are so charmingly and strongly developed among the Arab women, all tend to render them an easy prey." Males and females are said to marry for one or all of three reasons: (1) *behr*, pleasure; (2) *dehr*, convenience; and (3) *mehr*, money. Love is little understood as we in the West understand

* Hendrik de Leeuw, *op. cit.*
† John Roy Carlson, *Cairo to Damascus.* New York: Knopf, 1951.

it, therefore our judgment of their judgment is a waste of words.(4)

Occidental conservatives lament and lash out at the West's ever-increasing, seemingly rampant adultery and divorce rates; for they are convinced that we are blithely and blindly entering perilous straits. But one careful look at the Middle East makes Las Vegas look like a nursery school for naughty children. The same people who call venereal disease *dā'l-mubārek* (the blessed ailment), the mark of a virile man and a vital woman, also measure an individual by the number of spouses he or she has managed to exploit with impunity. The general feeling is that there is no disgrace in being a delinquent adult so long as one is not gobbled up by his own greed.

Dickson discovered that nearly every Arabian woman, by the age of thirty, has had two or three husbands—some taking and discarding as many as seven or eight. King Ibn Sa'ud and all government officials set the sexual example with a succession of over five hundred wives—"one- or two-nighters" they are called, being wedded, bedded, then divorced, a privilege and pleasure few will deny—as well as countless concubines or mistresses, perhaps a thousand in turn. The relative ease with

---

(4) *Paul Bowles, in his novel* Let It Come Down, *has admirably made this point. In the following exchange between an American male and an Arab female, the misunderstanding is axiologically fundamental, not just linguistic:*

> *He kissed her. "I love you." His open lips touched hers all the way around as he said the words. Hadija did not seem surprised to hear it. "Again?" she said, smiling.*
> *"Huh?"*
> *"You love me again now? This time quick one, yes? This time take few minutes. No take pants off. . . ."*

171

which a Muslim may marry and unmarry facilitates the fun of it all, especially since common-law marriage is the most popular form. *Zewāj el-mut'ah* (union of pleasure) originated in Iran and is now the most prevalent type of legal relationship in the Muslim world. Being a *mariage de convenance* as well as of *plaisir*, it lasts until the two "lovers" weary of exploiting one another for fun and profit.(5)

El-ihhlīl (the legalizer or liberator) is a common nickname for the penis because, by penetrating the vagina, it frees a female from her former husband or lover and makes her the lawful wife or mistress of her new paramour.(6) The legal meaning of *mustahhell* (variants *muhhellil* and *ihhlīl*) is "he who legalizes and/or liberates by way of sexual intercourse," an equivalent of the Talmudic "betrothal by copulation." According to old Muslim and Jewish law, a female becomes the legal wife of a male the very moment his penis enters her vagina, provided there is proof of consummation from four creditable witnesses. She remains his lawful spouse until such

---

(5) *It is certain that male potency is maintained by such frequent changes of sex partners at a higher level than would be the case if the stimulus of novelty were not so often provided. Female responsiveness, too, is probably heightened by the stimulus of novelty—a fact many Westerners are pleased to overlook or deny, while agreeing that such is the case with the male.*

(6) *In the West also the penis may be a "liberator," but of the "sinned against," rather than the "sinning," spouse. It might be that by adopting this Muslim custom entire, so that adulterous copulators became by their coition man and wife, the incidence of American extramarital activities could be drastically reduced. However, those whose main aim in life it is to hold all copulation to an irreducible minimum have surely examined this possibility and found the disadvantages to outweigh the gains.*

172

a time as another penis, the so-called *ihhlīl* or "liberator," penetrates her parts. Consummation now constitutes divorce, where before it had constituted marriage, and fornication and adultery are therefore legitimate forms of making and breaking a marital contract in the *mut'ah* or short-term "shackup" of expedience and enjoyment.

In North Africa and the Sudan, where the system amounts to legalized promiscuity, most men and women "marry" from seven to ten times by the age of thirty; and not a few, especially Sudanis, boast about a succession of from forty to fifty or more spouses. Oddly enough, however, very few except the idle and newly rich exercise their legal and traditional right of sporting from two to four wives at a time. For both economic and individual reasons, the modern polygamous Muslim satisfies his salacity in a monogamic common-law marriage or, in an atmosphere of lecherous free enterprise, lives fast and loose.

Love, to the Arab, begins and ends in bed. This has always been true, and now that the feminist revolution has succeeded, it will continue to be so to an even greater extent. It is doubtless based upon Oriental man's ancient and inscrutable fear of being dominated and emasculated by woman. Under the real or phantasmic threat of losing his masculine and phallic identity, the Oriental male fancies love to be the female's most potent weapon. And the Oriental female, somehow ashamed of her nonphallic femininity, makes a self-pleasing and self-advancing fetish of "love" in a wasteland of impersonal lust. The cynic might describe it all as an eternal fight for penis survival in the timeless age of the castrating cunnus.

There is an old Arab saying: *Sūq en-nayk dāyim qāyim* (The Tent of Fuck is never struck). The famous Arabian physician and philosopher Avicenna (Ibn Sina) declared that the human female is able to copulate dozens of times a day without any other inconvenience than that resulting from the continuous friction of two natural parts. When she participates in the

173

voluptuous sensation, receiving repeated orgasms therefrom, she may only feel exhausted and is able to stand additional stimulation almost indefinitely—until she faints. In other words, the female is sooner fatigued than satisfied! This physiological theory, allegedly gleaned from long and laborious experience, is found to contain many a grain of truth when we examine the average Arab female.

From about the age of ten, the ordinary Muslim girl is expected to learn her own way in life; and she does so in a fast-and-free manner that would shock the "living daylights" out of the model Western conservative. For by the age of twenty, the Muslim girl has as a rule experienced sexually all there is to experience; and she is then ready to decide what she wants to do with her exhaustive fund of knowledge. She may continue to be polyandrous or even promiscuous, or she may experiment with monogamy and acquire fastidious discrimination; but whatever she decides, the choice is hers and hers alone, and whatever she does is her own personal business and nobody else's. It is the same with her Jewish cousin; the Talmud tells us:

> There was no prince or ruler who had not possessed Rahab the harlot. It was said: "She was ten years old when the Israelites departed from Egypt, and she played the harlot the whole of the forty years spent by the Israelites in the wilderness. At the age of fifty she became a proselyte."

Thus *jeune coquette, vieille dévote* is a rule of the world, both East and West. But before she becomes the least bit ascetic, if she does so at all, the average Muslim female is married from two to five times—or even, as Dickson discovered, from seven to ten. And with the wildest passion she indulges riotously in genital intercourse, for sex is to her the supreme joy of life.

174

Arabia is a land of sexual license, hence Muhammed's traditions that "gossamer was invented so that women could go naked in clothes" and that "the emission of semen at the sight of a strange female does not violate the Fast of Ramazan." Since the time of the Prophet, when the unveiled feminine population fared about stark naked beneath their wispy chemises and sleazy culottes, fabulous Araby has reeked of aphrodisiac excitement. The women still wear very little clothing, perhaps a single garment to cover their nudity, and with one tantalizing lift all is bared before the admiring eyes. This parade of natural parts is significant; for the Arabians, far from being an effeminate breast-conscious culture of adult sucklings, glamorize and glorify the hairless cunnus "wherein man's pleasure doth lie." And since the women are wont to shave their pubes, the smooth vulvar cleft is emphasized and eroticized above all else.

Arabia is as wild and woolly today as it was thirteen centuries ago. It is one of the last outposts of raw and unrefined Islam which, when in its glory, was characterized by slavery, eunuchism, harems, and sexual anarchy. Among the "hottest" towns are Mecca and Medina, symbolically the holiest. Dickson writes that "Mecca is recognized as one of the most immoral towns in Arabia. If one can believe the Bedawin, every form of foul vice prevails there." There's an old saying: *El-hherām fi'l-Hharemayn* (Whoredom in the two Holy Cities). In Mecca and El-Medina, many are the Muslims who will openly boast of an abundance of "gay" *mujāwirīn* (squatters) with the characteristic comment that "each *hhājj* (pilgrim) is in the anal orifice of the other." A well-known verse has it:

A certain person the Pilgrimage made,
And for all his *anusing* escapade
He now lives at Mecca and thrives at his trade!

175

Male and female prostitutes are plentiful in the two Holy Places, where they serve a multitude of pilgrims who are willing to abandon their vows of abstinence and indulge their desires before returning home. This general sexual riot is symbolized in the following saw: *El-Hhejj mā mekmūl bela jimā' bi'l jemūl* (The Pilgrimage is not perfected save by copulation with the camel).

Both male and female homosexuality run rampant in Mecca and Medina. The local ladies are said to be passionate for sapphism (*qirādz*, cunnilingus) and tribadism (*sihhāq*, rubbing), while the local gents are notorious *istānīyeh* (analists) and *qerrādzīn* (fellators). Both men and women, as well as boys and girls, do a running business.

Heterosexual promiscuity is also prevalent, not only in the Holy (Whoredom) Cities but throughout the peninsula. Little girls erotically tease and entice little boys in the back streets and alleyways, pulling up their smocks and poking their fingers in their vaginas. Even adolescent girls will lift their *thōb* or long shirtlike garment and point to their hairless parts, sometimes rubbing them with their hand. Bands of boys copulate with groups of girls in secluded places. If a boy wishes to "lay" a girl, he comes up behind her and thrusts a couple of fingers between her buttocks; but if facing her he will raise his middle finger and then push it up and down toward the girl to intimate intercourse. Girls often grab a boy's genitals underneath his frock, which is why newly circumcised lads steer clear of libidinous little lassies. Following circumcision the small Arabian boy's penis is very sensitive to the slightest irritation, stiffening repeatedly as the tender glans rubs against his garment, and for at least a couple of weeks after the operation it is somewhat painful for him to play with himself, much less allow a mischievous girl to lay her hands on him. However, when the wound is thoroughly healed and the glans hardens, the little

176

lecher actively masturbates and copulates with vim and vigor; for he need no longer nurse his "little prickle."

Custom and inclination are such that most women surrender themselves to men on short notice, entertaining on-the-spot stimulation, and any female who is caught completely nude by any male is usually obliged by tradition to abandon her body to him. In other words, now that he has seen her nakedness (*'ōreh*) he might as well enjoy it! While in Arabia, Burton observed that "stealing women's clothes is an old trick and has often induced them, after having been seen naked, to offer their persons spontaneously."

The primordial desire of the Arabian female for polyandry is satisfied in an erotic parlor game wherein one woman has sexual intercourse with several turn-taking males. The Japanese call this sport *enza-bobo* or "rotation copulation," while to the Arabs it is commonly known as *el-istibdzā'* (the club lay or clique coitus).(7) In this Eastern variation of group therapy, the lusty female invites her little circle of equally lusty male friends to an evening of round-robin riding. This "taking on" of a small number of men by one woman is extremely common and customary, for it originally constituted a popular form of legal relationship in pre-Islamic times. About ten or twenty gigolos serve the woman turn by turn, both anally and vagi-

·†·

---

(7) *In the United States this practice, mainly confined to teenagers, is popularly known as a "gang bang" or, less commonly, "gang shay" or "gang shag."*

There are few American high schools or colleges without their legends of the girl who would "take on the football team" after a victory, and also, sometimes, "consolingly," after a defeat.

Gang bangs are presently rather commonplace among the teenage gangs of the larger cities, where the girl is usually willing but sometimes is not. Nelson Algren, in Never Come Morning, provides a realistic account of the rape of a young girl by an adolescent gang.

nally, then the female favors each of her boy friends with fellatio. The orgy rages all night long, its raucousness often creating a scandal in the neighborhood. For while outward decorum is enjoined unto all True Believers, what an individual does in private is his or her own personal affair. As long as public decency is not debauched, the Arab attitude is: "What I don't see, I shouldn't and needn't worry about!" But if he has an "accident," such as an involuntary erection, he excuses himself with the exclamation *Māshā'llāh* (What has Allah willed!) and clears his conscience.

Coitus à cheval is a favorite sport among the Arab Bedawin and the Muslim cavaliers of the vast Sahara and Central Asia. The classic Moghuls and Cossacks first popularized equestrian copulation, involving a variety of coital postures and erotic acrobatics, and the marauding Turks were notorious for running down and raping women and girls while on horseback.

We find a vivid description of *coitus à cheval* between two young Arabian lovers in Lord George Herbert's *A Night in a Moorish Harem*, serving to show that the desert Casanova, unlike the town Romeo, does not need an automobile in order to enjoy "forbidden" premarital fornication. The Bedawin teenager takes his sweetheart for a unique ride far more thrilling and much better adapted to the daring amorous designs of youth than what can be enacted on the seat of a parked car:

> We were borne along at an unflagging gallop. Hasan held me in front of him like a baby in his arms, often kissing me, his kisses constantly growing more ardent; and then I felt his stiff shaft pressing against my person. He suggested that I ride astride for a while and rest myself by a change of position. I obeyed his suggestion, turning with my face towards his and putting my arms around his neck, while my thighs were spread wide open over his own. He let the bridle drop over the horse's neck, whose headlong pace subsided into a gentle canter which was like the rocking of a cradle.

178

Hasan put his arms around my loins and lifted me a little, and then I felt the crest of his naked shaft knocking for entrance between my naked thighs. I was willing to yield to Hasan anything he wished; but no sooner had the lips of my sheath been penetrated than I involuntarily clung more tightly around his neck and, sustaining myself in that way, prevented him from entering further. Hasan's organ seemed adapted to the place and excited a sensation of pleasure. I offered my mouth to Hasan and returned his passionate kisses with an ardor equally warm. A desire to secure more of the delightful intruder overcame my dread of the intrusion.

I loosened my hold on Hasan's neck; my weight drove his shaft so completely home, notwithstanding the tightness of the fit, that his crest rested on my womb. It felt so unexpectedly good as it went in that I gave a murmur of delight. The motion of the horse kept partially withdrawing and completely sending it in again at every canter. The first thrust, good as it was, was entirely eclipsed by each succeeding one. I could have murmured still louder with delight; but what would Hasan think of a girl so wanton? But he was in no condition to think. He was fiercely squeezing and kissing me; while at every undulating movement of the cantering horse he seemed to penetrate me farther, and my womb was deeply stirred. The pleasure was too exquisite to be long endured. It culminated in a melting thrill, and my moisture mingled with the sperm that gushed from Hasan's crest. He reeled in the saddle, but recovered himself. The cantering motion drove his shaft less deeply in as it became more limber. It finally dropped out of me, a limp little thing drowned in the descending moisture.

"What a conquest for a slender girl to achieve over such a formidable object!" I thought. Exhausted, but triumphant, I laid my head on Hasan's shoulder. Twice more during the night he slackened the speed of his horse, and each time we completed an embrace equally satisfactory.

179

Other Arabian customs include a man's lending his wife or daughters to his best friends, thereby honoring the latter. The children of such unions are thought to be of superior blood, having been bred out of charity. Sexual hospitality is sometimes honored to such an extent that a man with many friends rarely sires his wife's offspring, for he impregnates all his friends' women while all his friends impregnate his. Under laws recently abolished by the former United Arab Republic (Egypt and Syria) but still extant elsewhere in the Islamic world, a group of men may verbally divorce their wives, swap them among themselves for a night of promiscuous pleasure, and then take them back again in the morning as legal spouses —absolved from any charges of adultery. Along with legalized wife swapping and three-second divorces, the hedonistic Arabians also enjoy common-law marriages of convenience, polygamy, concubinage, leviration, child prostitution, and many other free-for-all fashions of formalized fornication.

The Babylonian Talmud boldly states that "there is no adultery as flagrant as the adultery of the Arabians."

> Ten measures of immorality descended to the world; nine were taken by Arabia and one by the rest of the world.
> *By swearing and lying, and killing and stealing, and committing adultery, they spread forth and blood touches blood* (Hos. 4:2). As Rabbi Joseph translated: "They beget children by their neighbor's wives, thus piling evil upon evil."
> *That lie upon beds of ivory, and stretch themselves upon their couches* (Amos 6:4). Said Rabbi Abbahu: "This refers to people who eat and drink together, join their couches, exchange their wives, and make their couches foul with semen."

Muhammad Mazheruddin Siddiqi, in his thought-provoking *Women in Islam*, writes the following:

Women in pre-Islamic Arabia enjoyed a measure of sexual freedom amounting to license which led to widespread illicit unions and promiscuity in sex relations. The sexual morality of the Arabs had sunk so low that women were viewed only as a means of sexual gratification or at best a vehicle of procreation. Marriage ties were very loose and there was not much stability in family life. Women moved out of their homes with a style of dress that afforded unlimited occasions for sexual excitement to strangers; their looks and manners too were ill-calculated to ensure a healthy standard of sex morality.

Women in pre-Islamic Arabia did not observe any rules of decency while going out and dressed themselves with great ostentation with the intention of looking attractive to the male sex. Similarly . . . the rude and barbarous Arabs did not know even the ordinary rules of propriety and freely entered each other's houses without permission.

In these conditions, Islam found it necessary to impose certain restrictions on the dress and movement of women with a view to preventing the formation of illicit sexual relations and ensure a healthy and stable family life.

When the Prophet came to power, a revolution in public morality constrained women to cover themselves in substantial clothing and to refrain from displaying their bodily ornaments (zīnāt) to anyone save their husbands and closest relatives. Muhammed said: "When a female has reached the age of puberty it isn't proper that her private parts should be seen by the eyes of men. Women who remain naked even after putting on clothes lack wits and faith. What is above the knees and below the navel should be kept covered." Some say the Prophet made these recommendations after experiencing numerous erections and emissions at the sight of lovely young females wearing thin dresses. He added: "May females protect their private parts, and thus they will not be molested."

Soon after the Prophet died, social conditions slowly but

181

surely reverted to their original state, as exemplified by Shaykh 'Omar en-Nefzawi, who proclaims that when a beautiful woman walks, her *zīnāt* (ornaments) should stand out visibly under her clothes. Today, according to the most careful observers, conditions are almost exactly the same as they were in pre-Islamic times.

The women and girls of modern Arabia disport themselves in much the same manner as other Muslim females. The streets are aswarm with lissome creatures in light attire; and the never-ending array of smooth bellies, round thighs, and swelling breasts besieges even the most reserved and restrained males in a reign of passion. The womenfolk delight in donning thin dresses or gowns without any underwear for five reasons: (1) to show off their bare and beautiful shapes, (2) to keep cool but make the menfolk hot, (3) to attract lovers, (4) to defy and destroy ancient attitudes of propriety and self-control, and (5) to facilitate sexual intercourse in a standing position. Some willowy girls wear wispy petticoat panties beneath their outer garment, while others fare forth in tight or baggy pantaloons under a light chemise or even chemisette, but in nearly all cases these trousers are provided with an open crotch for admission of the male organ. Gay and fashionable belles will keep by their waistband or flutter about between their fingers a couple of gaily-colored silken handkerchiefs. After amorous activity, the girl will use this *mendīl* as it is called to wipe off her vulva as well as the boy's penis; whence "semen-soaked silk" has become proverbial. In Mecca and Medina, where young females fellate and masturbate males, they are wont to catch the seminal ejaculations in tinted handkerchiefs which are later washed and reused.

The sexual standards of primitive Arabia were such, according to several Muslim historians, that most females entertained erotic contact with a variety of males both day and night. There has been very little change in the past thirteen or so centuries. Married men and women sport a minimum of from one to three paramours, while unmarried girls open their thighs to literally dozens of attractive boys. Both premarital and extramarital petting are extremely popular, especially between "platonic" lovers. A great percentage of Arab women prefer *hhemsh* (sex-play, genital stimulation by hand) to vaginal intercourse because it affords them a more rapid and powerful orgasm which can be sustained or repeated by direct and continuous digital friction of the clitoris. Not wishing to risk the chance of impregnation, and desiring a discreet as well as direct means of expressing their affection for each other, the adulterer and adulteress will fondle and manipulate each other's genitals to orgasm. Oral excitation is commonly held in higher esteem by many lovers than is manual manipulation because "the mouth is more like the vagina."

Thousands of married men visit thousands of married women every day and night, and the professional prostitute can scarcely hold her own save among pilgrims and travelers who are not familiar with the underlying sexual freedom (or anarchy) of the country. If they are sensually attracted to the male, nearly all females offer their favors for absolutely nothing; the only immediate payment they seek is physical satisfaction. Economic gains, as much to be desired and even demanded as sensual gratification, follow in due course if the woman wishes to continue the relationship. Complete strangers, assigning each other in the street, will slip into a secluded spot to satisfy their senses and emerge going their separate ways. In "on-the-spot" activity, the male usually leaves the female with some monetary token of his appreciation.

In times like these, were a young girl to ask her mother, "How far should I go with my boy friend?", the reply might be: "Six inches!" Two maxims of the Arabians are *El-fehhl telq* (The stallion is free), meaning that any female is any male's fair game, and *Būseh bela zubb zay ma'mūl bela rubb*

(Kiss without futter is like bread without butter). *En-na'jeh telq li-dhīb* (The sheep is free to the wolf) means that men and boys may take women and girls and use them for sexual satisfaction in any way they wish. The female certainly favors this state of affairs, for she has all to gain by it and nothing to lose.

To the Arabian, the three pleasures of life are "eating meat, riding meat, and thrusting meat into meat." In Arabia, *el-khaiyāl* (a good and hard rider) is the delight of most damsels; for the Muslim female desires the most vigorous and continuous thrusting to achieve orgasm. Dickson notes that the Arab male and female "indulge riotously" in sexual intercourse. "So wildly passionate is their love-making that I have known of a man breaking two of his wife's ribs on the first night of their marriage." About a minute or two of violent jousting may leave an Arab woman swooning with orgasms. The shrill and vibrant *zeghārīt, zerāghīt,* or *zelāghīt* (trill of joy) is a manifestation of overwhelming ecstasy in the Arab female. It is provoked by vaginal stimulation, a rapid and forceful stroking, which builds tension and titillation to such an unbearable pitch that the woman, her thighs raised wide open and agitating, grasps the man hungrily and begins deliriously to pipe at the top of her lungs, kicking her legs and clawing the man's back and biting his shoulders. And at the instant of orgasm, if the sensations are powerful enough, she may lose her senses for a few seconds. Should the man continue thrusting or withdraw his member and start to rub her clitoris rapidly with his finger, thus sustaining the sensation or producing repeated orgasms, the woman may eventually faint for a few minutes, which is taken as nature's warning signal that she has had enough.

Muslim women do not ordinarily "lay like a log," (8) nor is

(8) Such arboreal apathy on the part of the female is not infrequent in the United States, judging by the traditional complaints of husbands who tell of wives, passionate enough before the marital knot

their response feigned, for they throw themselves heart and soul into the act. The highly passionate do not require any special precoital preparations for the attainment of orgasm; they merely tell the man to "stick it in and start thrusting," and almost in the same breath they are ranting and panting in orgastic ecstasy. The less sensitive, who take from two to ten minutes, develop receptivity by concentrating upon the tickling in their genitals and upon the penile penetrations producing this titillation, and they do whatever their impulses prompt them: writhing, wriggling, lurching, sighing, shrieking, clawing, biting, etc. With practice, the "slow" Arab female can amplify her feeling to the point where she experiences a paroxysm in at least and often less than one minute flat. This she achieves after a short period of foreplay involving general bodily caresses, while direct handling of her genitals heightens her capacity for rapid response in vaginal intercourse.

An Egyptian proverb has it that "the women of Cairo flatter themselves that their *ghunj* (coital shimmying and shaking) is superior to that of all other females in the Levant." The sinuous and sensuous writhing and wriggling of the belly dancer is equalled by that of the *ghenūjeh* or "wiggler woman" who sits astride a man and gyrates, contracting her pelvic muscles and wresting or "milking" the penis, thereby achieving orgasm herself. This is the famed *tertereh* or "milling movement" of Sudani, Somali, Swahili, and Ethiopian females. The *qebbādzeh*

---

was tied, reading confession magazines and chewing gum whilst irritated spouses belabor them to no avail in terms of awakening a feminine response.

It might be added that while comparisons to logs are probably favored in the U.S., perhaps because of the familiarity with the recumbent recalcitrance of such objects achieved by our forebears while clearing the continent, belly-minded Germans more often liken the unresponsive female corpus in coitus to a bag of potatoes.

185

(clutcher) is noted for the length and narrowness of her vagina and the strength and contractility of her genital muscles. She can literally strangle the penis and cause a man to lose his senses, so powerful is her *constrictor cunni.* By squeezing and compressing her genital sphincter and vaginal walls, she can induce orgasm in herself very quickly. Constriction of the pubic and anal muscles causes instant erection of the clitoris in the "she-milker."

The Hindus call a passionate and promiscuous female *jānghāmathānī* (churning thighs), because the pleasure of vaginal stimulation by the penis is so intense and intolerable that her thighs agitate up and down and round and round like churning sticks. Thus a long-legged girl is deemed exceptionally desirable, both for size of clitoris and rabid receptivity.

Muslims commonly consider the *hazzeh* (quake or explosion), which constitutes the feminine venereal climax, to be an ejaculation rather than a paroxysm. This idea may be attributed to the abundance of Bartholinian lubricant discharged by Eastern women during coitus and forced out of the vagina at orgasm by its violent muscular action, thus resembling an ejaculation. Hence the word *menī* (water of life) is defined in the dictionaries as "the seminal fluid of man or woman." The amount of mucus and lubricating liquid expelled from the *mehbil* (steam place) depends upon the intensity of the *hazzeh* or "genital earthquake." Many women, the moment they become sexually excited, experience a steady stream of "love fluid" which soaks their panties. Arabs term the provocation of this precoital flow "turning on the tap." *Medhī* (sticky juice) also runs out of the "faucets" of excited Muslim males.

As we have noted, North Africa is another stronghold of polysexual anarchy and promiscuity. The frenetic orgies of Canopus and Carthage are as real today as they were centuries ago. Burton aptly observed that extensive social intercourse with Occidentals "has produced not a reformation but a certain reticence amongst the upper classes; they are as vicious as ever, but they do not care for displaying their vices to the eyes of mocking strangers." India and Pakistan, which have not forgotten the fanatic debaucheries of the Moghul Empire, also enjoy a virtual free-for-all of fornication.

There is much jealousy and competition among Eastern females for possession of the male, and this jealousy and competition is heightened by widespread homosexuality. A woman will indulge in anal intercourse, however painful, just to hold her man. Although the Eastern male can no longer subjugate the female socially, he can control her sexually, exploiting her as she exploits him. Although the modern feminist can legislate monogamy and civil rights, she cannot legislate love or fidelity; thus the Muslim woman married to a man who runs around with other females is no better off than when these rivals of hers were legal concubines. Whether or not the self-appointed moralists like it, polygamy will always exist either licitly or, in the forms of adulteries and divorces and remarriages, illicitly and by legalistic device. Moreover, endemic homosexuality seems to represent a massive masculine reaction to the threat or reality of feminine domination. This reaction has always existed in the world. Males and females have probably always been, consciously and/or unconsciously, afraid and distrustful of each other. Civilization has only increased rather than decreased the range and intensity of the primitive "battle of the sexes," making it more subtle, more complex, and more mutilating.

Sophisticated Muslim women who still wear the veil often do so for erotic reasons. Facial concealment adds an alluring spice of aromatic mystery and savory excitement to what has now become, in these seemingly stereotyped and sterile times, a routine meal. A veiled woman can openly get away with more than an unveiled one, and because she cannot be recog-

187

nized, she avoids all scandal and can cuckold her husband or sweetheart as much as she pleases.

The observant often see a veiled female signaling to a young man whose looks she likes, then ducking into a dark alley or doorway with him. There, standing with parted thighs against the wall, she will lift her gown or let down her slacks and allow him to rub his penis against her vulva or partially penetrate her with his glans, which he works up and down between her labia, or completely penetrate her until he nears his ejaculation, when she, by long experience, will know just when to withdraw from him before he pays his tribute—and then only a second before.

Others, however, love to feel the exciting surge of seminal fluid against their wombs. The (to them) wondrous feeling of this fecundating fluid gushing in and oozing out is an extreme erotic excitation and thrill. Van de Velde writes that "there are women who decisively affirm that they only experience the orgasm if and when they feel the impact of the seminal fluid against the *portio vaginalis*." Many Muslim females will risk impregnation if only to savor the ineffable sensation of semen spurting into their sensitive organs, such being the final and most favored complement of a rapid round of phallic thrusts. In such women, so adapted are they to the male organ, only upon sensing the oncoming of the man's climax, the pulsations and distention of the penis followed by an explosive discharge, do they achieve their own orgasm; and for a man to withdraw prematurely would mean for them little enjoyment. Some females admit that the sensations in their "sheath" at the instant of the male's emission are so acute that they nearly lose their senses; their legs tremble violently, their wombs seem to leap within their loins, and they can scarcely keep from sagging to the ground in a voluptuous languor. Such women can never understand why other females (or males, for that matter) use

188

contraceptives which dull (condom) or hinder (diaphragm) this natural feeling.(9)

The Talmud states that "we know by tradition that a woman cannot conceive in a standing position," the idea being that the male fluid ebbs rapidly out of the vagina and is given no chance to penetrate the uterus. This assumption, however, does not prevent Muslim and Jewish women from carrying contraceptives along with them wherever they go. The most common article, which is worn at all times by some females for on-the-spot activity, is the *mās* or "absorbent." These are tufts of oiled cotton or wool, sponge, or some other substance, somewhat like a tampon or diaphragm, which are inserted and removed in a matter of seconds with the fingers or with a small silver probe which is generally worn in the hair. The *mās* serves to block the semen from entering the uterus, and it won widespread popularity in the cities of North Africa and Arabia several hundred years ago. The Talmud comments: "Rabbi Jose is of the opinion that a woman who plays the harlot makes use of an absorbent in order to prevent conception." Other fast-and-loose fillies carry the common male article, the condom (*kīs*, penis purse) or prophylactic sheath, which they are wont to slip over and roll onto the erect organ of their partner prior to penetration.

Dr. Jacobus, who spent several years in the Far East, noted that "the Chinese and Japanese girls simply use little round plugs of oiled silk paper, which they insert in the vagina to cover the mouth of the womb." For hundreds of years, in order

---

(9) *Even the best of condoms is, of course, a bar to maximum sensation. There must be a "contact of epidermises" if sensory rewards are to be undiminished. However, the insistence by the female upon experiencing the male ejaculation (referring here to the emission of the semen and not to such other effects as may be present in the penis) is rare, especially in the United States.*

189

to prevent impregnation, Oriental females have used diaphragms or uterine plugs made of various oiled materials; and
their facility and effectiveness are proved by their tremendous
popularity. The classic condom or "silken cap" enjoyed little
success because it blunted sensation in both partners, and the
rubber article is no less scorned as a "cuirass against pleasure."
The use of the *mesīr* or "sheep's gut penis pouch" is almost
exclusively confined to the vice-infested cities of North Africa
and Arabia. After their menfolk have slaughtered a sheep or
goat, Bedawin women and girls will remove the long intestine,
manipulate it until it becomes thin and supple, soak it in oil,
and then sell it to pimps or prostitutes in the towns. Girls of
the Ulad Nayil, the great whoring tribe of Algeria, are noted
for making and carrying these disease-preventing sheaths,
which they fit over the man's phallus prior to penetration.

The Jewish and Muslim females of North African and Arabian cities notorious for on-the-street intercourse are wont to
call their standing position in coition *el-kirshī* or "the belly-to-
belly." *El-kirshī* has long been an erotic art cultivated by young
and old alike, from the five-year-old boy rubbing his glans
penis against the little vulva lips of a three-year-old girl in a
doorway to the fifty-year-old man completely penetrating a
thirty-year-old woman in a dark alleyway. The action employed
in the "belly-to-belly" or standing position involves a wide variety of deep and shallow movements, among which the most
common are (1) *delā ed-delō*, the "bucket-in-the-well motion,"
wherein the male and female alternately thrust to and from
each other "like the plunging of a pail into the water of a
well"; (2) *en-nitāhhī*, the "mutual-butting motion," in which
the two amorous actors in mated measure pound each other's
pubes like two butting beasts; (3) *el-khīyātī*, the "tailor's motion," wherein the male inserts his glans penis between the
female's labia and initiates a rapid and shallow poking, then
with a single stroke plunges deep in the vagina to ejaculate,

"like the pricking and pulling movement of the needle and thread"; (4) *es-sewākī*, the "toothpick motion," in which the male exercises a deep and dynamic circular probing of the vagina and a grinding of the pubes, thereby exciting the clitoris; (5) *sebk el-hhubb*, the "fusion of love," wherein the male introduces his member full length and firmly without moving, while the female squeezes and milks it by contracting her vulvo-vaginal muscles; (6) *el-hhiddādī*, the "blacksmith's motion," in which the male lunges deeply several times, then withdraws to glide his glans penis over the vulva, "like the blacksmith who pulls a white-hot poker from the furnace and thrusts it into cold water"; and (7) *deqq el-bāb*, the "knocking-at-the-door motion," wherein the male rubs and drubs his glans penis against the clitoris, over the labia, and in the vulvar vestibule and vaginal orifice.

Shallow or surface friction, involving merely the glans penis and the labia and clitoris, is said to be popular with young women and girls; while deep or interior friction, involving complete penetration and vagino-uterine stimulation, is the preference of older and more experienced females. Those attuned to rapid and satisfactory orgasm through primarily internal rather than external strokes almost invariably employ contraceptives.

The Fellahin girls of Egypt are among the most accomplished sirens in the Muslim world, and they often put their talents on a paying basis, the profits being very noticeable in their summary rise from rags to riches. They often say: "Earn your bread and butter; just learn how to futter!" In 1888 Sir Richard Burton had occasion to write:

> The last time I visited Cairo a Fellah wench—big, burly, and boisterous—threatened one morning, in a fine new French avenue off the Ezbekiyeh Gardens, to expose her person unless bought off with a piastre. The Cairenes, especially the feminine half, have always been held exceedingly de-

bauched. With civilization, they become worse; and the Kazi's court is crowded with would-be divorcées.

Burton does not mention whether or not these lusty females ever pursued sexual promiscuity at the same time they carried on their extortion activities, but a hint that they did (and that Burton, disguised as a Muslim, had erotic experiences with them) is couched in the following note:

> The *mendīl* or kerchief is mostly oblong, the short sides being worked with gold and colored silk, and often fringed, while the two others are plain. Women usually carry such articles with them when "on the loose," and in default of water and washing they are used to wipe away the results of carnal copulation.

In Burton's time, thousands of Muslim and Jewish women roamed the bazaars of North Africa and Arabia in quest of extemporaneous intercourse; and in El-Medina the Hindu women, who like the Egyptians did not wear veils, performed a sexual service for cunnus-starved pilgrims fresh from Mecca. These doe-eyed, beautiful Indians advertised their trade by "wearing tight, exceedingly tight, pantaloons" and by carrying several tinted silk handkerchiefs. In the crotch of these pantaloons, concealed between the thighs, there was usually a small slit or hole to allow immediate entry of the male organ.

What can be more revealing, but at the same time sensuously if not esthetically suggestive and concealing, than the skin-tight trousers and panties that many Muslim, Jewish and Indian women wear? They are so close-fitting, and mold the flesh so perfectly, that the vulvar cleft is clearly seen in smooth outline. It is said that Arabian women remove all their pubic hair in order to make their *kus* (crack) or *ferj* (slit) more visible. Moreover, these pantaloons of the fair sex are so tight that some men cannot help but imagine they cause an almost

192

constant irritation to their wearers. Many Muslim females are anatomically altered by clitoridectomy and/or nymphotomy, which means that such trousers may be practical in their particular case, but uncircumcised girls need not seek artificial excitation. They do, nonetheless, for skin-tight panties and pantaloons have a peculiar effect upon the little head of the clitoris. They wear these pants not only to excite the sexuality of men but also to keep themselves in a state of exquisite sensitivity, since the heated friction of the tight-fitting fabric tickles them whenever they walk or run.

To say that exceedingly snug panties or trousers are comfortable is to cloud the issue. Many Eastern females first learn to rub their genitals for sexual satisfaction by way of their clothing, towels, bedsheets, or some other fabric with which they come into direct contact between the thighs and which produces pleasurable sensations when pressed and pulled against the vulva. So it is not at all unusual that these same females, when they are past the age of puberty and once having formed the habit, unconsciously like to keep such significant material in constant and closest contact with their genitals.

The Bedawin point with pride at the fact that their women's *sirwāl* or petticoat trousers are baggy and loose, while the city women wear them skin tight, saying that these close-fitting pants are the vehicle of their continuous masturbation and the excitant of their lascivious thoughts, habitual lesbianism, and excessive sexual intercourse. But city ladies note the "looseness" of Bedawin drawers, the ease of removal, and speak of "slackness of slacks" and "laxity in the trouser string."

"May my rival find his snare in her bushy pubic hair!" is an old Egyptian saying. Muslim women traditionally shave or pluck the pubes for hygienic and esthetic reasons. A smooth vulva makes them appear girlish and therefore more desirable to the menfolk, who admire a "hairless peach." This craving for depilated genitals often has its origin in early erotic experiences. Since prepubertal children customarily observe each other's nakedness and engage extensively in genital play, the smooth symmetry of the sexual organs remains impressed in their minds. Masculine partiality to depilated pubes may also reckon in the powerful nymphophilia complex, and a hairless vulva naturally enhances the girlishness of a slender woman's form.

Jacobus and Stern saw both veiled and unveiled women and girls standing in the back streets of Alexandria, Port Sa'id, and Suez with their robes pulled up above their thighs, rubbing their vulvas and inviting passing men to serve them sexually. Homosexuals spat at their feet and offered them icy stares. In front of their houses and brothels, both veiled and unveiled females assumed the *mejlis* (sitting) or *muqerfis* (squatting) positions of coition. They reclined with legs splayed and thighs spread wide apart, completely exposing their hairless vulvas, which in some cases gaped because of nymphotomy or were held open to reveal the red vestibule and vagina. Modesty, cultivated by the Bedawin, is virtually unknown to other Arabs and Jews. North African Jewish girls frequently lift their dresses to scratch their hairy sex organs, and the same is true of bare-faced Fellahin females. When Muslim males behold a female scratching her vulva they often say, "O bitch! does your slit itch?" (*Yā qehhbeh, shī jerbān ferjik*), meaning that the prurience goes far deeper than the outer parts.

5. ANAL INTERCOURSE

The female is your field;
Till her in whatever way you will.

EL-QURĀN 2:248-9

Dr. Jacobus notes that "the Arab is an active pederast and a sodomist, cultivating with an equal taste the male and female orifice. It matters little to him which it is." In seeking to explain the popularity of *coitus per anus* in the polysexual East, Jacobus adds:

> It is certain that the friction of the penis against the anal sphincter, which possesses great contractile power, is greater than it would be in a vagina dilated and relaxed by the heat of the climate.

Since physical pleasure in the male depends upon friction of the penis, the desire for anal intercourse is readily understandable.(1) The genital organs of Middle Eastern and African

---

·ľ·

(1) *The desire for anal intercourse and the pleasure found in it, by both the active and the passive partners, are readily understandable*

195

women, often large even in the virginal state, exhibit great
looseness and lack of elasticity following childbirth, constant

---

on a physiological basis. However, where most Europeans and Americans are concerned, psychical factors often override the physical ones to make the pleasures of anal intercourse both impossible and incomprehensible. As should by now be plain, the Arab, much more than the typical Westerner, seems to be able to approach his erotic acts on the basis of sensation, excluding or at least drastically minimizing the effectiveness of the psychical elements.

The heterosexual Westerner tends to avoid anal intercourse on both positive and negative grounds. That is to say, "positively" he is much more attracted, partly as a consequence of conditioning, and perhaps partly as a consequence of reproductive instinct, to the vagina and to coitus. "Negatively," and in accordance with the values he has been conditioned to accept, he thinks of sodomy as an unnatural and/or sinful act. Also, he thinks of the anus, from which excrements are voided, as dirty; and of anal intercourse as a dirty (unhygienic and unesthetic) act. He has largely or altogether excluded from consciousness the erotic titillation he once received from the passage of his phalliform feces through his rectum, and which to the adult conscious of the titillation would inevitably suggest the possibility of repeating the sensation, and intensifying and prolonging it, by means of pederasty.

The combination of positive and negative psychical features mentioned above results in the individual's either not desiring anal intercourse in the first place or in his failing to achieve maximum physical rewards from it if the act is attempted. On the other hand, psychical factors may increase the pleasure he receives in coitus (though probably not on a sensory level). Unfortunately, the very same sex-is-sin conditioning that inhibits desire for and pleasure in anal intercourse often results also in negative attitudes toward the vagina and coition. This has the effect of diminishing sensation and may easily result in more serious impotence.

196

copulation, and (as Jacobus noted) the effects of climate. Moreover, a physiological fact is that the *sphincter ani,* a ringlike
contractile muscle surrounding the anal orifice, far surpasses
the typical *constrictor cunni* in strength.

The lustful Oriental, by virtue of his bisexual and sadomasochistic nature, seeks the most intense and vigorous stimulation
of the penis. In boyhood he is an ardent masturbator; in manhood he is an ardent fornicator. This not only explains in part
the Oriental's preference for girls, whose little vulvas are tight
and narrow; but also for boys, whose anuses are selected for
the greater narrowness they afford the voluptuary.

Eastern languages emphasize this desirable diameter in their
words for anus; e.g., Turkish *byūzyūk* (that which is contracted), Persian *chusteh* (that which is tight and narrow), and
Hindustani *gāndh* (knot). The Arabs say facetiously:

> The penis, smooth and round,
> > Was made with anus for to fit;
> It would look just like a hatchet
> > Were it made for sake of slit.

Although the penis of the Muslim may be quite large, the
common aim is not to desire a proportionate receptacle. The
more fashionable ideal is to force it into the smallest possible
orifice and then to thrust unmercifully until the ejaculation
occurs. Hence the Hindu *gāndhmārā* (anus beater) or *gāndhū*
(anuser), having a little penis, may be justified in asking his
wife or sweetheart to present her buttocks; but what excuse
can the *kher-nefseh* (mule-membered man) offer in defense of
his addiction to anal intercourse?

However, when the roué wearies of conventional copulation
there is always a new approach to be considered. Consequently,
istāneh (analism, from the Arabic *ist,* anus) first became a
sexual fad in classic times; for an *Arabian Nights* satire on the
subject runs thusly:

197

> She offered me a tender coynte;
>   But I, "I will not swive," replied.
> She drew back, saying, "Destiny
>   Turns him from truth who's turned aside,
> And futtering frontwise in our time
>   Is fain abandoned and decried!"
> So round she swung, showed shining rump
>   Like lump of silver, her backside.
> "Well done, O mistress mine; no more
>   Am I in pain for thee," I cried,
> "Whose hole of all Allah's openings
>   Is sure the tightest, never wide!"

Mardrus and Mathers translate the following variation of this well-known gem from the pen of the pederastic poet and lampooner, Abu Nowas:

> The other day, or rather night,
> She showed a grotto sweet and tight;
> And when I said, "That's out of fashion,"
> Instead of flying in a passion
> She turned quite round and smiled. "I know
> That modern men do not do so;
> See, I am up-to-date," she said.

Throughout the Muslim world there are women and girls who, competing *à la aversa venus* with men and boys, love "buttockry." In fact, according to many observers, the incidence of heterosexual sodomy and the feminine fancy for sodomitic excitation of the anus are widespread and well-nigh universal throughout Africa and Asia. Sundry Muslims told Jacobus that at least three out of five of their females actively solicit anal intercourse, while the remaining two only experience it incidentally. With their extensive sensitivity and far-reaching receptivity, Arab women generally regard *istāneh* as an extremely enjoyable method of preventing pregnancy, pleasing their menfolk, and achieving orgasm. From all accounts, there is little doubt that anal activity runs a very close race in popularity with vaginal intercourse, followed by oral and manual pursuits. Thus a man who loves anal intercourse, but who is not esthetically attracted to members of his own sex, will play at ducks and drakes by plying his particle of copulation in the posternal conjunctive of the female; and he needn't look long and far to find one as avid and eager as he is for this type of sport.(2)

·ᐟ·

(2) While today's Western female is less than avid for anal activities, and may find them thoroughly repulsive, this was not always the case. Heterosexual sodomy, like some other erotic practices, is subject to alternating periods of fad and disfavor. The matrons of ancient Rome, for example, at one period notoriously and deliriously delighted in anal intercourse; and the same was true of both the high- and the low-born Parisienne in the time of Napoleon. It is worthy of remark that such predilections have traditionally been more common among the higher levels of society, so that Kinsey's finding that the better educated are the more likely to engage in erotic refinements came as no surprise to historians.

Psychological motivations to anal intercourse are many and various. The fact that sodomy, as compared to coitus, is so often painful, is of major significance. So is the association of the anus with the elimination of "filth" of great import. This last is particularly true in the Western world.

Just after World War II, as one of the authors (R. E. L. M.) personally observed and was advised by informed students of sexual behavior, there was a remarkable increase in the practice of anilingus, or tongue stimulation of the male anus, by German females. This activity occurred almost entirely among women having sexual relations with members of the armed forces of the occupying Allied powers.

The pleasure derived by German females from this practice seems

199

The Kabuli, notorious for heterosexual sodomy, lives only for the orgastic ecstasies derived from "raking a woman's rear end." Hence the famous ditty, *Qedr-i-kus Afghān dāned; qedr-i-kunrā Kābulī dāned:*

> The worth of crack the Afghan knows;
> The worth of hole the Kabuli chose!

The word "boy" in *Zekhmī Dil* (Wounded Heart), the pederastic love song of the Pathans, is altered to "girl" by the *ist-zen* (anus beater) of Kabul: "There's a girl across the river with a postern like a peach, but alas! I cannot swim."

The *ghulāmīyeh* or "she-boy" has become an institution in the Islamic East. She is the sister of the *ghulām* (catamite), for the *ghulāmīyeh* is a girl ordinarily dressed as a boy and employed for "homosexual" purposes in the houses of enter-

---

to have been quite masochistic, and to have aimed at and successfully evoked a sadistic response in the male participants. The act symbolized the total subjection of the conquered to the conquerors, and it was an extreme manifestation of a much broader psychosexual disturbance.

There were a considerable number of German women who would have nothing to do sexually with their own defeated troops, but who were thoroughly promiscuous with the occupation forces. This seems not to have meant, as some supposed, that the German males, erstwhile supermen, were regarded as emasculated by their defeat. The German females, rather, were in many cases unconsciously (and sometimes consciously) attempting to share the degradation of their men. Some, feeling great guilt at having remained home in comparative safety while so many millions of males died in combat, felt unworthy of their own men. Doubtless, too, they were in part obeying the age-old impulse of conquered female populations to redress the balance of power by castrating the victors.

tainment and refreshment.(3) Abu Nowas was the first to extol the "she-boy" in verse:

> Wine comes from coynted one
>   Dressed as if she had a peeter;
> She has two lovers, cunnuser
>   And anus beater.

These serving girls, many of whom are lesbians, generally wear their hair bobbed like that of a boy—and for all outward appearances they are effeminate males! The *ghulāmīyeh* keeps

---

.T.

(3) *The girl who dresses as a boy to engage in anal and oral inter-course with males is a comparatively rare phenomenon. She is not entirely unknown to the brothels of France and Germany, but she is much harder to find than in the East. On the other hand, boys who dress as girls, and men who dress as women, for the purpose of homosexual prostitution are to be found throughout the world.*

The term "she-man" ("she-boy" very rarely) is sometimes used in the United States to refer to the effeminate or "swish" type of homosexual male. In U.S. women's prisons, the same term is used to designate a lesbian, usually of the masculine or "butch" type, who takes the male role in female homosexual intercourse.

Among some primitive peoples, the "she-man" is a male used by other males for homosexual purposes. Such she-men are usually dressed as females and do the work of women, and in many cases they have been "castrated" by systematic masturbation, which is performed on the she-man-to-be by relays of women over an ex-tended period of time. Certain American Indian tribes are said to have manufactured their she-men by binding naked youths to wild stallions. This is said to have had the effect of provoking repeated seminal issues, which resulted eventually in permanent impotence followed by a feminizing of both body and mind. Probably the long jolting ride on the stallion destroyed the capacity of the tes-ticles to function.

201

her pubes and anus plucked clean and smooth of hair, and every day she conscientiously exercises her anal sphincter to strengthen and retain its superior muscular tone. Sometimes, if the price is right, she will submit to bilateral fornication; whereby she becomes "apt for two tricks," per anum and per cunnum, taking two males at one time.

We know that the pelvic musculature of the female is greater and stronger than that of the male. The powerful *constrictor cunni* and *levator vaginae* muscles are closely connected with the *sphincter ani* by a network of fibers which encircle and reinforce the rectum and which, by reflex action, transmit the voluntary and involuntary spasms and contractions of one into the other. Thus many Muslims note that the venereal endurance of the female, coupled with the intensity of her internal muscular action, make her indispensable for anal intercourse. It is also observed that erotic excitation is more rapidly and readily radiated from the vagina to the rectum than it is from the penis to the anus by reason of the connecting and corresponding structures of the female reproductive and excretory organs.

The *ghulāmīyeh* will assume in analism (*istāneh*) the same squatting posture as the *ghulām*. The active partner, called *el-istānī* (the analist) or *el-fā'il* (the doer, counterpart of *el-mef'ūl*, the done), will squat close behind the passive partner and insert his glans penis between her buttocks. Then, as he embraces her, she will lower her posterior and, by twisting round and round, gradually force his glans penis inside the anal orifice. Penetration having been effected, the girl will begin to "grind" by lurching and swiveling her buttocks; while the man, reaching around with his hands, will tender a continuous rubbing of her vulva, particularly the clitoris. Tremorous undulations and rippling constrictions stir her vaginal and rectal tracts, touched off by the clitoral titillation and masturbatory manipulation of her cunnus, followed by a violent and pro-

202

longed convulsion of the pelvic muscles at the approach of, during, and just after the orgasm.

These muscular pulsations and paroxysms are felt to be longer and stronger in the female than those experienced in the male during genital excitation and the spasms of ejaculation. Most important of all, the average male commonly loses his erection and sensation after the first, second, or third emission; while the average female who is attuned to protracted sexual excitement can endure and enjoy at least twice if not three times that number of climaxes. Thus the active and passive partners need never move alternately or simultaneously, but may remain perfectly still and rely solely upon reflex action to supply the pleasurable agitation. Involuntary muscular movements are then reinforced with voluntary motions, or a forceful squeezing and pumping of the penis by the anal sphincter, in such a manner as to milk the virile member to orgasm. During all this time the male will continue to masturbate the female and fondle her breasts until satisfaction is achieved. The Japanese term this erotic activity *mitokoro-zeme* or "attack on three parts"; for the man penetrates the woman's anus, fingers her clitoris, and handles her breasts.

Some Persian physicians, in seeking to explain the prevalence and popularity of *istāneh* in Iran, blame it upon "excessive" boyhood masturbation. They remark that in *jelq* (jerking) or *musht-zenī* (beating by hand, clutching the penis in the fist and pounding or flipping it) there is more vigorous stimulation than that experienced in vaginal intercourse, and that the velvety and slippery walls of the vagina cannot equal the energetic rubbing and manipulation enjoyed by the masturbator. Hence the claim to fame of heterosexual and homoerotic sodomy is often attributed to the intense pressure and friction accorded the penis of the Irani masturbator by the narrow anus of a girl or boy. Pederasty in Iran is therefore often a purely physical phenomenon, which may have nothing to do with

psychic homosexuality. Paolo Mantegazza termed this "lustful sodomy," due to a desire for vaginal narrowness and mas-
turbation-like stimulation. Mantegazza's analysis of Oriental
analism has never been refuted, and those who ignore it have
no realistic understanding of Oriental sexuality. He writes:

> It is easy to explain the voluptuous inclination of the active
> sodomist, who derives from the act a true erotic pleasure by
> way of a path selected for the extreme narrowness of diameter
> it affords. This explains why it is that in many countries sod-
> omy is practiced only upon boys, and it likewise explains
> why this vice is a good deal more common in warm countries,
> where the woman is often dishearteningly large in her sex
> organ and where nudity is ever visible and women are easy to
> be had, all of which circumstances are but spurs to lust.(4)

---

(4) In the past, southern Europe was notorious for its high incidence
of homosexual intercourse. However, at the present time homosexuality is at least equally and possibly even more rife in northern than
in southern Europe, and in the north there is a strong predilection
for boys. This is, of course, relevant only to the extent that psychical
homosexuality, as distinguished from the predominantly physical
craving for greater friction, motivates the Oriental sodomist. Similar
effects need not imply similar causes.

The preference of a great many Western adult homosexuals for
boys has, in fact, little or nothing to do with the dimensions of the
anus-rectum. Large numbers of homosexuals notoriously tend to
prefer youthful sex partners (though not necessarily "boys"), and it
is well known that older homosexuals have a difficult time acquiring
lovers and often have to resort to male prostitutes. It would not be
amiss here to remark that heterosexual males also appreciate youth
in their sex partners; and that the burden upon the wallet of the
heterosexual male also tends to increase commensurate with the
number of his years and the expansion of his waistline.

Again, this search after more intense friction, leading to anal inter-

Before one attempts to analyze Oriental sexual behavior, one must first be fully impressed with the fact that all is grist to the Oriental mill which finds something good in every grain. Julius Rosenbaum also considers this "luxurious sodomy":

> Pederasty appears, as is the case with all sexual perversions, to owe its origin to the stimulation of the Asiatic climate, the mother of exuberance and voluptuousness. The primary condition of its genesis may be easily traced, if side by side with the dictum of Forberg (*Hermaphroditus:* "The pleasure of the sodomite is readily intelligible, since all voluptuous pleasure depends on friction of the penis"), we take into consideration the fact that the genital organs of Asiatic women—a fact true also of Italian and Spanish women—like their whole bodies, exhibit great looseness, and further note that the *sphincter ani* muscle far and away surpasses the *constrictor cunni* in strength.*

course, is very largely alien to the contemporary West. A "tight" vagina is commonly preferred over a loose or "sloppy" one, but that is about as far as the matter goes. One is tempted to propose an "obvious explanation"—that the penis of the Western male, either naturally or because it is subjected to less abuse, is more sensitive than that of his Eastern counterpart, so that such vigorous stimulation is not required. However, any conclusion of the kind must remain only speculative.

There is the (mentioned) possibility, too, of a greater general Eastern anatomic disproportion, structural or climatic, between the male and female parts. And one must also reckon with the possibility that the Western male, as well, would often prefer the greater friction afforded by anal intercourse if he were not conditioned to avoid and condemn such activity.

* Dr. Julius Rosenbaum, *The Plague of Lust.* Paris: Carrington, 1910.

Whether pederasty did or did not originate in the East is unimportant—and unknowable. What the Orient did is to legitimatize and systematize man's other nature, which explains modern attitudes of tolerance and acceptance, contrasting queerly with Occidental hatred and hysteria. The fatalistic Easterner is less afraid of life, less afraid of his own bisexual nature, than is the humanistic Westerner.

Burton observed in Turkey, Persia, Afghanistan, and Kashmir, countries proverbial for heterosexual sodomy, two peculiarities of the feminine figure: hanging breasts and slack vaginas. While Hindu and Arab women, even after parturition and lactation, appeared to have the firm vaginas and high breasts of virgin girls (in Arabic *meflūkeh*, she who has round plump breasts), those of the so-called "Sotadic Zone" seemed to lose all the fine curves of the bosom and elastic tightness of the vaginal orifice, sometimes even before the first child. Burton concluded that these anatomical peculiarities are more hereditary than climatic, citing as an example the women of South India who, inhabiting a damper and hotter region than Sind or the Punjab, are noted for firm rounded breasts and narrow tensile vaginas even after parturition.

Burton, in his observations of young Irani analists, found that "most actives end within the nates [achieve orgasm by rubbing the glans penis between the buttocks], being too much excited for further intromission [responding without actual penetration of the anus]." In this connection, after noting that sodomy begins in boyhood, Burton adds that "onanism is to a certain extent discouraged by circumcision." Little boys, finding *musht-zenī* (jerking off) somewhat painful for several weeks following circumcision, resort to *elish-tekish* (give and take), wherein they take turns rubbing the glans penis between the buttocks. Response is rapid, for the *hheshfeh* (head) is very sensitive. Riza Bey, a Turkish physician, writes that "the pain involved in the masturbation of those who are newly circumcised is much too severe not to outweigh the pleasure combined with the act; but this pain must be all the greater and inevitable, the more sensitive the corona or rim of the glans is, and the higher the tension caused by the shortened foreskin in erection as it resists the pleasurable friction of the glans." Were a newly circumcised boy to penetrate another's anus, the friction and pressure would be so intense (affecting the tender circumcisional cicatrice as in manual manipulation) that pain would overcome pleasure. Hence a new pattern of pleasure is established to replace the old. Moreover, since anal penetration is often a difficult procedure for the active and a painful experience for the passive partner, the contact is customarily exterior. Many anoerotics need only insert their organ between the buttocks, and orgasm occurs immediately or very quickly after a few seconds of friction.

The Arab is not as fastidious as the Irani; for if he can effect it, he almost invariably enters all the way. This is one of the reasons why more and more Muslims are having their male children circumcised in infancy, after the Jewish fashion, not wishing temporarily to deprive them of any erotic pleasures when they are old enough to indulge in sexual stimulation. Over the centuries, the age at which circumcision is customarily performed has become lower and lower. It was originally a puberty rite, practiced between the ages of twelve and fifteen. When its primitive significance was lost with the advent of civilization, the age of operation dropped to ten, then eight, then five. Now it is extensively enacted at age three, sometimes at one or two, and in a short time to come the many who are circumcised within three weeks after birth will form the majority and finally the totality. This will mean that every sexually active little boy, having undergone the operation in early infancy, may freely experience erections and play with his penis without fear of pain or discomfort; for a circumcision wound is thoroughly healed by the time a baby is a month old, the actual cicatrization taking place within a week or two. Thus compassionate Muslims, anxious not to interfere with their little sons' autoerotic impulses and pleasures, have the operation enacted in infancy (just after birth or a bit later) to insure an uninterrupted development of active and intensive sexuality: the Islamic ideal.

Dr. Jacobus, who examined hundreds of Muslims from Malaya to Morocco, reports in his *L'Ethnologie du Sens Génitale*:

> The costume of the passive pederast presents a peculiarity worthy of being noted. Their Turkish pantaloons frequently have an orifice behind on a level with the anus and perfectly dissimulated by the folds of the garment. This enables them commodiously and without undressing to abandon themselves to their shameful trade.
>
> An examination of the clothes of sodomites may lead to interesting discoveries. Very often a hole is found in the trousers at about the level of the genitofemoral fold.

This genitofemoral orifice, which Jacobus discovered in the *sirwāl* or "bag breeches" of nearly every non-Westernized Muslim, is the original trouser fly as invented by the Turks and introduced into Europe from Turkey between the eighteenth and nineteenth centuries. Its purpose is not only to facilitate urination (since modern Arabs, like the Westernized Turks, make water in a standing position) but also to facilitate the active analism, fornication, rape, and mutual fellatio or masturbation so common among them. So-called "passives" have both an open crotch and a small fold or fly in the rear of their drawers to allow free egress of their own erect penis, which the so-called "active" clasps and manipulates, as well as free ingress of their partner's phallus per anum. To facilitate intromission by dilation, the passive "forces" himself as in the act of defecation; the active's penis is thereby directed and drawn in until the glans is past the anal sphincter, which tightly grips the organ below the corona. While the *fā'il* masturbates him, the *mef'ūl* runs through his erotic routine of rotations and gyrations, lurching and shaking, pumping and squeezing.

In examining the sexual and anal organs of Muslims who engage regularly in active and passive sodomy, Jacobus found nothing unusual. In some, the folds of the anus were slightly obliterated and the sphincter a trifle lax, admitting one or two fingers without the usual involuntary constriction; but in most analists there was absolutely no sign of sodomy. The sphincter was strong and difficult to pass, reactive to penetration by powerful contraction.(5) The penis ordinarily hung smooth and "semierect," expanding and elongating very little when perfectly stiff; the glans was normally large, the cicatricial skin fully retracted as a narrow ring of scar tissue rather than forming a fleshy collar under the corona. This phallic semierection

---

·T·

(5) *This would, if true, be remarkable. Western physicians who have examined large numbers of passive sodomists are almost unanimous in declaring that such an individual may be detected with the greatest of ease. There is a characteristic reaction to digital penetration of the anus which is impossible to suppress over any period of time.*

Many physicians, since the days of ancient Rome (if not earlier) up to the present, have claimed to be able to recognize practitioners of passive sodomy by visible external signs (as well as by reaction to penetration). Others, however, have found no such signs, or have not recognized them, so that external alterations resulting from anal intercourse remain, if held to be universal or general, not conclusively demonstrated.

(Particularly fanciful-sounding are the reports of those [for example, Tardieu] who assert that the anus of the catamite comes to resemble the external genitalia of the female. If the phenomenon they describe exists, it is far from commonplace.)

209

is a racial as well as an individual peculiarity, Jacobus thought, while extreme heat and humidity tend to weaken genital muscle tone and produce flaccidity.

When Hendrik de Leeuw heard a Frenchman say, "*Hein, monsieur*; the Moor attacked her with the frenzy of an Arabian steed," he learned his first lesson in Arab psychology. De Leeuw observed how Muslims will "forsake home and family and will fall into a life of the most debauched savagery." Astounded by their "barbaric amorous violence" and "almost bestial passion," he remarks:

> Their satiety then breeds demands for novelties. . . . With passions unhampered by moral restraint, the Moor indulges, and does so wildly, in dissipations of the worst nature. Often he admits to incest, which seems to have for him a most captivating fascination. And, a more common abnormality, Moors and Arabs are abject homosexuals. . . . And there is probably no person elsewhere in the world who enjoys sex gratification with animals—dead or alive—in such a measure as do the Moors of the Maghreb. . . . It is understandable that many develop into sadists who delight in inflicting cruel and degrading acts on others. . . .
>
> Knowing nothing of morality, they have no strength of will. They resemble animals in their repeated yielding to impulse.

Dr. Jacobus, considering "the ferocious lust of the African Arabs," concludes that "the Arab is the greatest pederast in the whole world." He elucidates:

> The Arab is an inveterate pederast, even where there is no lack of women. He is not particular in his choice, and age or sex make no difference to him. Boy or girl, anus or cunnus— they're all the same to him, and he loves each with an avid passion.
>
> Woe betide any handsome young man who falls into the hands of Bedawin rapists. They will commence by robbing

him of all he has, not leaving him even a shirt. What follows need not be described, but they take turns abusing his anus and penis—and sometimes even his mouth!—and after having thus tortured him, they will leave him naked.

I have in my possession reports concerning atrocities perpetrated by rebel tribesmen under the leadership of Sheykh 'Abdel-Krim during the recent campaigns in Morocco [the great revolt of 1919–26]. The fanatic Riffs, Berbers, and Kabyles castrated every French and Spanish soldier, wounded or dead, whom they found uncircumcised. The English encountered similar acts during their Egyptian and Sudanese wars of the last century; all uncircumcised soldiers left wounded or dead on the battlefield were later found mutilated between the legs and their foreheads slashed or throats slit. The Arabs are in the aberrant habit of pulling a wounded or dead Infidel's trousers down and examining his genitals as to size and shape, dissatisfaction resulting in mutilation. An entire company of Zouaves was found with their penises cut off, indicating that the Berbers deemed them praiseworthy trophies to show to their women and children. Signs of unnatural rape were also prevalent; numerous dead and wounded troops, as well as live prisoners, were buggered by Moroccans, who held daggers to their throats. Two Spanish seamen, captured by Bedawin after the annihilation of Spanish forces at Anual in 1921, escaped death after a harrowing experience. They were stripped, raped anally, and masturbated by about a dozen rebels. Stark naked, nearly dead from thirst and heatstroke, they finally reached safety. A patrol of spahis [Algerian native cavalry] and their French lieutenant, captured by Riff horsemen in 1926, suffered a similar fate. The officer later reported: "They unceremoniously stripped us, jerked us off, and nearly staved our fundaments in with their large weapons. We escaped castration only because I, being a European, was the only uncircumcised Infidel in the lot." Circumcised prisoners, whether European or Muslim, although they did not suffer mutilation, were nonetheless, as one captain of the

211

Foreign Legion expressed it, "jerked off in front and jabbed behind so fiercely as to ruin one's copulatory and excretory functions."

El-Ghīlān (The Ghouls) are bands of professional raiders, slavers, and rapists who operate in the vast Sahara from Timbuktu to Libya and the Sudan. They are mostly Berbers and half-breed Arabs, numbering among them a few Negroes. They rob, strip, analize, and masturbate (then sometimes castrate and sell) their male victims; while unfortunate females, whatever their age, are no less savagely received. They gloat over a captive's genitals, handling and measuring them, often taking photographs of their prisoners in the nude. The Arabs and other Muslims are notorious for carrying pictures of naked men as well as women. The most common pose is a large Negro standing and lustily grasping his stiff penis, often holding and brandishing it with both hands if it is long enough, as if in the act of masturbation. Other popular photos show lusty-looking Arabs sodomizing grinning Negroes, the while clutching their rigid penises in a scene of passion.

The ghoul (*ghūl*, mischief maker) is the ravishing phantom of the wasteland. Robbers and rapists, thought to be possessed by the evil penis genie and demon of debauchery *El-A'wer* (The One-Eye), are therefore named after various species of ghouls and jinn which roam and ravage the deserts of North Africa and the Middle East. *Es-sa'lāh* (the seducer) is an insidious creature which entices lone travelers, captures them, and plays with them as the cat plays with the mouse. *El-gheddār* (the trickster) is found throughout the Sahara and Arabia, as first reported by Edward William Lane: "It is said that it entices a man to it, and either tortures him in a manner not to be described, or merely terrifies him and leaves him." * *El-kābūs* (the assaulter) is the Islamic incubus. So does the Arab

* Edward William Lane, *Notes on the Arabian Nights*, London: 1898.

find an outlet for his exuberant sadomasochism in the realm of fantasy as well as in that of reality.(6)

"Shallehhūh tishlīhh!" (They stripped him totally) is a common exclamation among traveling Arabs. The verb *shallehh,* "to rob or strip," also means "to make one undress himself." Every month, numerous wayfaring African Muslims are waylaid by plunderers and made to remove all their clothes. Outside the oases, young Negroes are a favorite prey. Assailants will seize a black youth, pull off his pants, handle his penis until it is erect, then suck it ravenously and repeatedly, spitting his own sperm in his face after each ejaculation. Having fellated him to exhaustion, they take turns furiously attacking

·ⲓ·
_____

(6) *Malign and lustful spirits are to be met with in the past, and to some extent in the present, of every nation of the West. They were common among the Greeks and Romans of the ancient world, who had a whole menagerie of such creatures. Incubi and succubi, werewolves and vampires, were abroad in Europe well up into the last century, and in some rustic regions the belief in their existence is still prevalent today.*

Slavic peoples are particularly victimized by spirits comparable to those which roam the deserts of North Africa and the Middle East. Most commonly—reversing the situation encountered in Europe in the Middle Ages and during the Witch Mania—such demons and depraved spirit entities are of the female sex, or at least are feminine in form. They prey upon males who travel by night, or who become lost in the woods or in remote mountainous regions. The East has no monopoly on strange sexual beings who seduce or ravish their human victims in dreams, daydreams, hallucinations, trance states, narcotic visions, etc.

(The sexual intercourse of Arabs with demons is discussed by Allen Edwardes in The Jewel in the Lotus *[Julian Press, 1959]. The same phenomenon as it occurs in the West is dealt with at great length by R. E. L. Masters in* Eros & Evil *[Julian Press, 1962].)*

213

his buttocks, fastening their greedy hands hungrily on his genitals in an effort to extract the last drop of desire from his body. Having drained him completely dry, as it were, they then force their organs into his mouth for a final foray and leave him stark naked and well-nigh senseless in the sand.

El-Lewātī (The Men of Lot) are sex clubs of fanatic homophiles against whom the Prophet Muhammed wrote: "Do you approach lustfully unto men, and lay wait in the highways?" The *lūtī* is a thief, a pimp, and a prostitute by profession; but for the sake of amusement, or "kicks," he devotes his attention to sexual assault. Jacobus received the personal testimony of a dozen or so Muslim merchants and travelers who had been robbed and raped by the *lūtī* outside oases and other dangerous areas of the Sahara. For example, of a small party en route from Khartum to Tripoli he writes:

> A young businessman, his twenty-year-old wife, their three-year-old daughter, and her nine-year-old brother were attacked by seven sodomists near the Sudanese-Libyan border. After robbing them of all their valuables, they made their victims undress at gunpoint; then four of the marauders seized the man's wife, their daughter, and his brother-in-law. While two of them held his arms with demonic strength, one of the sodomists pulled down the young man's underdrawers and forced his penis into his anus. Doing so, he grabbed hold of his victim's penis and rapidly masturbated it. The others followed him, raping the man five or six times. Three of the others took turns ravishing the man's wife in a natural and unnatural manner, treating her so brutally with violent thrusts that she fainted. They then assaulted the little girl. Not bothering to remove her panties, they pushed their penises fiercely between the poor child's thighs and buttocks. They did jerk down the boy's underpants and abused him again and again; in fact, all seven sodomized and masturbated the young lad.
>
> When I examined them, I found anal fissures in the young

wife and her small brother; the man's anus was merely sore and irritated. The wife's sexual organs were abrased. Because they did not remove the little girl's panties, she suffered no genital or anal injury. If they had, as in other cases I have seen, they may have driven their instruments of torture all the way into her little organs. The persistent masturbation did no harm to the boy, although it was forceful and abusive. His sister did not fully recover from the terrible shock of this attack for several days; moreover, she required the most medical treatment. The others were very sore and irritated. They were stripped and robbed of everything except their underclothing. If what one hears and sees is to be believed, these outrages occur every week throughout the desert areas and oases, where bands of plunderers and pleasure seekers pounce upon men, women, and children.

Similar situations are encountered in other parts of the Muslim world, and Pakistanis present a warning to all traveling females lest they suffer anal abuse: "Though of men there be famine, steer clear of these three: Afghani and Sindi and Kashmiree!"

Indian women and girls are frequently raped both anally and vaginally by lustful Mussulmans, hence a female who fares forth unescorted in "dangerous territory" is generally looking for what she eventually gets—and perhaps far more than she bargained for. A gang of Muslim boys may rape one or two Hindu girls all night long without stopping, and there are cases on record of five or six boys keeping two or three girls captive and attacking them repeatedly by turns for at least a couple of days. According to recent reports, this is extremely common in Japan, where almost every night young girls stagger home or to the local police, telling how they were picked up by older boys, promised a few hours of innocent fun, and finally forced into a place where they were raped again and again for what seemed an eternity. The beach house is a common site. Two thrill-seeking girls between the ages of ten and thirteen often find themselves trapped in a beach house with a half dozen once-friendly boys who now, with lustful fury, strip off their bathing suits, force them to the floor, pull their legs wide apart, and rape them continually and violently for nearly twenty-four hours. What begins as innocent fun inevitably ends as worldly folly.

The physical benefits of phallic stimulation during anal penetration were well known to the ancient Orientals, and the modern *istānī* or "anuser" of the East has retained the old technique. The *fā'il* (active) will squat behind the crouching *mef'ūl* (passive), introduce his penis into the anus, then elicit his partner's semen by hand. As previously noted in the case of females, genital excitation causes pleasurable contractions of the anal sphincter, a kind of milking of the penis. At the onset of ejaculation, the passive swings his buttocks to and fro or rotatively, which heightens the tension and provokes an explosive orgasm.

When a lieutenant in the Bombay Army, Richard Burton discovered that Karachi supported no less than three brothels "in which not women but boys and eunuchs, the former demanding nearly a double price, lay for hire." Burton, disguised as a Persian merchant, visited these *bechcheh-khānāt* (boy brothels) and satisfied his curiosity as to why the uncastrated catamites brought more for their favors than the castrated ones. What was true then is true today. The eunuchs of India and Pakistan are nearly all of the *sendelī* class, the "flat and smooth ones" or "human anvils," having had both penis and testicles cut off in infancy or boyhood by the barber's razor. Consequently, connection between the delicate nerve structure of the genitalia and that of the rectal tract is severed and destroyed. In old Karachi, unmutilated boys between the ages of six and twenty were better paid and preferred because they did not lack the "weights of the weaver" and because masturbatory

216

manipulation of their genitals provided pleasant results. Moreover, one of the strongest impulses of the homosexual is to masturbate anther male and play with his penis. Many Muslims
therefore choose the masculine *mef'ūl*, whom they can masturbate as well as analize, instead of the effeminate *hijrā*
(eunuch) who is "less than a woman between the legs." (7)

'T'

(7) *Brothels staffed with young male homosexual prostitutes are
rare in the United States, where they are called "peg houses," but
have long been known. Most prostitution of this (homosexual) type
is carried on instead by streetwalkers—youths and older males who,
by costume and hairstyle and mincing manner, and sometimes by
open approach, make known to other men their availability for
intercourse at a price.*

*A few male prostitutes are available in some "gay bars," but they
are seldom able to solicit openly for the reason that bars permitting
such activity are liable to loss of operating licenses and other penal-
ties. Massage parlors also occasionally provide male prostitution, as
may a few public baths and "health clubs."*

*Some juvenile street gangs procure or provide boys for homo-
sexuals, and often the gangs either terrorize neighborhood children
into engaging in such prostitution or else make participation a
requirement for membership in the gang. Funds taken in become
the gang's property, and then may be used to purchase the services
of female prostitutes for the gang's members.*

*Further, in recent years there has been an increasing amount of
male prostitution by high school students, usually on an individual
or small group basis, who provide such sex service to suitable adult
homosexuals whom they have met in various ways. Youths of this
type rarely solicit openly on the streets, but sometimes they loiter
around public latrines and are receptive to homosexual advances.*

*Despite all this, male prostitution is somewhat less than common-
place in the United States, although the continuance of present
trends may make it so.*

217

When King Richard the Lion-Hearted jestingly asked Sultan Saladin which he preferred, girls or boys, the Sword of Islam solemnly replied: "Girls? Allah forbid! It's as if you were to serve me a leg of lamb without the bone!" Saladin later added that he liked having something to hold onto while at work, explaining to the amused Infidel that the genitals of a boy can be used as a kind of bridle which directs the movements of an animal. Richard was not so partial as not to agree.

Anal intercourse, be it heterosexual or homosexual, was quite common if not customary in ancient Israel. It was just as popular among married lovers as among unmarried, for in the first case it was employed contraceptively and in the second to preserve virginity. A well-known *mishnāh* (oral law) which is recorded in the Talmud states:

> Even if ten men copulate unnaturally with a betrothed maiden, she is still a virgin.

The *gemārā* (commentary) explains this law:

> If injury to the anus is to be subject to the same restrictions as injury to the hymen, if the disqualification [with regard to virginity] should be extended to unnatural intercourse also, you will find no woman eligible to marry a high priest, since there is not one who has not been in some way wounded [deflowered anally]!

From this we learn that anal masturbation and copulation were endemic among classical Jewish girls, which led to the rescinding of the Mosaic prohibition against high priests marrying females who had been deflowered front and rear.(8)

---

(8) A case was recently reported of an American high school girl, up before a court on a charge of sex delinquency, who admitted to anal intercourse on a number of occasions, but who defended herself

Stimulation of the female anus is widespread and well liked among the modern Jews of North Africa. By the age of five, nearly every little Jewish girl has inserted one or two fingers or an object into both her rectum and her vagina. From about the age of three, females experience male penetration of buttocks and anus by older brothers, cousins, and other boys; hence many little girls come to identify the rectum with the vagina,

---

on the basis that she wanted to please her boyfriend without "doing anything wrong" (that is to say, without copulating and so sacrificing her virginity). Many other girls perform fellatio for this same reason, and countless others engage in mutual masturbation.

The practice of "petting" among United States teenagers has this primary objective—to provide sexual gratification for the boy and girl "without doing anything wrong." Breast-fondling and oral stimulation of the breasts, along with "French kissing" and other embracing are the methods of choice, closely followed by masturbation. Where coitus is taboo, fellatio and cunnilingus come next in popularity, with anal intercourse running a poor last.

Thus, the virginity taboo, and the insistence that premarital coitus is a heinous evil, tends to result in young people engaging in practices (to them) less satisfying and less conducive to the development of healthy sexual attitudes and adjustment to a normal (satisfactory) sexual life.

While many, and probably now a majority, of teenagers do copulate, it is plain that for many others the sexual values of our society are sufficiently confused and confusing to lead them to embrace, as a lesser evil, practices which are branded as "perverted" by many individuals and by the statutes of most states, and which probably ought logically to be regarded as greater, not lesser, evils in the social context. It is evident from the Talmudic law that the problem is not a new one, and that we have not come very far over the centuries in bringing custom and statute into alignment with the realities of adolescent (or adult) existence.

219

and friction of the anus produces erotic sensations similar to those resulting from friction of the vulva. The Talmudic injunction that "Even if ten men copulate unnaturally with a betrothed maiden, she is still a virgin" is a sanction of popular custom; for ten males often analize a betrothed girl when she is brought into her fiancé's house. The boy's brothers and other male relatives and friends besiege her buttocks so as not to deprive him of the right of "natural" consummation. Nonetheless, there are few virgins above the age of five—not even the daughters of rabbis. For if Jewish boys do not enfilade Jewish girls, Muslim youths introduce them to repeated rape both fore and aft. The daughters of rabbis are the prime targets of Arab penises. Fierce forays are made in mouth, genitals, and buttocks. They are abused in the most merciless manner, and these early erotic experiences ofttimes determine their sexual behavior later on in life.

Reporting on India and the Far East, Jacobus writes that "nearly all the Hindu and Muslim prostitutes allow themselves to be sodomized."

> The anal (as well as the vaginal) sphincter in the Indian and Mussulman races possesses less tonicity than in the European, consequently the sphincter is dilated more easily. I have always found the anus dilated and not affording the finger, when introduced into it, that sensation of constriction which it meets in those who do not allow themselves to be sodomized. I have always observed a relaxation of the sphincter and an effacement of the radiated folds in those females who give themselves up to excessive sodomy.

Jacobus adds that "all the women who practice sodomy lubricate the anus, in order to render coition easier, with an ointment composed of banana or olive oil and the juice of a plant which possesses emollient properties." Arabian women commonly use olive oil as an anal lubricant. Coconut oil is also popular in some areas, and frequently the inside of a banana skin is rubbed between the buttocks to facilitate intromission. Saliva, Vaseline, and numerous other natural and artificial ointments and emollients are popularly employed. Our industrious Frenchman continues:

> It cannot be questioned that the compression of the virile member by the anal sphincter is far more forcible than by the vaginal sphincter, especially if the man has a medium-sized penis. Thus the Hindu seeks boys for coition, enabling him to increase his venereal pleasure by a greater compression of the penis. The Indian boy usually begins very young, and has the path first opened out by a youthful companion, to whom he does the same in return [the Irani *elish-tekish* or "give and take"].

Jacobus found that in many cases he could introduce three fingers into the rectum of an Indian girl addicted to *gāndh-mārī* or "anus beating," but comments that this extreme dilation is due to the admission of such very thick penises as are found among Muslims and Negroes rather than Hindus. Women whose anal sphincters are large and loose from extravagant use are wont to exercise them with voluntary contractions; and as an adjunct to vaginal application, Arab females commonly anoint the anus with alum or some other astringent for the sake of tightness and tonicity.

The popularity of heterosexual and homoerotic analism is vividly unveiled in Chinese literature. The following excerpts from *Chin P'ing Mei* reveal pederastic pleasures which are as prevalent today among the Muslim and Buddhist Chinese as they were in classic times, when servant boys between the ages of four and twelve were pleased to satisfy their masters' insatiable desires by abandoning themselves to orgies of masturbation and anal copulation:

221

Hsi-men opened the boy's robe, pulled down his pants, and gently stroked his penis. . . . While the boy surrendered his bottom to a mighty warrior, Hsi-men stroked his stiff penis. . . . Said the boy: "He pushed his poker so violently between my buttocks that today they are swollen with great pain. When I ask him to stop, he pushes his poker in and out all the more." (9)

The Chinese girls of Southeast Asia often take a little opium with their boy friends, which enables them to abandon their bodies to raging and repeated bouts of sodomy. The drug anesthetizes and dilates the anus, facilitating painless penetration and pleasurable pummeling. The Chinese, like the Muslims, delight in "back-door blossom beating" because the woman's buttocks can be pressed tight together to squeeze the shaft of the penis while her anal sphincter firmly grips the neck of the glans. Thus, with a little lubrication to prevent abrasive friction, the most complete and vigorous masturbationlike stimu-

---

(9) *In both China and Indochina, facetious hosts are wont to keep little boys and girls hidden under the dinner table. It is the duty of these carefully trained children to entertain the male and female diners secretly. They do this by reaching into their clothes and manipulating their sexual organs—or, as Guyon puts it, they "discreetly masturbate the guests."*

Small children, as well as somewhat older ones, also served at the banquets of the ancient Romans, where they would circulate among the guests during the feasting and provide such titillations as might be desired. Nor were the old Romans satisfied by the use and abuse of children. In the Roman brothels, at one period, babes in cradles suckled the penes of adult customers. Throughout the world there are and always have been those adults who crave or require the sexual services of children, and there has always been at least some supply to answer the demand.

222

lation of the penis is effected as the active male, inflamed to passionate frenzy by the drug he has taken, forces it to and fro with all his might. Those who frequently masturbate by rubbing the glans rather than by manipulating the shaft do not ordinarily enter the anus but are wont to insert the head of the penis between the girl's buttocks, have her compress them, and then make the necessary motions. Manual and gluteal rubbing of the glans penis is practiced by those males who are "nonsensitive" and slow to respond.

Anal intercourse is eminently common and customary among the peoples of Indonesia and Malaya, who take their cue from the numerous anoerotic episodes in *Chin P'ing Mei:*

Porphyry stroked his warrior, and soon it arose proudly. The veins stood out and it appeared to be a liver purple. His passion blazed like fire. His spear was exceedingly hard. He told the woman to lift herself up on hands and knees like a mare, and he thrust himself forward into the flower at the rear. He did this one hundred and fifty times, beating the woman's bottom with a loud noise. She, with her fingers between her thighs, played with the stamen of her frontward flower and called him endearing names unceasingly.

Still Hsi-men was not content. He bade the woman turn over and tied her feet with two ribbons to the bedposts. He began by playing the game of the golden dragon stretching its claws; and he drove himself hither and thither, now this way and anon that way. He brought the lamp nearer and bent his head to watch the movements. As often as he drew out his sword, so often she resheathed it to the very hilt herself; and they did this one hundred and fifty times. Porphyry, her voice trembling, called him every endearing word she could think of. Soon he drew it out entirely, and he put a considerable amount of red powder upon the top. Then, when he again pushed himself into the woman's blossom, he tickled her so much that she was hardly able to endure it. Lifting herself up,

223

she implored him to push deeper; but the man deliberately played at the opening, gently rubbing the heart of the flower, for he did not wish to go down any deeper. Love liquid flowed from the woman like sap oozing from a tree. Under the light, Hsi-men beheld her dazzling-white legs as they lay raised and wrapped around both sides of his body. When he felt her tremble, his own legs trembled also; and feeling this made him even more savage than before.

The woman received his lotus stalk into her bud at the back door and spoke very pleasant words. Hsi-men, incited by the wine which he had been drinking, held her legs tightly together and lunged violently forward. Proceeding with greatest force and fury, he entered her almost three hundred times; while the woman's tongue was so cold that she could not speak. Hsi-men was hardly breathing himself, but suddenly the essence shot forth and he enjoyed the utmost pleasure.(10)

Hsi-men set the woman on the edge of the bed, pulled down her trousers, took his member in hand, and attacked her blossom at the back door. He pushed himself to and fro more than a hundred times, making a loud noise. From their rapid breathing and their behavior it looked as though they wished to break the bed in pieces.

---

(10) This oft-reported "cold tongue," if understood at all literally, is baffling. It should be noted that the coldness is during coitus and not at or just after climax—when it might seem more intelligible.

Many persons report sensations of warmth when "in the heat" of coition or sexual arousal. To "be hot" means to be erotically stimulated. Body temperatures of lovers probably rise in most cases. It is also the case that a loss of temperature sense is often reported to occur simultaneously with erotic excitation. Coldness, however, is another matter; especially when associated with full arousal. Apparently this must remain another "mystery of the Orient."

He took a little of the red powder from the silver box and put it into the horse's eye. Immediately the medicine took effect. His member stood straight, an amazingly terrible sight; its head swelled and the eye opened wide; the purple veins stood out; it was a dark reddish-brown color like the liver, nearly seven inches long, and much thicker than usual! Hsi-men Ch'ing was highly pleased; he decided that the medicine was a very fine thing. The woman, sitting naked upon the man's knees, took his weapon in her hands.

She said in a choking voice: "O my dearest man, your marvelous member will be the death of me." Soon she murmured again: "My life, my joy, wouldn't you again like to pluck love's fruit at the back door?" He turned the woman over on her belly and advanced his mighty warrior. His attack was so violent as to produce a loud noise. "Push in, push in, my darling," cried Porphyry; "don't hold back! Thrust home as hard as you can; your pleasure will be the greater!" Hsi-men pulled her thighs wide apart and plunged furiously forward; while the woman, murmuring tremulously, fingered the stamen of her little flower.

"Today," the man said, "I want to play with the flower in the back court. Will you let me?"

"You shameless fellow," the woman said, "you have played that game often enough."

Hsi-men Ch'ing laughed. "Little oily mouth," he said, "don't you understand that I am particularly fond of this kind of play? I will only put it there for a little while."

Thus urged, the woman said: "I don't believe you can do it. Your thing is too big. But take the ring from its head and I will try."

Hsi-men Ch'ing took off the sulphur ring and left only the clasps at the root. He bade the woman to get on the bed, to raise herself on her hands and knees, and to lift her buttocks high. He put some spittle on his spear and moved slowly forward. But the head of his member, haughty and unyielding,

225

was willing to go in only a short distance. The woman knit her brow and bit her handkerchief. "My darling," she said, "do not go in too fast; my back door is not like the front door. I feel you inside as if I were afire."

He plunged violently forward.

The woman turned her head and looked at him. "Darling," she said, "it is painful enough. Why are you so violent? Won't you let yourself come now?"

But Hsi-men Ch'ing would not. He held her legs, while he watched his weapon going to and fro, and cried: "Be kind to me, you little whore, and call me your darling; then you will take me entirely."

The woman closed her eyes and said something like the whisper of a bird. She gently shook her willowlike waist and thrust her sweet body forward to meet his. The sound was so soft that no words can describe it. After a time, Hsi-men felt that the essence of his manhood was ready. He pressed his thighs together and thrust forward with such an awesome sound that the woman said she could bear no more. When the time came, he pulled her backward towards himself; he plunged into the depths of her bottom, and he enjoyed the greatest pleasure. She took him entirely into her rearward receptacle; he spent profusely, and then they lay interlaced upon the bed.

6. MASTURBATION

Masturbate, and then you can wed the wind!

ARAB PROVERB

Whether owing to the effects of physical and psychological environment, temperament, or whatever, the African in many cases early acquires and makes use of a powerful libido. The same may be said of the Asian.

One may scarcely declare with assurance in these cases that an inherent sex drive has been prematurely awakened; for it seems active from the start. Almost from the time he emerges from the womb, the infant's erections are spontaneous and frequent, his tiny hands instinctively reaching down to touch and fondle his genitalia. These erections, with fondling and general pursuit of sexual sensation, continue throughout boyhood.(1)

_____

(1) American and European infants also, of course, have erections, spontaneously fondle their genitals, and may be observed in the throes of their erotic pleasure. However, it is almost precisely from the moment that the infantile sexuality begins to make itself manifest (to the parents), that the Western mother begins her antisexual crusade of interference by distraction, by physical force and, later on

227

The casual eroticism of the three-year-old Arab boy is further activated and particularized when an older and more knowledgeable boy, playing with the child's penis and provoking an erection, instructs him in systematic stimulation by repeated

---

in childhood, by admonishments against naughty and dirty behavior.

The consequence of such interference is that the Western child, by contrast to his Eastern counterpart, has a long and comparatively asexual period during childhood. This asexual period is seldom ever, even in terms of overt behavior, "perfect." There is almost always a certain amount of exhibitionism, of mutual inspection of genitalia, and in some cases of attempts to emulate the observed erotic activities of parents or other adults or older children. That such childish behavior is necessarily carried out in secrecy, and that it tends to be "forgotten" as the child grows older, makes extremely difficult the task of the researcher seeking to learn something about the true amount and character of childish sex practices in the West.

An important question raised by this book is the extent, if any, to which the sexual activities and development of American and European children would differ from those of African and Asian children if the former were as unimpeded in the exercise of their sexuality as the latter often are. And we must wonder, too, whether the effects would be—as seems likely—more beneficial than damaging were Western youngsters permitted to develop along somewhat more natural lines. In recent years there has been a certain amount of encouraged experimentation in the West with parental permissiveness in the area of overt childish sex expression. However, it is still impossible to speak with assurance about what is desirable or undesirable in the way of regulation and self-regulation; and it remains true that even the most sexually unfettered children of the West must contend with an officially antisexual society, which introduces an element less often present in Afro-Asian societies where the sexually free child is not perpetually at odds with his environment.

228

manual manipulation. From Morocco to Malaya, unless they learn spontaneously or "by accident," little boys of only three or four years are taught methodic masturbation by their older brothers or companions; and they in turn pass their knowledge along to other boys. Almost without exception, the technique is the so-called "jerking off" of the Western world: The shaft of the penis is gripped in the hand or with the thumb and fingers and vigorously agitated until the orgasm arrives.

Like little girls, small boys experience erotic titillation and numerous erections due to retention of urine, excitement, anxiety, fear, and other acts and emotions. Stiffness, and especially urethral tickling, draw the boy's attention to his penis, which he momentarily (often unconsciously) clasps and fondles underneath his clothes. If distracted, he usually loses his erection and discontinues further handling, despite the fact that his penis may have been perfectly rigid and tense. Boys often masturbate before they urinate, spurred by the intense titillation produced by retention. The erections caused by a full bladder are quite rigorous; the little lad's penis is stretched tight and strained to stiffness. He almost compulsively clutches it in his hand or with his fingers and rapidly manipulates it to relieve himself of erotic tension. Then, and only then, does he urinate, having first satisfied his sexual instincts. Urination eliminates all remaining titillation.

Sleeping customs and living conditions in much of the East are prime factors in encouraging prepubertal and adolescent masturbation. Two or more boys in one bed or even one room sooner or later means genital play, and patterns of behavior are thus formed. Before going to sleep, and often upon awakening, boys freely follow a regular routine of manual and oral "give-and-take." The nudity and/or proximity of one boy excites an immediate erection in the other, and their hands reach down and touch each other's genitals. When one boy is not particularly inclined to "play," or displays very little or no desire for

229

mutual exploration, his bedmate takes the initiative by handling and squeezing his penis until it stiffens; hence a boy who would otherwise experience from one to three orgasms a week may under these circumstances be urged to enjoy from three to five or more. If he refuses, he is laughed to scorn as an impotent misfit or a sexless hermaphrodite.

Muslim and Jewish boys actively and exclusively engaged in solitary and/or mutual masturbation do so on an average of from three to five times a week during their adolescent years (ages 11 to 18). This estimate includes all classes, but of course there are many exceptions to every rule. Unless he practices premarital intercourse, a young male may feel the urge to masturbate from eight to ten times a week. Generally speaking, such high performers invariably seek substitute or supplementary outlets to break the monotony of masturbation; and if girls are not available for sexual relations they naturally turn to members of their own sex. Because of its peculiar taxing effect upon the nervous system, ofttimes reported as equaling two masturbations or copulations in its single power, fellatio is frequently the choice of those males who are endowed with a dynamic sex drive. Many of them find that after being fellated two or three times they are thoroughly satisfied if not utterly exhausted, while otherwise they might have striven for twice or three times that number of orgasms.(2)

Because most Asian and African boys are erotically active

---

(2) *The idea that a greater amount of energy is discharged in fellatio, or that the effect of fellatio is more enervating or sapping than that of coitus or masturbation, is almost universally encountered. If the idea has any basis in fact—and one should not casually dismiss, in the absence of evidence to the contrary, so omnipresent a belief—then the explanation might possibly reside in the vigorous sucking of the fellator, which precipitates a more intense and powerful ejaculation.*

230

previous to or long before the advent of puberty and the appearance of ejaculation, only a slight increase in activity is noticed at the time when sexual maturity customarily makes itself known in the West. Frequency of outlet tends to reach its zenith between the ages of sixteen and twenty, and thereafter slowly declines. Reversions to the original high frequency pattern then become the exception rather than the rule, occasioned by ultraexciting circumstances. That is why aphrodisiacs of every variety are all the rage throughout the East.

Bernhard Stern notes that in Arabia masturbation "has become almost the custom of the land." Indeed, the first sexual trauma of the male infant or the small boy occurs when his little penis is rubbed to erection, his foreskin forcibly retracted, drawn tightly forward again, clamped, and cut off. Parents who do not have their sons circumcised soon after birth, but who wait for a couple of months to three years, make a custom of repeatedly pulling down the long prepuce, thereby denuding the glans, which the boys themselves do when they are old enough. Both the act of circumcision and that of preputial retraction seem to cause an intense concentration of erotic sensitivity in the penis, resulting in repeated erections and arousing the child to genital handling. Almost without exception, all Muslim and Jewish boys masturbate in one form or another from earliest infancy. During erections occurring spontaneously (without external or imagistic erotic stimulus) or due to chance rubbing, the delicate and sensitive glans of the circumcised infant is wholly denuded and fondling produces such acute sensations of titillation that frequent masturbatory activity is almost inevitable.

During the circumcision ceremonies, little Arab boys awaiting their turn will allay their fear of the operation by pulling down their pants and each playing with the other's penis. Before circumcising a child, the surgeon systematically examines the child's penis by retracting and manipulating or stretching

231

the prepuce, looking for adhesions and cleaning away any smegma, and to facilitate this procedure an erection is induced. Thus, since tumescence is necessary for a precircumcisional examination, striplings do not hesitate to stimulate themselves and one another just before the operation.

The Muslim and Jewish methods of circumcision are essentially the same throughout North Africa and the Middle East; age is the only difference worthy of note. All Jewish males are circumcised in early infancy, within a week after birth. Many Muslim males are also, especially if they are born in hospitals and their parents are Westernized.

Among the Jews, the *mōhēl* or circumciser takes the infant's penis by his thumb and forefinger and gently rubs it several times to produce an erection; then he proceeds with the examination and operation. The Muslim *khettān* or circumciser fingers the little child's penis until it is erect; then he pulls the prepuce all the way down, completely exposing the glans, which he examines, and removes any sebaceous matter. There are several ways of clamping, tying, or compressing the foreskin after it is drawn tightly forward, whereupon it is removed with an expert flick of the blade. Now comes the delicate procedure. When the clamp is removed, the integumental skin or outer layer of the prepuce retracts as far as or sometimes beyond the rim of the glans. The sheath of the penis is thus shortened by the removal of its forward fold, which is now a mere remnant, the so-called preputial root. The thin inner layer of the foreskin is then lacerated and turned back over the corona to join the thicker outer skin and form a kind of cicatricial ring or narrow band of scar tissue around the neck of the glans. The wound is now anointed and bandaged, healing in a week's time.(3)

·ȷ·

(3) *The merits and demerits of circumcision are periodically and heatedly debated by Western physicians. Some regard the operation*

The inimitable traveler and Arabist, Wilfred Thesiger, recently observed the barbaric rite of *es-selkh* (the flaying) which is practiced by many Bedawin tribes in western and southern Arabia. *Selkh*, which has been vainly forbidden by every Wehhabi (Orthodox) Government from that of Muhammed 'Ali Pasha to that of Ibn Sa'ud, is a puberty rite or test of manhood enacted on boys between the ages of ten and fifteen. As the name implies, not merely the prepuce but the entire sheath of the penis is longitudinally slit and sliced off, leaving the *qedzīb* (rod) like a skinned eel. As a rule, youths look forward to the ordeal with masochistic enthusiasm or fatalistic abandon. They pull down each other's drawers and stand proudly naked, not daring to move a muscle or cry out. Thesiger notes how they look like girls with their flowing hair and delicate features; for

---

as no more than a barbaric mutilation, receiving its impetus from a residue of antique superstition; others would justify it on hygienic grounds. It has been argued that circumcision diminishes sexual sensation, and that it enhances it. By some the operation is seen as a traumatic experience for the infant, and by others as being of negligible importance in this respect. It is certain that it leads to much comparing of organs by circumcised and uncircumcised youths.

There is no doubt that the practice historically was bound up with magic and with the worship of the generative powers. Alleged foreskins of Christ were the proudly owned properties of any number of churches and monasteries, where those who touched or looked at them were miraculously healed.

As recently as the time of Napoleon, it was still common practice for a Roman Catholic priest, in connection with the circumcision ritual, to take the penis of the infant into his mouth—an act possessing at that time definite sexual content for many a priest, and probably for the infant as well. Napoleon ordered an end to this practice, because the priests were so often syphilitic and infected the infants during the performance of the rite!

the young Arabian male with his handsome statuesque body has a classic effeminate beauty, and one need not wonder why (as in ancient Greece) homosexuality is so common and customary in a land of "beautiful beardless boys." Thesiger adds that each youth stood with legs apart, "while a slave handled his penis until it was erect and then flayed the entire organ." (4)

Dr. Jacobus, when in Egypt, discovered what he calls "three causes of the development of the virile member of the Arab: (1) Circumcision, which allows free development and enlargement of the penis; (2) Wide garments, which do not prevent the development and enlargement of the genital organs; and (3) Habitual boyhood masturbation." He adds, speaking of all Muslims in general:

> The genital organs of the Arab, particularly the penis, generally attain dimensions which differ but little in the flaccid condition to that when in a state of erection.
>
> It may be taken as a rule that the penis of the Arab, compared to that of the European, is at least one third longer and thicker. In fact, this member is allowed to develop itself in entire liberty from the earliest infancy. Nothing contributes to confine it, as European dress. The air can freely flow through the simple *ghendūreh* (ample shirt) which is the sole vestment of the child and which still accompanies him in later life, tucked into the vast recesses of his Turkish pantaloons. It must also be borne in mind that the Arab is at an early age addicted to manual excitation of the genesic sense, which largely contributes towards the development of the organ.
>
> Among the African Negroes, and among the Arabs, the majority of travelers have pointed out the considerable de-

─────────────────

(4) *An even more gruesome operation formerly was performed, and may still be performed, in China. The flaying begins just below the navel and is continued almost down to the knees.*

velopment of the penis in proportion to the large vagina of the Negress and how the scrotums among them are more voluminous and pendant. But here we must bring in the influence of costume. In the case of the man who walks along scarcely covered with a slight loincloth, just as in the case of the Arab clad in the *ghendūreh*, the genital parts have no support and are influenced by their weight. Moreover, habitual handling of the penis is influential in increasing its size with the aid of circumcision, which frees the glans from its preputial imprisonment.

In a report entitled "The Effect of Circumcision on the Size of the Penis of the Sudanese Boy," Jacobus writes:

In part, I attribute the size of the Sudanese Negro's penis to the operation of circumcision. The early removal of the foreskin, which caps and compresses the glans and often prevents it from coming out even when in erection, eliminates all interference with the free development and enlargement of the young boy's organ.

A fairly large cushion of flesh is removed in circumcision, and the retraction draws the skin of the penis behind the crown of the glans to the extent of two-fifths to four-fifths of an inch at least. When the penis afterwards develops, the glans, having nothing to check it, will assume its normal size. Cicatrization, assisted by the healing growth which repairs the loss of the skin and mucous surface taken away in circumcision, causes the largest part of the member to correspond with the circular scar caused by the operation. Although the glans may be much developed, its diameter [the circumference of the corona] still remains slightly inferior to this part of the penis, which on the whole greatly resembles a large fish with a round head and a short tail. We can then understand why the Negroes call their member a "fish." It is not a little fish either which these good Negroes possess, but a big eel with a black or brown head.

235

Finally, from his earliest years, the little Sudanese boy is addicted to shaking his penis repeatedly to produce the tickling sensations of masturbation; and this vigorous manual manipulation exercises his organ and aids in its growth.(5)

The little Muslim boy looks forward to circumcision with great anticipation, because it means that masturbation will then be more pleasurable to him. The foreskin is an interference, frequently too long and too tight, and the orgasm is hastened by its friction against the glans. This rubbing irritates and often inflames the delicate and sensitive corona, especially if the opening of the prepuce is very narrow or if there are adhesions. Within two or three weeks after the operation the little fellow is masturbating regularly again, this time with his "new" penis. The skin is now tense during erection, resisting friction of the glans and making the manipulation more pleasingly vigorous and prolonged. All previous discomfort is replaced by continuous titillation.

Jacobus observed that in Arab circumcision "the skin of the sheath of the penis and the mucous membrane are cut at the same level, and after the operation is completed there is absolutely no prepuce." This is the desired result. The penis is lit-

------

(5) *It is the general position of Western scientists that nothing may be done to increase the size of the penis. However, this dictum should perhaps be understood as applying to the penis of the mature male rather than to that of the child. While it seems certain that circumcision does not contribute discernibly to genital size, we are able to speak with much less authority on the effects of early and oft-repeated masturbation, and of costume allowing freedom from restriction to the genital organs. This is not to say that Jacobus is correct in his theories; but it is to allow for the possibility that there may "be something" in what he says. The matter must be regarded as for the present not proved one way or the other.*

236

erally strained to stiffness when erect, for the skin is stretched tight; and the entire glans, including the corona and the "neck" of the corona, are fully exposed by the retraction. The ring of cicatrice which is formed at the junction of the inner and outer flesh now forming the preputial root is the principal target of stimulation in the circumcised, necessarily taking the place of the glans in the uncircumcised.

The Arab word *jeld* (stripping) refers to the method of milking a cow by hand as well as to the most common process of manual masturbation. It is similar to *zelq* or *zerq* (jerking or shaking). Technically, *jeld 'omayreh* means "drawing or pulling the erect penis, between the forefinger and thumb, through the closed hand"; in short, "flipping the phallus." This is the "milking" or cow-stripping manner of masturbation employed by the circumcised Muslims and Jews of the East. The Arab inclination for anal activity may be traced to the habit of *zelq*; for in sodomy, like "self-abuse," the pleasure can be prolonged in that the sphincter ani clasps only the upper part of the penis (as happens in masturbation) and leaves the glans free in the rectum. When movement is effected, only the sheath of the penis or the band of cicatrice is masturbatorily forced to and fro or up and down as the case may be.

Jacobus' belief that circumcision, masturbation, and other artificial factors affect phallic proportions is purely empirical and without scientific basis. A circumcised Semitic masturbator will reveal a small and retracted penis just as an uncircumcised Negroid onanist will reveal a large and protracted penis. One thing is certain: Eastern and African boys, because of environmental and psychophysiological factors, begin their active sexual life in early childhood. Continual masturbation and vaginal and anal coitus prevail during the prepubertal years. Boys and girls enjoy regular erotic intercourse between the ages of eight and ten, sometimes earlier, and until she is married almost every girl is common property. She sleeps with all the

237

boys and all the boys sleep with her. Heterosexual promiscuity is supplemented by homosexual experimentations.(6)

Arab boys wearing nothing but a sleeveless, shirtlike, knee-length garment or *ghendūreh* (fop frock) are not allowed to wear trousers and underdrawers until after they are circumcised, which operation, as already noted, usually occurs between the ages of three and five. Those who are circumcised in infancy may begin wearing grownups' clothes at any time, thus

---

(6) Nor, in Africa, does being "common property" always cease with marriage. A recent study of sexual behavior in the Sudan advises that brides celebrate their weddings by copulating all night with the assembled male guests. As reported in the August 1962 issue of Sexology:

> Women in the primitive society of Africa's Southeast Sudan are, surprisingly enough, practically equal to men in their sexual and matrimonial privileges. This seems to be the finding of recent research completed by Dr. Herbert Hilke of the University of Bonn, Germany, and published in Umschau (Frankfurt A/M) 1961, issue 19.
>
> For one thing, marriage can only take place by mutual consent, and instead of the prospective bridegroom purchasing his wife he is required to perform a considerable amount of service on the land of his future in-laws before he is accepted. He must be helped by his closest relatives, and at the end of his labors he can still be turned down by his future mother-in-law.
>
> "After the wedding," writes Dr. Hilke, "the woman enjoys great sexual freedom. During the wedding night, the young bride runs away to the woods with her husband's friends and is possessed by all of them."
>
> All children born to the couple, regardless of doubts concerning their paternity, are unquestioningly accepted as legitimate.

238

the operation of preputial amputation represents a young male's inauguration into the adult community. As an example of the use of the trouser fly in circumcised boys, the observant often see Muslim youths, their little organs erect outside their pants, mutually fingering or manipulating each other. Young scamps commonly pull their penises out of their trousers and make water against a wall, a kind of game to see who has the best aim and who can urinate the farthest.(7) Little girls look on with admiration or envy: "The boys are making rainbows again!" Some of them turn their little hoses on their female spectators, knowing that they have no manner of redress. Another common occurrence is a boy and girl in sexual experimentation, he with his penis outside his pants and she with her panties pulled down to her knees. Lifting her dress, she says: "You may touch my turtle if you let me touch your snake." She straightway holds his penis, and he has no alternative but to finger her vulva. Two or three boys pouncing upon a little girl and raping her one after another, front and rear, may occasionally be seen; and in every case, the trouser fly makes what would otherwise have been difficult extremely easy and inviting.

In a tract entitled *Fī Tetwīl wa-Tesmīk el-Qedzīb* (On the Lengthening and Thickening of the Rod), Ibn Kemal Pasha quotes the old Arabian physicians as saying that "rubbing and constant handling doth make the virile member longer and thicker." He continues:

---

(7) *This is a childish game not at all uncommon in the United States and Europe, though probably more commonly it is conducted on a sexually segregated basis. In the past, some investigators found a relationship between (male and female) sexual vigor and the ability to urinate forcefully. This finding seems not to have been checked in recent years.*

239

For my own part, I warn parents to give heed during the infancy of their children to the making of their boys' members bigger. Persistent shaking and jerking will make the monkey's prickle longer, and so it is with little boys.

Kemal Pasha adds, however, that if a man's penis is too big it makes a woman "unable to live without constant intercourse!"

Much consideration is given to the development of the penis in little boys, and both circumcision and masturbation constitute common practice and custom in many Muslim countries. The child's foreskin is repeatedly retracted after birth until the time of circumcision, a process unmistakably masturbatory in nature and intent. This constant forcible retraction has for centuries been customary among the Islamic peoples of Central Asia (e.g., the Turkomans, Kurds, Uzbeks, Kazak-Kirghiz, etc.), who methodically masturbate their sons from early infancy in order to expose the glans penis, dilate the preputial orifice, and stimulate growth and development. Rubbed erect, the infant's penis is clasped directly under the corona by the parent's fingers; then the foreskin is jerked fully down again and again, stretching the frenum and uncovering the crown. All the members of the family, young and old alike, take turns performing this denudation of the glans on the new baby for at least an hour every evening.

The Muslims of Central Asia are habitual masturbators from the very cradle. They indulge passionately, compulsively, and one of their most familiar sayings is: "The mutual penis stroking is sweeter than cunnus poking!" The baby's genitals are continually congested; he has erections every hour, especially at the approach or touch of one of his relatives; and unless he is thickly swaddled, he handles himself almost constantly. When swathed in tight cloth, the infant, unable to reach his genitals, kicks about frantically in an effort to produce

240

the pleasurable friction, experiencing one orgastic spell after another. When the older folks are out of the house and the children are left to baby-sit, they frequently remove their little brother's diapers (under a pretext of changing them) and play with his penis for hours at a time. Both male and female babies are traditionally masturbated when they begin to cry, for the tickling of their genitals takes their minds away from previous displeasure.

Manual manipulation persists even after circumcision, which is supposed to discourage the habit by the removal of this retractable skin. Those boys who are circumcised shortly after birth become no less addicted than those who remain uncircumcised until their first or second year. Muslim babies circumcised forty days after birth continue to be masturbated on the sly by their little brothers and sisters, who seek every opportunity to fondle each other's genitals. Kurdish and Kazak boys, for example, masturbate at a minimum of from two to three times a day. They indulge mutually from the day they are able to walk, experiencing erections every hour at the slightest provocation. When they weary of mutual masturbation they turn to anal intercourse, a practice extremely widespread among both married and unmarried males in Central Asia, who see in it a perfect substitute for manual stimulation:

> O little boy in colored cloak,
> Let me push it in your poke!
> I'm sick and tired of jerking off;
> While I jerk you, I'd rather stroke!

The Turkomans sing:

> One mane, one rein,
> Two penises at her anus;
> I pulled the mane—
> My penis rode into her anus!

241

Jacobus remarked that "among the North African Arabs and Jews, many of the former being circumcised in infancy like all of the latter, the masturbation habit is not only common but customary." Our Frenchman found the same situation in Islamic India (now Pakistan) "where *jelq* or *jerq*, as it is called, is usually performed by jerking the band of cicatrice about until the orgasm sets in, which circumcised Aryans also do in Europe."

Having examined hundreds of Muslims who were circumcised within three weeks or three months after birth, Jacobus found that each had a history of habitual self-stimulation from as far back as he could remember. All were of the popular opinion that masturbation is eminently instrumental in phallic development, observing by way of explanation or analogy how frequent exercise enlarges a muscle. This is what the older boys told them when they were little; for while a few of them learned to manipulate their penises quite by accident, the majority presumed that they were taught to masturbate sometime between the ages of two and five by their playmates.

Middle Eastern mythology tells us that the Phoenician phallic god Baal made his penis enormous by constant copulation with heifers. The Muslims of Morocco have a similar belief, doubtless a throwback to ancient phallicism, whereby fathers encourage their little sons to practice anal and vaginal intercourse with donkeys in order to make the penis grow big and strong. Boyhood masturbation is scorned in favor of bestiality, and the spectacle of a bunch of young Moroccan boys taking turns mounting the rear end of a donkey is truly comical.(8)

---

(8) Historically, bestiality has commonly been put to more therapeutic uses in the West, especially as a remedy for venereal diseases (to which end it is also employed by Muslims). Europeans have further attempted by bestiality to cure cases of satyriasis and nymphomania. And aging males, brooding regretfully over their declining

The Sudanis, Somalis, and Swahilis are masturbators from their earliest boyhood. In order to appear circumcised, little boys smear the irritating juice of the Euphorbia on their glans, which then swells up and holds back the prepuce. This chemical denudation or artificial paraphimosis is reported by Felix Bryk: "In small children there often occurs a morbid swelling of the glans, which probably arises from putting poisonous saps on the penis." Once he has effected this artificial retraction, the little two- or three-year-old Negro boy will clutch his penis and masturbate. The use of euphorbium often has a pernicious effect on small boys, for it provokes a severe priapism or persistent erection of the penis that even the most strenuous manipulation cannot alleviate.

Bryk asked a young circumcised Swahili to demonstrate the effects of euphorbium by smearing some on his glans; the Negro politely refused, turning in his lips as if he had tasted something tart. He well enough knew the results, either by observation or experience. Circumcised boys love to torment one another with the caustic juice, which causes a fierce half-burning half-itching sensation. A boy's friends will seize him, pull his penis out of his pants, and rub euphorbium on his glans. The sap produces a violent erection almost immediately; his glans throbs and swells; and the other urchins watch with amusement as their pal impulsively clutches the shaft of his *mboro* and rapidly, repeatedly masturbates in primitive abandon right in front of them.

Bryk, while studying the Muslim Swahili of East Africa, found that manipulation of the penis is practiced by little boys in order to retract the prepuce and give it a circumcised ap-

---

virile powers, have also sought to find in intercourse with various beasts an improvement of their potency—a search sometimes crowned with temporary success, since any novel erotic act may in some cases, and for a time, revive flagging appetites and capacities.

pearance, make the member grow big like that of an adult, and produce the highly pleasurable tickling sensations:

> Children practice masturbation more from the desire of having the foreskin drawn back, in order to resemble the older folks, than to satisfy awakening desires. It is common practice for the boys to smear the sticky, milky juice of a euphorbiaceous plant on the glans and to masturbate [in Swahili, "pound the root"]. The juice of this plant is quite caustic and causes the glans to swell strongly, so that the foreskin can easily be held back beyond the corona, which is what is wanted. During this process the boys call out: "Become large, and I'll give you something to eat." Then the little boy can go to a girl and try it out.
>
> Onanism is very widespread among the young people. Boys often masturbate in groups; if they are caught by their parents they are punished. "How can you take your penis into the same hand with which you eat?" they hear in reproach. Little girls run away from masturbating boys out of fear of being raped.
>
> The boys often masturbate in a crouching position. If he wants an erection, the small boy rolls his little rod between the palms of his hands until it stands up. Then he draws the skin down and spits on the glans with perfect precision, using saliva to lessen the friction. They are so young that they have no ejaculations in this "game" as they call it.

Jacobus, who visited Zanzibar to discover unusual sexual customs, found the following:

> There is prevalent among the Swahili the remarkable custom of fathers massaging the penis of their little boys. They sit on the bed and take the member of the boy between their big and second toes, or if they sit nearer they sometimes knead it with their hands also, which the boys do not at all object to. I observed this custom several times. That is probably the reason why the little fellows, though only four to

244

six years old, had erections every moment which were not very noticeable but often slyly hidden.

He adds that "these massages of the penis among the Swahili of Zanzibar are not for the purpose of denuding the glans, a reason why many Kazak elders masturbate their children, because circumcision takes place at or before the age of three."

This systematic masturbation of their little boys by Zanzibari fathers does not begin until after their sons are circumcised; any autoerotic activity before the age of three is self-enacted. Between the ages of three and six, boys have the penis manipulated for about an hour every evening before going to sleep. The purpose is to stimulate growth, develop the erotic instincts, and insure sexual potency. The Swahili hold that masturbatory exercise strengthens the penis, even enlarges it in some cases, so that when the little lad has arrived at puberty he is twice as vigorous as one who did not handle himself habitually from earliest boyhood.

At Siwah, a tremendous oasis on the Libyan border in northwest Egypt, ancient phallic worshipers reveled in nocturnal orgies of ritual masturbation, sodomy, and promiscuous copulation before the great shrine of the Nilotic god of propagative power, Amen-Ra. It was believed in popular myth that Osiris, an avatar of Amen-Ra, creates all living creatures by an infinite act of masturbation. The royal and religious rites which evolved from this legend, wherein the young pharaohs on the eve of their enthronement practiced self-stimulation before the idol and wherein the hierarchy of Heliopolis indulged in sacrificial orgies of mutual masturbation in honor of Osiris, soon spread into public worship and led to the emergence of many homosexual cults. Egyptian hieratic records reveal the following: "Osiris became a masturbator while he was in Heliopolis. He seized his phallus in his fist in order to satisfy his lust with it."

245

From this tradition stems the ancient belief that the Nile River arises through the continuous masturbation of Osiris. Ritual masturbation was instituted in Egyptian, Phoenician, Babylonian, and Assyrian sacred ceremonies to expel evil and to honor the gods of generation. Representations of Osiris clutching his huge semen-ejaculating penis in his left hand decorated the temples and tombs of the Land of the Pharaohs.

In modern times, these antique orgies have survived among the bisexually oriented Hamitic or Arabo-Negro populations of the Libyan and Egyptian oases. In Siwah, one of the largest of these areas, anal intercourse is known as *ed-dūdeh* (the worm) because the probing glans penis feels like a worm in the rectum. In honor of masturbation and anal copulation the males of Siwah hold special rites which are celebrated in conjunction with the customary marriage of men with boys recently outlawed by the government.

As soon as a boy is circumcised he becomes a member of *Ez-Zeggāleh* (The Berserkers), a word derived from *zegl* (uproar, play). In this homoerotic sex club, both men and boys of all ages forsake the womenfolk except for propagative purposes. During the initiation ceremonies and on general occasions, the boys masturbate and sodomize the men and the men in turn masturbate and sodomize the boys. It often happens that a *shaykh* or local patriarch homosexually famous for his superior potency cannot procure an erection while in bed with his wife to beget offspring, so he customarily has a handsome boy come in and lie beside him to handle his penis until it is perfectly stiff; then he mounts his wife and makes quick work of it. A woman's hands or mouth do not ordinarily evoke such electrifying results as will the touch of a beardless and round-bottomed youth. The Hamites of Siwah do not excise the glans clitoris of their little girls. They want their females to be quickly and easily satisfied in sexual congress or self-stimulation, so that they can devote their more passionate attentions to boys.

During a *zegl* or orgy the men and boys strip each other stark naked and, inflamed by stimulants, attack one another passionately. Having effected anal penetration, the active partner rotates his penis as energetically as possible; at the same time, he masturbates his passive lover. There are two methods of manipulation commonly employed. In the first, the erect male organ is clasped firmly by one or both hands and the skin of the shaft forced up and down; in the second, the penis is clasped at the base by one hand while the palm of the other slides rapidly up and down the sensitive underside of the glans. Both "shaking" and "rubbing" are applied to the *zubb* (prickle). Each partner assumes an alternately active and passive role. This same pederastic pattern may be found throughout the oases of Libya and Egypt, in the Sudan, and along the old slave routes to Timbuktu. It is difficult to determine why these Hamites are so addicted to mutual masturbation and sodomy, for their womenfolk are allowed complete freedom and equality, suffer no social or sexual suppression, and are in fact very promiscuous. They try every known way to win their menfolk, but with slight success. Males have no unnatural fear of vaginal intercourse, nor are they misogynistically prejudiced against heterosexual relations. All of them marry at the age of puberty, and all of them experience marital as well as premarital coitus, but most of them seem to prefer homoerotic activities when all is heterosexually said and done. Consequently, females are obliged to have all their sex fun in girlhood, before the boys become overly attached to their older companions. The married but neglected women traditionally prostitute themselves to outsiders, travelers, and the like.

Ritual masturbation reckons in the initiation ceremonies of Sudani sex clubs. Every new member must submit to the secret *sunnet es-samek* or "rite of the fish," whereby he proves his

247

potency in a seminal sacrifice. The "fish," one of the most ancient of phallic symbols, is the circumcised penis of the Sudani.

The initiate, surrounded by the other club members (both male and female), is stripped naked in the room where the orgies take place. Then a lovely nude girl approaches him from behind, slips her arms around his waist, firmly grips his erect penis with her hot moist hands, and starts to stroke it hungrily. The initiate is told to be seated on the floor with his knees bent and his thighs open. The girl continues to grasp and fondle his sexual organs with delirious delight. Squatting beside him, she writhes and rubs her vulva against his arm, clasping and squeezing the shaft and head of his phallus. She moves her hands up and down in a rapid and rhythmic manipulation until the initiate ejaculates; but not stopping there, she bends over and begins to fellate him feverishly, holding and agitating the shaft while she sucks the glans. Her mouth and hand play havoc with the young initiate, thereby measuring his manhood, until he can stand no further stimulation and loses his erection. Three successive ejaculations are necessary to pass the test.

When Yahveh forewarns Hagar about the babe in her womb (Genesis 16:12), "He will be a wild ass of a male, his hand upon every male and every male's hand upon him (*yādō be-kōl veyād kōl be-ō*)," He means to convey that Ishmael will be a compulsive masturbator. Thus in Genesis 21:9 we read: "And Sarah saw the son of Hagar the Egyptian, whom she had borne unto Abraham, playing [Heb. *metzahhēq*, rubbing repeatedly]." The Greek and Latin versions add, after Hebrew commentators, "with her son Isaac." Sarah saw thirteen-year-old Ishmael persistently masturbating her little three-year-old son Isaac. Interestingly enough, "Isaac" (*yitzhhāq*) bears the cabalistic connotation of "he is rubbed." Out of jealousy and scorn, Ishmael wantonly masturbated his little step-brother, who was the true heir of Abraham. Through Ishmael's repeated rubbing, Isaac became permanently addicted to masturbation. We learn this in Genesis 26:8: "Abimelech, King of the Philistines, looked out of a window and saw Isaac playing [metzahhēq, petting repeatedly or immoderately] with Rebekah his wife."

This Biblical episode is most significant, for it exemplifies the fact that masturbation has for centuries been extremely widespread among Jewish children. The Sephardic Jews of North Africa are dubbed "habitual masturbators" by their Muslim neighbors. The autoerotic practice begins in earliest infancy, becomes intense between the ages of three and ten, and is mildly recurrent throughout married life—varied only by mutual manipulation, which husband and wife commonly perform for contraceptive purposes.

Active masturbation is aroused in many male infants among North African Jews by their mothers, nurses, older sisters, and other attending females who pacify and soothe the displeased baby by tickling his genitals. This method of becalming is not only common but may indeed be considered quite customary. Most families employ it at one time or another, especially if all other means of quieting and humoring a bawling babe have failed and the well-nigh sleepless household as well as neighborhood complain of the noise.

The young girls of the family usually take turns attending to their new brother, cousin, or whatever the child may be. For example, they bathe him, change his diapers, and if he has no wet nurse or if his mother is not inclined to be milked, give him his bottle. Seeing that he enjoys it, they fondle his genitals repeatedly. This is not always a casual tickling of the testicles, but a steady stimulation of the penis. He has repeated erections, particularly when he is approached by one of the girls, and his little organ stiffens instantly whenever he is touched or his swaddling clothes are taken off. When he is naked, his hands immediately reach down to play with his penis; but the impish girls, pulling them away and slapping them slightly,

249

say, "You mustn't do that!" and do it themselves. Nearly every Jewish girl has touched or held a baby's penis by the age of ten. In fact, they make it a point to do so; it is a little erotic thrill for them.

The popular technique of manipulation is to take the infant's penis between the thumb and forefinger and gently or rapidly rub it up and down. As among the Muslims of Central Asia, this stroking involves moving the skin or sheath of the penis in an up-and-down agitation. The Muslims do it to retract the prepuce, but because the Jewish infant is already circumcised (since eight days after birth) this motive has no meaning to the Jews. They do it merely because it is superexciting to the suckling; the exposed glans is therefore rarely if ever touched or rubbed by the fingers.

Male infants are masturbated almost every day and night by their female nurses. This is especially the case in orthodox and rabbinical families, who hire "outside" women to perform the necessary services. These females, frequently from the "ordinary" or middle and lower Jewish classes, freely introduce their uninhibited sex habits into the homes of the upper or élite classes, who are characterized by a classic and traditional puritanism. The erotic custom begins with a casual fingertip titillation of the infant's testicles and perineum, which provokes a sudden erection and an enthusiastic response. The nurse will then press the little penis between her thumb and forefinger and gently stroke it. If the baby's response becomes even more ardent, she will now encircle and clasp the shaft (a mere inchlet) entirely as though by a ring with the same thumb and forefinger and rapidly jerk it up and down. This third and superstimulating manipulation will thenceforth be her usual practice with the child, and he will experience it several times every twenty-four hours. Perhaps two or three orgasms may be achieved over the same period of time if the stimulation is prolonged.

250

Having been so conditioned from his earliest days, the Jewish child invariably adopts this technique when he is able to manipulate himself. Numerous nursemaids are fired every month as a result of being caught playing with a baby's genitals; but the girls of the family, having learned the "trick" from the domestic, continue to apply it without their parents' knowledge. Little boys are left in the care of servant women till the age of three or four, sometimes five at the latest; and because orthodox children are ordinarily bathed once or twice a day, morning and/or evening, their naked bodies are continuously exposed to the wanton handling of lustful females. Without exception, washing and drying of the genitals induce repeated erections; and all during the bath the stripling's penis is flipped and frictionized until he has an orgasm or two.(9)

---

(9) *There is a rather extensive literature of English and European complaints about the masturbation of infants by domestic servants. The act is most often performed ostensibly for the purpose of stopping the baby's crying or restlessness, although it seems obvious that the servant often derives erotic titillation from her behavior.*

Later, these same servants, or their successors, frequently initiate the male children into other mysteries—copulation, fellatio, and cunnilingus; and, sometimes, perversions.

Sexologists of the nineteenth century were rather unanimous in deploring this very widespread practice of masturbating infants and of seducing adolescent boys. One hears fewer complaints nowadays, mainly because servants are now more rare.

Dire results were held to be forthcoming, and whatever "depravity" a youth later exhibited was likely to be blamed upon his introduction to vice by lewd and bawdy wenches in the domestic employ. Doubtless such experiences were sometimes traumatic, and aided in the development of a craving for forbidden fruits, but almost certainly the part played by the experiences in the development of such

251

Arabian and Negro women frequently play with their infant sons' genitals, but not systematically. It is an occasional and often unconscious expression of affection, for they fondle and tickle the penis and testicles for only a few seconds.

Masturbation represents a form of psychophysical pacification for the Jewish boy thus soothed in infancy. Anxiety and excitement result in spontaneous erection, and impulsively the boy takes hold of his penis underneath his clothes. Orthodox parents are perpetually stopping their little sons from playing with themselves, but the urge to rub and manipulate and evoke throbbing sensations of pleasure is too overpowering to be quelled by the threats of others. *Ghulām yehūdī jeld zubbō fi medkhel* (A Jewish boy jerking off in a doorway) is proverbial among observant Arabs.

Among the Sephardic Jews, manual masturbation is commonly called *zelb* or *zelābāh* (Arabic *jeld*) and *shlek* or *shelākāh* (Arabic *zelq*). *Zelb* and *shlek*, like *jeld* and *zelq*, may be translated "whipping, flipping, stripping, jerking, skinning, milking, beating, shaking, churning," etc. A letter in *Real Life Guide* (August, 1961) is relevant in that it relates of a condition that is extremely common among the Jews of North Africa:

> Since puberty I have been bothered by quick, strong erections which occur every morning, as well as during the day, and are usually not associated with erotic thoughts. In the mornings before I am even really conscious of it, I flip my erect penis rapidly to increase the pleasure. By the time I am fully awake, the glans is so congested and sensitive that only a few light touches are needed for ejaculation.
>
> Is flipping an unusual condition? Are nerves or muscles responsible? Can some men ejaculate by flipping alone? Can

---

cravings was greatly overrated—as was the importance of the subsequent indulgence.

it enlarge the glans or penis in time? Is flipping of any benefit in marital relations?

The editor answers:

> Flipping is certainly not a usual condition. [!] It is masturbatory in nature, and as such is not a very desirable practice. [!] In this process both nerves and muscles are involved by being mechanically overstimulated. It has no effect upon the size of the glans or the penis.

"Flipping" is not only usual but universal, as any knowledgeable student of sexual behavior knows. Therefore it must be a very desirable practice! (10) Manual manipulation of the shaft

---

(10) *Desirable to whom would seem to be the question!*

In discussing masturbation pro and con, it is customary presently to assert that the practice is not harmful. It would be more accurate to say, however, that the benefits usually far more than counterbalance any damage.

It is well known that masturbation is most harmful to those who believe that it is wrong or sinful, and who as a result develop guilt feelings about the practice. Masturbation is probably most helpful to those who consciously use it as a stopgap device when a sex partner is not available, and who readily make the transition back to coitus whenever that is possible.

Guilt apart, masturbation may be harmful if so long practiced that the individual comes to find his own phantasies more stimulating than the reality of a fleshly companion. However, when this occurs it is probably usually the case that the long-time solitary gratification is a symptom, not a cause, of the individual neurosis.

Obviously, the young masturbators described in this book do not share the anxieties that are the lot of many of their Western counterparts. No guilt is attached to the practice; on the contrary, it is

253

of the penis is perhaps the most common masturbatory technique among both circumcised and uncircumcised, for it supplies a brand of physical stimulation and psychic response not realized in vaginal intercourse. Of course, many males (especially those who are relatively insensitive) obtain little or no pleasure from "flipping," which to them is hard and frustrating labor, and prefer direct manual or digital friction of the glans or frenal area. In the sensitive, however, direct rubbing of the underside of the glans causes a rapid climax; and this is unsatisfactory to those who like to prolong the act and at the same time maintain a certain amount of vigorous manipulation. In any case, according to information based on the most exhaustive anthropological studies, those Asians and Africans who prefer and practice manual friction of the glans certainly do not outnumber those who practice and prefer manual manipulation of the shaft. The former are, in fact, in the minority, although many alternate from one type of stimulation to another.

Many Muslims and Jews use the morning erection, which is usually not sexual in origin, for erotic purposes: masturbation or sexual intercourse. A full bladder induces tumescence and produces a mild urethral titillation which is relieved by urination. Married males often employ the morning erection for satisfying their impulse to play with themselves. Since stiffness is "involuntary," and since the faint tickling is not of their conscious creation, they take advantage of the situation on a "pleasure-without-responsibility" basis. They masturbate, rapidly flipping the phallus to increase the tension and titillation, but not always to the advent of ejaculation. Unless an "acci-

---

regarded as a desirable and essential one; and neither is there any lingering folklore to the effect that masturbation will thicken the lips, dry up the brain, cause the spine to cave in, make the masturbator a "sex fiend," etc., etc.

dent" occurs, they turn to their women or get up and empty their bladders.

Masturbation often occurs in semisleep. Jewish boys, sleeping together, stimulate each other at or just before dawn. The boy who is awake will handle or mouth the penis of the boy who is asleep, either evoking an erection or making use of one already in existence. When he begins rapidly to manipulate or vigorously to suck, his bedmate becomes either semiconscious or fully awake. Hence, after repeated experiences of this nature, a pattern of behavior is established. Self-stimulation in semisleep may in many cases be traced to masturbatory experiences in early infancy or boyhood. When encountering erections during the day, while sitting in school for example, the boy will (if he can without being noticed) put one or both hands in his pockets and clasp and manipulate or rub his penis in this manner: the so-called "pocket pool." Prepubescent boys will masturbate surreptitiously any number of ways and times a day; for if they cannot pull the little penis out of their pants, they will stand with both hands pumping up and down in their pockets.(11)

·T·

(11) The bottomless pocket is equally legendary among American schoolboys, and probably among schoolboys everywhere (where boys have pockets). The pockets of boys' pants wear out with remarkable speed, not only because of the variety of objects crammed into them, but also in part as a result of thrusting the hands deeply into the pockets for the purpose of fingering the penis. The boy is often only vaguely conscious, or not conscious at all, of this tribute he pays to his awakening or just awakened and exceedingly ravenous sexuality; and there is a sad moral in the considerable longevity displayed by the pockets of older males.

Masturbation in semisleep is also a common Western phenomenon. Sometimes it is stimulated by the "morning erection," sometimes by hypnagogic erotic images, and sometimes simply by healthy

Let us now examine the "hands-off policy" of the Talmudic rabbis:

> Rabbi Eliezer said, "Whoever holds his member in his hand when he makes water is as though he had brought a flood on the world." Women, in this respect, are not sensitive; but in the case of men who are highly sensitive, their hands ought to be cut off because of masturbation.

In rabbinical tradition, one of the four hateful types of men is "one who holds the virile member when making water." One of the four types said by Rabbi Simeon ben Yohai to be hated by the Holy One (blessed be He!) is "the man who holds his penis when he makes water." The Talmud continues:

> Rab Judah and Samuel once stood upon the roof of the Synagogue of Shaf-Weyathib in Nehardea. Said Rab Judah to Samuel: "I must make water." "O man of iron endurance," the other replied, "take hold of your member and make the water over the roof." But how could Rab Judah do so, seeing that it was taught: "R. Eliezer said, 'Whoever holds his mem-

---

animal appetites. Sometimes the boy ejaculates without being conscious of the fact that he has been masturbating, and passes off the ejaculation as a wet dream. On other occasions, his movements will suffice to awaken him when he is likely to finish off the process in full consciousness (and be faced with the problem of how to dispose of the semen without being caught).

Some boys are much troubled when they awaken to find themselves masturbating; and parents observing such behavior in their sons may also become disturbed and consequently engage in the lamentable American practice of making a psychological mountain out of a biological molehill. But neither child nor parents should take any alarm at this phenomenon, which is an altogether natural one.

ber when he makes water is as though he brought a flood on the world' "? Abaye replied: "He was a married man, and concerning such Rabbi Nahman ruled: 'If a man is married, this [holding the penis in the hand while urinating] is permitted.' If you prefer, I might say that which Rabbi Abba the son of Rabbi Benjamin ben Hiyya learned: 'But he may support the testicles from below.' Or if you prefer, I might say that which Rabbi Abbahu stated in the name of Rabbi Johanan: 'It has a limit; from the corona downward touch is permitted, but from the corona upwards in the direction of the body it is forbidden.' "

When R. Abbahu (after R. Johanan) ruled that a man may only touch his penis "from the corona downward" (i.e., the entire surface of the glans) and not "from the corona upwards in the direction of the body" (i.e., the entire surface of the shaft), he wished to prevent the most common form of masturbation from occurring. His premise was that if a man held the shaft of his penis with his hand rather than the corona of his glans with this thumb and forefinger when about to urinate, the heat and pressure of his palm would produce an erection and lead to manipulation. Hence we have the recommendation that men who are apt to be inflamed to self-stimulation at the moment of urination should wrap a thick rag around the penis in order to intercept the warmth, the direct pressure, and the tactile excitation of the hand.(12)

·T·
_____

(12) *In reading such injunctions one might well be moved to wonder if the sexual sensitivity of man has not seriously degenerated over the centuries. Few today are very often moved to masturbate simply by holding the penis betwixt the fingers while urinating.*

The gravest risk undoubtedly is run by the male whose urethra habitually continues to dribble after termination of the mainstream of urination. Such a man customarily and of necessity performs a few "masturbatory" movements in order to avoid dampening his

The orthodox Sephardic Jews, who settled by the thousands in North African cities after the Spanish Inquisition, still recognize these Talmudic rules and prohibitions with regard to touching the penis and masturbation. All the little boys of the rabbinical and upper-class families, from the time they are five years old, are advised or warned not to hold the penis in the hand when they make water. Middle-class parents caution their nine-year-old boys against touching or holding the penis when about to urinate. They reason thusly: Retention of urine in young boys commonly causes erection, which leads to handling. Even if erection does not occur, the mild urethral tickling makes the boy impulsively want to finger his penis. He presses and squeezes it, trying to hold back the urine and retain the titillation, and from this forceful fingering an erection results. If he is excited enough, he will now carry the act to its natural conclusion by indulging in repeated manual manipulation, after which he will urinate.

In order to discourage erections, genital friction and irritation, and masturbatory fondling, the Sephardic Jews customarily swathe their sons in *miknās* or "briefs," the abbreviated (skin-tight) underpants common in the Western world. These close-fitting underpants confine the genitals, but they do not in any way discourage masturbation or erections. Briefs for boys necessarily have an open crotch or fly for urinary purposes; and even if the youngster is not in a position to "pull it out," he will put his hands in his pockets and do all he can to clutch and agitate his erect penis as it is pressed up against his belly by the tight underpants. In other words, difficulty increases desire!

---

drawers and visibly and disgracefully wetting his trousers, and these movements may in fact be sufficiently stimulating to lead the dribbler to finish off in lust what he began by way of paying homage to modesty.

258

Non-Westernized Muslim children do not wear underclothing of any kind; they are dressed either in a loose frock or
trousers, and their genitals are easy of access. When a boy
wants to masturbate yet remain concealed, he merely slips his
hand into his pocket or inside his frock (sometimes gripping
from the outside) and clasps his free and unrestrained organ.
But again, difficulty increases desire; for the Westernized boy
likes his tight-fitting briefs. When he clutches the shaft of his
penis by way of his pockets or even outside his trousers, and
jerks energetically up and down, the sensitive underside of his
glans is rubbed continuously against the fabric of his underpants, which increases the pleasure twofold, making him manipulate all the harder and faster until his arms are tired from
the extreme effort. Boys do all in their power to get a good
hold on the penis while they sit in school or some other place;
and one may see them, with one or both hands in their pockets,
stirring and squirming in their seats. Retention of urine also
causes a great deal of fingering and squeezing and fidgeting and
squirming. The little fellows, with their legs pressed together,
grind away at the crotch with nimble fingers. If their underpants are drawn up too tight around the waist, they cause considerable discomfort and constriction; thus the boys are continually pulling at the crotch to loosen them and ease their
genitals, which sometimes makes the penis stiffen as a result
of friction and irritation.

Middle- and upper-class Jewish girls also wear *miknās*, but
in feminine style, with closed crotch. These panties are often
drawn up so tight around the little girl's waist that her vulva
cleft is plainly visible, making them a source of constant friction and irritation between the labia and against the clitoris.
Nearly all young girls masturbate by yanking their panties up
and down again and again until the rubbing of the fabric produces an orgasm. This forceful movement draws the crotch of

their briefs sharply, with a fiercely pleasant shock, between the lips of the little vulva and against the clitoris, causing them to squeeze their thighs close together and yank even harder and faster. Sometimes, while sitting down, the child will pull her panties up as tight as possible and then rapidly rub her thighs together till she is overwhelmed by the intense thrill.

Every orthodox Jewish boy and girl of North Africa is cautioned against playing with Muslim children and allowing anyone to remove their *miknās*. These warnings are useless, however, as evidenced by the number of small Jewish girls who permit Arab boys to pull down their panties, finger their genitals, and then "rape" them. Several Muslim urchins often seize a couple of Jewish boys bound for their religious lessons or returning from the Talmudic schools, force them into a dark place, and stuff their black skullcaps into their mouths to stop them from crying out. Yanking open their trousers and pulling down their underpants, the Arab boys will examine and handle their genitals, remarking about size and shape, rolling each Jewish boy's penis vigorously in their palms till it is perfectly rigid and then taking turns manipulating it. At times they run off with their pants and briefs, leaving the little Jews in what is Islamically considered a most shameful circumstance. Similarly, impish boys will sneak up behind a small girl whom they see pressing her fingers or hand between her legs, flip up her dress and jerk down her underpants, and cause her to wet herself in fright.

Jacobus learned that the Mussulmans of India and Pakistan frequently refer to the Hindu as a "human monkey." There are three reasons for this: (1) the Hindu male has the smallest genitals in the world, comparable in size and shape to those of an ape; (2) the Hindu is as lustful and prolific as a monkey; and (3) the Hindu, like the monkey, habitually masturbates whenever he is without a woman. So saith Dr. Jacobus!

260

Jacobus found that the erect penis of the prepubescent Hindu boy is barely the size of his little finger, which in a child is about an inch and a half long, while the Muslim boy's *kīr* (prickle) measures from 2½ to 4 inches in length. At puberty, the erect penis of the Indian is about as large as his forefinger (2½ or 3 inches) while the Mussulman's *zekr* (pecker) is five or six inches. Jacobus adds that "the preputial ring of the Hindu penis is generally narrow, the foreskin long and tapering. As nearly all the boys practice masturbation from the age of fourteen or fifteen years, this ring enlarges and permits the free egress of the glans." The penis is very slender, not much thicker than the two fingers mentioned above (between one-half and five-eighths of an inch), and to increase both girth and length the little boy pulls down the prepuce and executes the most violent jerking action.

The Hindus call masturbation *mathōla* (churning), the masturbator *mathōliyā* (jerker). Brahman or upper-class fathers are wont to detect habitual masturbation in their young sons by a bared glans or retracted prepuce, believing that "excessive self-abuse" causes semierection of the penis and retraction of the foreskin. Many uncircumcised Indian boys find manual manipulation somewhat difficult, frustrating, and even painful owing to adhesions and/or a long and tight prepuce. Erection does not free the glans, and dilation of the narrow orifice as well as stretching of the frenum are very discomforting. Uncircumcised Oriental masturbators almost invariably draw down the foreskin and fully expose the glans in order to prolong the energetic operation and prevent abrasive friction of the corona. Thus circumcision is highly desirable in that it removes the troublesome foreskin and facilitates the kind of vigorous masturbatory manipulation that satisfies the Easterner's senses.

Older but still prepubertal Muslim boys, when they masturbate little Indian lads, will execute this preputial dilation and frenal extension with one or two violent downward tractions that lay the glans, its corona, and the neck of the corona completely bare and, if not slightly bleeding, sorely abrased. Jacobus writes that he often found in very young boys "signs of masturbation characterized by a glans very easily stripped (the prepuce being retracted with ease), the mucous surface red, and the penis becoming erect at the least touch." This irritating hyperesthesia is induced in little Hindus by frequent and frenzied rubbing of the phallus. Not stopping at dilation and extension, and before the child has even begun to recover from this traumatic experience, the Muslim youth wrenches the foreskin fully upward again and proceeds to flip the little boy's penis, which (because it is so small) his hand completely and firmly encloses, as forcefully as he can. The Indian urchin lurches convulsively and lets out a cry at the piercing sensations of pleasure and pain. He will never forget this masturbation, fierce and intense, for it is instrumental in his becoming permanently addicted to the practice.

Far Eastern Muslim youths derive cruel and probably sadistic delight out of forcefully masturbating Chinese and Indian boys between the ages of three and five. They will firmly grasp the little lad's erect penis at the top and rapidly frictionize the foreskin over the glans and corona. Because a great many Chinese boys are born with a very short skin or no prepuce at all, this deliberate rubbing of the penis' head is made more difficult when the shaft is in erection and the sheath fully retracted.

Mussulman boys and girls will pounce upon a little Hindu, hold him down with legs outspread, and take turns mercilessly masturbating him. They call this manual rape *zerdek-zenī* or "pounding a carrot." Jacobus examined three little Tamil boys in Malaya who were ravished thusly by a band of Muslim boys and, as a direct result of the persistent stimulation to which

262

their penises were subjected, found their foreskins easily retractable, their coronas reddened and abrased, and a certain
psychophysical erethism or hypersensitivity which manifested
itself in tense erections the very moment he touched them for
a genital examination. When Jacobus flicked each boy's foreskin up and down several times to bare the glans and note
physical reaction, he observed in about ten seconds a vigorous
throbbing of the penis clearly indicative of orgasm. The doctor
immediately applied a local anesthetic, anointing the boys'
organs with the ointment until the effects of the abuse finally
wore off. In retaliation, a bunch of Tamil boys seized a couple
of Muslim lads and masturbated them repeatedly until they
began to bawl. Since their penises were circumcised, Jacobus
found nothing to indicate that they had been forcefully manipulated except for a slight redness and swelling of the shaft,
which had suffered all the squeezing and agitation. A third
Muslim boy later complained that several Tamil boys, having
taken him prisoner, rubbed *kapīkachchū* (monkey itch) or a
cowhage pod all over his glans penis. The tiny irritating hairs
covering the cowhage pod cause an intolerable itching which
is only increased by friction. Jacobus found the youth's penis
in violent erection and dark red from tip to base; the glans was
swollen and throbbing. He said he had masturbated repeatedly
without relief, and had even raped a little girl in her anus. An
anesthetic ointment soon altered the situation.

Throughout Southeast Asia, all children begin active masturbation during their first year at school, where they learn
about and are taught the habit by the older boys, who either
demonstrate before them or upon them. While mutually masturbating, the youngsters fully observe genital differences and
become engrossed in noting nuances of manipulation and sensation peculiar to circumcised and uncircumcised organs. For
example, the Muslim boy sees how the prepuce completely

263

covers the glans of his Indian friend's penis and how this "hood" may therefore be used to stimulate the "head." He sees how the short prepuce of his Chinese pal's penis merely caps the corona without covering the glans and how, in erection, it is fully retracted. He compares this penis, "circumcised from the womb," with his own artificially circumcised organ, which has a circular scar or ring of cicatrice around the cervix or "neck" of the corona, noting how this band of tissue fully retracts during erection and how he is therefore unable to do what his uncircumcised classmates can do.

The manner in which circumcised Mussulmans masturbate is greatly influenced by a method commonly employed by the uncircumcised Indians and Chinese, who grip the upper part of the penis' shaft so that the rim of the prepuce rubs over the rim of the glans, thus evoking the most acute sensations. Imitating this technique as best he can, the Muslim encircles and clasps the circular circumcisional cicatrice with his thumb and forefinger at the same time he holds the shaft in his hand; he then jogs the skin up and down, bumping up against the corona at each jerk. They call this *jalkh* or "jiggling." The *jeld 'omayreh* (whipping up an erection) of the Arabs or manual manipulation of the shaft causes the glans to react through sympathy; the nerves and tissues of the penis are superstimulated and the pleasure prolonged as compared to direct friction of the glans or frenal area.

Many Mussulman males are active masturbators from earliest infancy. It is customary for the mother, nurse, or some other attending female to tweak and jiggle the little penis to amuse them. We find similar habits among the Hindus. Jacobus writes:

> Masturbation is prevalent and even customary not only among adult males who cannot get women but also among those who have access to sexual intercourse, and it is ex-

264

tremely widespread among boys before puberty; for it is quite common for little sisters to pull the penis of their little brothers, or for boys to do it to one another or to themselves.(13)

'I'
_____

(13) *A point this book repeatedly makes, and it is one that the reader should not neglect to reflect upon, is that masturbation in the East, much more than in the West, is engaged in not as a substitute for some other sex act impossible at the time, but as an alternative method of gratification freely chosen and of merit in its own right. Thus, masturbation has a status in the East such as it does not often enjoy in the West.*

The masturbator engages in his practice because it affords different titillations from those available in other types of erotic behavior. He considers masturbation as one of a variety of possibilities open to him, each offering its own unique advantages. He is seldom a masturbator exclusively any more than he is likely to be a copulator or a sodomist exclusively. While the individual does not often work everything out so exhaustively as do the Oriental erotologists, he seems to give at least some thought to which type of stimulation he prefers at the moment. Then, having made his choice, he engages in the act best designed to provide him with food for his sexual hunger.

In the West, by contrast, even today masturbation is regarded as sufficiently disreputable that the masturbator must usually persuade himself that he is masturbating only because the presence of desire has unfortunately coincided with the absence of a sex partner. To masturbate under such a circumstance is surely to deprive the experience of some of its sensual and tension-discharging rewards, since the individual is settling for half a loaf and his expectations are not high.

Needless to say, African and Asian children are seldom faced with the necessity of participating in that dismal Western game where the parent attempts, by spying and other techniques, to catch the

Sisters, in order to tease and torment their brothers when in the nude, will snatch at the penis and pluck its prepuce forcibly until erection occurs. Small girls are wont to grab and pull the penises of their little boy friends when they see them naked. The girl will reveal signs of being jealous of the boy's penis and then suddenly catch hold of it with her hand and begin to jerk it to and fro. The boy, lurching back, will resist with all his strength; but she, struggling with him and giggling gleefully, cannot be made to loosen her grip. His little member stiffens instantly in her hand, and the more he pulls away the tighter she holds, until she finally feels sorry for him and lets him go. Because the method used to masturbate the penis is the same as that employed in manually stripping the teat of a cow or goat, the girls titteringly refer to their little trick as "milking." It is perhaps only natural that an imaginative girl just learning how to milk a domestic animal will want to make the same experiment with a boy's penis, which certainly resembles a teat. She is fascinated by the fact that nothing squirts out of the penis of her little playmate, no matter how much she milks it, but that when his older brother asks her to do it the milky essence spurts out within a few seconds after she begins to wrench away. This constant plucking of the penis activates and intensifies the masturbation habit in most Indian boys, for it greatly irritates the delicate glans and results in frequent erections.

The companion of the *fellatrice* (she who sucks the penis) is the *fricatrice* (she who rubs the penis), although both in many cases are one and the same. Perhaps the most famous fricatrices of the Eastern world are found among the Jews of North Africa; for they are like the fair females of Lesbos, whom

---

child masturbating; and it is up to the child to develop techniques for escaping detection.

266

Catullus described as standing at crossways and in alleys "to jerk off the high-souled sons of Rome." (14)

In the East, the harmless mutual fondling of the genitals during early childhood, becoming habitual, leads to more serious experimentation and actual intromission. Sometimes penetration of the penis into the vagina is enacted quite by accident among children, but more often it is the result of their having observed elders in the act or of their having been induced to perform it by older and more knowledgeable companions. This is the inevitable consequence of allowing children to witness adult coition, of which they have little or no understanding, and of allowing children of both sexes and various ages to sleep together in groups, a custom arising from Oriental housing

·|·

(14) In eighteenth-century France the fricatrice was well known and her services were much in demand. Neither is she entirely unknown in Europe presently, although the demand for her talent is seldom sufficient to enable her to earn a living by that specialty alone.

In the United States, by contrast, the fricatrice has never enjoyed any vogue. Practical Americans, if they want to masturbate, do it themselves; or, mostly during boyhood, exchange manipulations with a friend. Later, young couples may masturbate one another as a way of achieving gratification without risking pregnancy. To pay for such a service would seem a waste ill-according with the thrifty principles of a do-it-yourself people.

More seriously, the relatively normal American who visits a prostitute seems to feel impelled to "go all the way," which usually means coitus, and may also mean fellatio and cunnilingus. Masturbation is regarded as affording a lesser titillation; but also, and doubtless more significantly, it is regarded as a "lesser offense." The American male patronizing a prostitute often approaches her with the attitude that if he is going to be damned, he will be damned the whole way. For him, the fricatrice cannot fulfill such a craving.

267

conditions and parental indifference. The indiscriminate erotic intermingling of boys and girls, sisters and brothers, during early childhood has always been the principal excitant to bisexuality and promiscuity in the East. Children are left to their own devices, their natural impulses are given free rein to develop, and it often results that "a hole is a hole and a pole is a pole" and that aimless experimentation leads to endless exploitation.(15)

Danger arises only when the element of force, no less than of destruction, enters into these promiscuous activities. Under a system of "pleasure at any price," selfish competition and lethal jealousy are prevalent; and the impulsive child, knowing neither self-discipline nor social responsibility, becomes a conscienceless victim of the most destructive fatalism and fanaticism.

Each female has her own reasons, both conscious and unconscious, for being a fricatrice and/or a fellatrice. These motives are her own personal business and nobody else's, and it is all too easy and typically smug for the authoritarian to say that she is "fixated" in her extracoital desires. But she must live her own life, not someone else's; and if she is relatively satisfied with herself and with the peculiar pleasures that make an otherwise unsatisfactory life worth living, it is often tragically stupid and hypocritical for the "therapist" to think he is doing her a great service by seeking to convert her to his way of think-

---

(15) Many sociological studies, in Britain and other Western countries, indicate that overcrowding of children and adults in rooms and beds invariably leads to promiscuous intercourse, including incest. The younger imitate the older, and not infrequently the older initiate the younger by seduction and rape. Probably no amount of countereducation would be sufficient to thwart the natural tendency of human beings to cohabit indiscriminately under such circumstances.

ing. Professionals who convert by emotional blackmail and intellectual brainwashing seem in many cases to be deeply dissatisfied with their own status quo. This tampering with the profound patterns of nature, although it is very faddish, may be nonetheless dangerously foolhardy. People naturally vary in innumerable ways, and what a boring world it would be if we were all made in the same mold.

In classical Israel, the *zārāh* (tight woman or adventuress) was distinguished from the *zōnāh* (loose woman or whore) in that she engaged only in extracoital activities with strange men. *Zārāh* stems from the root *zūr* (to press or squeeze, to take and hold in the hand). The *zārāh*, being married, pursued her illicit pleasures just for the pure thrill of it. She practiced everything short of vaginal coitus. The *zārāh* is frequently mentioned in the Book of Proverbs; e.g., 5:3, "The lips of a strange woman drip with honey, and her mouth is smoother than oil [an allusion to fellatio];" 7:12, "Now in the street, now in the market, and at every corner she lies in wait [to masturbate men];" 22:14, "The mouth of a strange woman is a deep pit [she will "swallow up" the largest penis];" and 23:27, "A whore (*zōnāh*) is a deep pit [she offers her cunnus], and an adventuress (*zārāh*) is a narrow well [she offers her anus]." (16)

---

(16) *The girl who will engage in many or all sexual acts with the exception of coitus was quite famous in Europe in the late nineteenth and early twentieth centuries. She was called a "half-virgin," after Prevost's novel. Such "Demi-Vierges" were not necessarily prostitutes, but might also be girls from middle-class families who sought to achieve sexual gratification in their love affairs without forfeiting the virginity essential to the making of a good marriage.*

Such half-virgins will be found among the girls of any country where a high premium is placed on virginity at the time of marriage. They are still common in the United States, although the great increase in premarital copulation is fast diminishing their ranks.

269

Unlike fast-and-loose Arab females whom we generally find to be vaginally and orally oriented in their sexuality, the promiscuous Jewish females are primarily interested in manual activity and receive the greatest sensations from external stimulation. They are by nature fricatrices rather than fellatrices, preferring mutual masturbation or petting to genital intercourse. They masturbate repeatedly by rubbing the clitoris, and each of them loves a man to apply extravaginal friction with his fingers until a number of orgasms are reached. Oral excitations are of some interest to them; they are passionate for cunnilingus or stimulation of the clitoris by the tongue, which sends them into orgastic ecstasies, but unlike Arab women they are not compelled by passion to apply their mouth to a man's sexual organ. Many will relate how and why they came to prefer mutual masturbation to vaginal copulation:

The typical young Jewish female expresses the belief that she was "fascinated" by the penis when she first laid eyes upon it. Naturally enough, she immediately wondered why she did not have a little "tassel" between her legs. This strong combination of fascination and envy manifested itself in the impulse to touch, hold, and even pull the little "tassel." When the girl did so, she instantly noticed the electrifying reaction in the young male, which resulted in an erection. The thrill was equally felt by both girl and boy; so she did it again, pinching the glans with a quick pull of the fingers. The tickling sensations were acute; the boy almost invariably asked her to do it again. However, before doing so, the girl would usually expose her little vulva and tell him to touch it. If he refused, she refused to touch his penis. Once he had touched it, giving her

---

On the other hand, half-virgin prostitutes are rare. Those who will not engage in coitus usually must specialize not in such commonplace acts as oral and anal intercourse, but in sadism, masochism, fetishism, coprophiliac practices, etc.

a little thrill, she would separate the outer lips with her fingers and tell him where the "water" came from. She was envious of his ability to make a "rainbow" while urinating, and that he was able to stand while doing so without wetting himself down the legs. She then continued squeezing and fingering his glans.

Pinching the glans is the most common form of contact at the first experience. While holding is also prevalent, actual handling of the penis ordinarily occurs later. Sisters will teasingly pinch a little brother's corona, which in a split second makes his penis stand perfectly stiff, then hold it and press it in the hand to make it "tickle." While pulling of the prepuce is the usual "game" played by Hindu girls with their uncircumcised brothers, who will in turn pluck at the sister's clitoris, this is of course impossible in the case of Jewish boys owing to circumcision of the foreskin in infancy. Thus the Jewish girl will squeeze the glans and wrench it in her fist, rubbing it rotatively. An extremely popular game involving manipulation of the shaft is to roll the penis rapidly between the palms of the hands, as one would a stick in an effort to produce fire by friction. However, when they observe the process of milking a domestic animal and come to compare the teat with the penis, imaginative little girls at once attempt the same stripping technique on their little brothers or boy friends by seizing the shaft of the penis and manipulating it with a rapid and repeated snatching or jerking action. The continuous shocks against the corona or base of the glans produce the pleasurable sensations and finally the spasms of orgasm. Girls often perform this impulsively, without any previous example, for while holding the penis the usual impulse is to pull at it; and when she sees that a quick flick is instantly appreciated by the boy, the girl will yank again and again as fast as she can until his little organ throbs in orgasm.

Wilhelm Stekel, in *Auto-Erotism*, notes that "masturbation among men is frequently called milking." Eastern Jews, tradi-

271

tionally a pastoral people, employ the world *zelb* (stripping) because the most common method of male masturbation is similar to that used in milking a cow or goat. *Shlek* (skinning) is a variant; "to strip" or "skin" the phallus is to hold it in the hand or between the fingers and force the integument up and down.

North African Jewish girls indulge in intensive masturbatory activity between the ages of three and thirteen. They generally do so with younger brothers or with boys at least a year below their age. Most fricatrices will admit that they fondled their brothers, cousins, and other male relatives, masturbating them as babies and as little boys. The occasional violence revealed in this habitual play, as in the *zelb* (stripping) or *shlek* (skinning) methods, bears evidence to the envy they felt toward the male organ. If they can, preadolescent girls will play with their little brothers' penises whenever they are in the nude; e.g., before bedtime, upon awakening, or in the bathtub. Orthodox boys and girls are bathed every evening, seated naked in the same tub together and left to play, during which time the girl will tweak and jiggle the boy's penis while the boy will finger and pinch the girl's clitoris. When they sleep together, which is commonly the case with small children rather than older ones in the upper-class families, it is their habit to handle and rub each other's genitals for at least an hour every night. One young female, who slept with her brother all during childhood, freely confessed: "I loved to play with it; it stiffened the moment I touched it. I would finger the head, pinching and tweaking it in different ways; then I would rub the whole thing and roll it around in my palms or squeeze it in my hand and jiggle it up and down as hard as I could. While I did this to him, he would poke his fingers in me and then pinched my tickler so much that I squirmed with the wild feeling. Sometimes we got on top of each other and made our parts fit together, pushing them all the way in, while at other times I

272

would put his penis in my mouth and he would lick my vulva like a puppy. We learned these tricks all by ourselves."

The fricatrice's sexuality is often enkindled between the ages of three and five, usually by some so-called traumatic experience. Older boys frequently take little girls into a secluded place, where they pull down their panties and perform cunnilingus upon them. When subjected to repeated licking and rubbing of the clitoris, small girls become habituated to masturbation. Occasional contacts seem to have little effect in determining the direction taken by subsequent desires. Almost every Arab child has had a boy lift her skirt and tickle her genitals, but the incident is of minor import and soon forgotten. Even if several boys finger her vulva, unless the excitation is persistent and piercing rather than quick and casual she may soon forget about it and only recall the episode in later years, if at all.

By the age of ten, the typical fricatrice has masturbated a large number of boys, both young and old, but upon reaching puberty she normally sets her sights upon postadolescent youths and men. She offers as her principal reason the fact that she was always "fascinated" by the mechanism of ejaculation, which is a "thrilling mystery" to her. Little boys and girls often masturbate dogs and other domestic male animals in order to observe the mechanism of ejaculation; meanwhile, the girls express their disappointment to the boys, because they are as yet unable to ejaculate like their older brothers. The fricatrice loves to see a man "shoot" (*shāfek*), as the Talmud terms it, to watch the sperm "come out in spurts from his shooter (*shāfkāh*)" and to observe the male orgasm and ejaculation from beginning to end. This revelation ofttimes unveils a deep-seated desire to drain the male of masculinity, for these females will avidly masturbate a man until he can bear no more. In fact, the man is frequently forced to grab the woman by the wrist in order to stop her from further stimulation.

273

The typical fricatrice acknowledges a sense of sadomasochistic satisfaction felt in mutual masturbation. It represents to her a powerful outlet for her aggressive and rebellious impulses. Nevertheless, she rarely assumes any personal responsibility regarding her preference for clitoral sexuality. When she was very young (she says), and playing in the back streets and alleyways, older boys would lift her dress, sometimes pull down her panties, and tickle her clitoris with their fingers. Then each boy would make her feel his phallus. Acute sensations of pleasure were experienced, leading her to repeat with her own fingers what the boys had done to her. She became "addicted" to masturbation, rubbing her little clitoris repeatedly whenever she could. Other girls claim they were raped externally, having had their vulvas forcibly frictionized by the glans penis; while a few admit that an older brother or some other boy pulled down their panties and performed cunnilingus on them, then took his penis out of his underpants and forced it into their mouth, often making them hold it in their hands as well. The explanations are many, but the results are the same.

Many Jewesses confess that they deliberately masturbated their little brothers, deriving therefrom a sadistic thrill. In fact, they kept up the manipulation even when the "tickling" had stopped and "it started to hurt." Some of them speak of an overwhelming desire to pull the penis off, to yank it right out at the root, just as we find many Arab fellatrices obsessed with the impulse to bite the penis very hard, to sink their teeth into it as far as possible, perhaps in an effort to castrate the "male animal."

Hendrik de Leeuw noted that the prevalence of rape in the *Mellāhh* or Ghetto of Tangier, plus the crowded conditions and consequent loose living, are instrumental in creating a large class of prostitutes and promiscuous females. The same is true in Tunis, Algiers, Oran, Fez, Marrakesh, and many other North African cities. Jewish girls, raped repeatedly by Muslim youths, paradoxically become prostitutes supported by Arab patrons or rent themselves out as mistresses to Muslim playboys. The name for such a kept or free-lance woman is *sehhīqeh* (she-rubber, fricatrice) or *sehhāqeh* (masturbatrice), from *sehhq* (rubbing, pounding).

The *sehhīqeh*, a dancing girl and professional entertainer by trade, seeks psychosexual satisfaction and profit on the side in the masturbation and fellation of men. She caters to upper-class, well-to-do Muslims: esthetes, sophisticates, and bisexual Hedonists who have long since wearied of vaginal and anal coitus and who are now seeking the "new thrill" in oral and manual excitations. The *sehhīqeh* thrives under the *zewāj el-mut'ah* (union of pleasure) system, living in luxury with each lover or libertine on a short-term basis. Out of bed, she is his fashionable showpiece; in bed, she plays with his penis, suckles it passionately, and does any other erotic deed he asks her to. He enjoys watching her masturbate herself; and when he has satisfied his voyeuristic impulses, he will masturbate her himself and then lavish upon her vulva the most avid caresses of lips and tongue. The *sehhīqeh* is devoted to lesbian techniques, whether practiced with female or male, is ardent for cunnilingus, and true to her nickname (*sihhāq* means "tribadism" or genital friction), she delights in rubbing her cunnus and clitoris over the man's thigh or against his arm. In a word, he and she indulge fervidly and feverishly in all the extracoital acts of love.

Riza Bey writes:

> These girls are exponents of an age-old art, and there is not one of the thousand and one sexual "exercises" set out in the *Kāmasūtra* which they do not know and do not practice.
>
> With these girls and their clients there is nothing of the gloomy, joyless union which comes of contact with a paid paramour of the West. They delight in subtlety, and the actual act of union is perhaps the least of the pleasures which they retail.

They are adepts at amorous intimacy, and they proceed to their assignments full of life and zest.

He adds, however, that their sexual life is not a long one, "because of the abandon with which they consume aphrodisiacs."

Honoré Gabriel Riquetti, Comte de Mirabeau, the notorious French orator, politician, and voluptuary credited with having fired off the petard of the French Revolution, entertained the amorous embraces of an accomplished *sehhīqeh* while visiting Istanbul (then Constantinople). Mirabeau learned from a prominent pimp that there were approximately 25,000 fricatrices in the city to serve him: Jewish, Armenian, Greek, and Turkish girls between the ages of ten and twenty. Our Frenchman made the necessary arrangements with a pretty and witty young Jewess, and he writes:

> A girl educated in the art of *zalaba* [*zelb* or *zelābāh*, skinning or masturbation in Hebrew] does not conduct herself with a circumcised man or one who has a very short prepuce as with a man who is uncircumcised or one having a long prepuce which completely covers the glans.

Mirabeau intimates that there were two distinct methods of masturbation employed by Istanbuli fricatrices on circumcised and uncircumcised males. Since Mirabeau was circumcised, we offer his description of the first method. In the case of the uncircumcised, the girl utilized the foreskin for stimulation of the glans by pulling it up and down over the corona.

> Imagine the two naked players in an alcove surrounded by mirrors and lying upon a gently sloping couch. The skillful girl at first avoids with the greatest care the touching of the generative parts. Her approaches are slow, her embraces soft. Her kisses are more tender than wanton, the strokes of her

276

tongue restrained. Her expression is voluptuous, the enlacements of her limbs full of grace and gentleness. She excites with her fingers a slight tickling sensation upon the tips of his nipples. Soon she sees that the eye of his organ has become moist. She perceives that the erection is thoroughly established. Then she lightly lays her thumb upon the tip of his glans, which she finds bathed in the clear liquid. From this extremity her thumb descends smoothly upon the root of the frenum, returns, redescends, then makes a tour around the corona. She now stops if she finds that the sensations have increased with too great a rapidity. She then makes use of more general titillations. It is not until after the simultaneous and direct touchings of her hand or more often of both her hands, and the approaches of all her body, that the erection becoming extremely violent prompts her to judge the instant in which she should allow nature to act, either to aid it in its work or to provoke it into arriving at its aim, because the spasms which are established in the man become so acute and the sensory appetite so severe that the erection will fall slowly in syncopation if she does not put an immediate end to it. And she does this by a firm clasping and a rapid manipulation of the shaft, which produces a powerful climax to the whole affair.*

While studying the sexual behavior of the Chinese, Dr. Jacobus observed that

Although they consider solitary pleasures to be the worst and the most immoral, yet children and grown-up people are much addicted to them. It is this shameful self-abuse that renders thousands of Chinese effeminate and fatalistic. Young men, from twenty to twenty-five years old, masturbate each other every night of the week. The bestial orgies to which they abandon themselves can find no analogies but in the history of the ancient Romans. They assemble to smoke

* Honoré Riquetti, Comte de Mirabeau, *Erotika Biblion*. Bruxelles: 1890.

opium and, with little boys to serve them, abuse their generative organs for hours at a time in a frenzy of mutual masturbation and anal copulation. I treated numerous cases of anal lesions and penial swellings in boys who joined these orgies and subsequently suffered unbelievable abuse in the embraces of bacchanals. The violent sodomy of Islamic Chinese injures the anus of many a Malayan or Indonesian boy, while violent masturbation often causes a temporary serous swelling of the skin of the penis. Swollen penis and sore anus are common complaints in the Far East, where Muslims and Chinese abuse their bodies with fatalistic and voluptuous resignation.

Jacobus found that the Chinese males of Southeast Asia are "compulsive masturbators." He could not find a man or boy, married or unmarried, who did not indulge in self-stimulation at least twice a week. He discovered that it was for centuries quite common for young males to assemble and, while leisurely smoking opium, to masturbate and fellate each other all night long. The anesthetic effects of the opium, taken in small and stimulating doses, enables them to enjoy prolonged erection and several hours of continuous manual and oral excitation without ejaculating more than two or three times at the most. Jacobus adds:

In the Chinese brothels and at private parties, rich voluptuaries take a few whiffs from the opium pipe between each masturbation or copulation; and up to a certain point they find themselves invigorated. The Islamic Chinese in Jakarta are said to prepare an electuary called *a-fu-yung* [from the Arabic *efyūn*, opium], which is chiefly composed of opium. It is said to cause such lust that the woman is often obliged to flee from the too energetic embraces of her lover, and it has driven many Muslims and Chinese into violent bouts of masturbation and anal copulation. The penis of the circumcised as well as the uncircumcised Chinese hangs smoothly, being somewhat bellied, the purple veins standing out beneath the yellow skin, revealing signs of repeated masturbatory manipulation. I once watched a Chinese Muslim masturbate himself; he grasped the shaft of his erect penis firmly in his fist and jerked it rapidly up and down until the ejaculation occurred. This forceful and habitual abuse produces a protraction or semierection of the organ when in repose, for it distends very little during tumescence.

Some Chinese physicians attribute the high incidence of boyhood masturbation and sodomy to the fact that nearly all males are born with naturally short foreskins. Many are entirely lacking this protective prepuce and, as in the artificially circumcised, the glans is exposed to direct friction and irritation which provoke frequent erections and lead to repeated handling and masturbatory rubbing.

Jacobus tells us that the Chinese are "immoderate masturbators from early boyhood." He ascribes this "premature addiction to onanism" to the physiological peculiarity that they are born with very short prepuces which barely cover and protect the sensitive glans from erection-provoking friction and irritation. When examining the penises of little Chinese boys, Jacobus found the foreskin freely retracted and the corona exposed. In babies it merely encircles the rim of the crown like a ring or cap, giving the appearance of circumcision, and during erection the corona is fully denuded. Jacobus observed genital manipulation in many infants, who commonly press and roll the little penis between the palms of their hands. Young boys often masturbate their baby brothers, teaching them a new movement. They clasp the suckling's phallus with their fingers and jiggle it up and down, or sometimes they press his little hands around the shaft and make the same motions of forcing the outer skin to and fro. Thus Chinese tots will with great frequency squeeze the penis between their palms and rotatively rub the glans or up-and-downly agitate the integument. Wearied of manu-

279

stupration, boys turn to analism and coitus; for the forceful friction and pressure supplied by the intensely tight anal sphincter, or by the vaginal constrictor of a little girl, approximate the vigorous rubbing and squeezing of the penis' shaft by the hands in masturbation.

Bathhouses are the favorite haunts of Far Eastern masturbators and pederasts. The same is true throughout the Near and Middle East. The *hhemmām* or public bath is one of the most favored luxuries of the Muslim, for it is a paradise of homosexual pleasure. The naked bather wears only a *fūteh* or towel around his waist when he enters the *hherāreh* or hot room, where the masseur awaits his command. The intense heat and humidity of the bath have an anesthetizing effect upon the genitals, which require a more strenuous and prolonged stimulation to produce orgasm, thus making it a masturbator's delight. Several minutes of continuous and vigorous manipulation may be needed to evoke sensation and finally ejaculation. Standing also seems to delay the orgastic reactions, which explains why pederasts and sodomists almost invariably operate in an upright position while the passive analist bends over and braces himself against a bench or the like.

Bathers who have taken hashish submit their penises to the most dynamic excitation, such as analism. The anus is penetrated and the passive partner's buttocks pressed firmly together, abrasive friction being lessened or eliminated by extreme moisture. Then the active partner forces his organ back and forth as fast as he can while the passive rotates his pelvis. When the *fā'il* stops for a moment's rest, he will squeeze and agitate the penis of the *mef'ūl* in his hand. The *fūteh* is used to catch the seminal ejaculations. Some men spend hours in the *hhemmām* engaged in homoerotic acts; and the masseurs are in great demand among bathers if they are young, handsome, and skilled in manual and oral stimulation.

Riza Bey, in his comments upon the Turkish bath, notes

that "homosexuality is not only frequent in practice, but is largely accepted as normal." He adds that among Easterners "homosexuality is innate, but . . . does not blind them to the attributes of the opposite sex." In other words, they "love to eat both figs (anus) and pomegranates (cunnus)!"

Riza observed that from two to a dozen naked girls, in lieu of beardless boys, are often in attendance.

> They descend upon the bather, and with an extreme delicacy of touch, remove his one feeble garment [the *fūteh* or towel]; and then they proceed to wash him and massage him.

He discovered that their technique of manipulation is lengthy and prolonged, adding suggestively that

> "always light, deft fingers are playing with some portion of his anatomy. . . . These young females, all of whom are selected for their looks and the symmetry of their bodies, are adepts. . . . Their province within the bath chamber is titillation."

Extensive oral, anal, and vaginal intercourse with each of these lovely girls may be enjoyed by the male bather, in which case he is offered *imsāk*.

> It is intended primarily for those who wish to prolong the sexual act, and to live a night of amorous delights without undue fatigue. In a manner it produces in men many of the characteristics of the eunuchs of Istanbul [i.e., the erotic imagination is superstimulated while the genital nerves are anesthetized; erection is violent and prolonged, psychophysiological pleasure intense and protracted, and the orgasm and ejaculation greatly delayed]. The sexual act can be prolonged for an hour, if need be, but in this instance it is the man who dictates the tempo and not the woman.

When a man is under the influence of *imsāk*, a woman may rub and suck his penis all night long for his satisfaction.

281

Bath attendants, especially those who do a running business, often take hashish to make them last the night; for many of them, offering themselves for anal intercourse, have their penises handled and manipulated almost constantly. To hide any continuous erection produced by the drug, they are wont to tie their virile member up against their belly underneath their towel. As a rule, Muslim male homosexuals who are promiscuous rather than selective are capable of repeated climax over a twenty-four hour period. The hashish, while deadening the nerves of the penis, also loosens the anal muscles and makes even the most forceful penetration by a big phallus easy and painless; so saith the poet:

> My prickle is big and the bathboy spoke:
> "Thrust fiercely up fundament with lionlike stroke!"
> Said I: "It won't fit!" Then he: "What a joke!
> I've had some hashish!" So I battered his poke.

The evil jinni *El-A'wer* (The One-Eyed), who encourages debauchery, is said to oversee the bath. *A'wer* is a stock nickname for the penis, which has only one eye (the meatus urinarius), and *yā a'wer* (O one-eye) or *yā bin 'aor* (O son of a prick) are common curses in the Arab world.

In the bathhouses of Arabia, sapphism or lesbianism is rampant. Muhammed said: "Whatever woman enters a public bath, the devil is with her." The *bellāneh* (tirewoman) is generally a Negress, and one of her duties is to remove the pubic hair. She does so with the maximum of fingering, so that the Arabian female becomes so sexually excited that the desire for orgasm is overwhelming. Cunnilingus, clitoral and vaginal masturbation, and tribadism (mutual apposition and friction of the genitals) are prevalent practices in which the *sehhāqeh* (rubber, fricatrice) is skilled. A vivid description of the erotic activities of the female bath attendant is found in the *Arabian Nights:*

She used to compel the young male slaves to mount her, and she herself loved to mount the young female slaves. Above all things she loved to tickle and rub herself against these virgin bodies; she was terribly expert in the titillant art, and could suck the delicate parts of a girl voraciously while rubbing her nipples in an agreeable manner.*

Habitual masturbation is so widespread among both married and unmarried Muslim females throughout Africa and the East that it is commonly regarded by the menfolk as customary and matter-of-fact. *Sehhq* or *sihhāq* (rubbing, pounding) is considered a natural manifestation of feminine nature, for "woman's passion is ten times greater than man's." Fatalistic philosophy therefore states that since it takes ten men to satisfy one woman, it is only normal that a female faithful to one male should occasionally or even habitually masturbate to answer her erotic needs when her husband is not at home.(17)

---

(17) *It is recorded that French troops marching off to war used to provide their wives with dildos or rubber verges, aimed at easing the loss of regular copulation and so preventing adultery. American husbands, on the other hand, are often horrified to learn that their wives masturbate, despite the fact that those same husbands may be inveterate masturbators themselves.*

The American male, who has only lately come to admit that sexual desire is possible in a good woman, is also likely to take his wife's masturbation (when he is at home) as a personal affront—that is, as evidence that he has failed to satisfy her (and so by implication is "not enough of a man" for her).

The Oriental and Arab view that woman is almost insatiably lustful, which used also to be the Christian view, may be less than accurate; but its resulting approval of female masturbation is far

* Mardrus & Mathers, *op. cit.*

Vaginal masturbation, either with fingers or with some penis-like object, is much more prevalent and popular in the Orient than in the Occident, for the simple reason that in most Eastern and African cultures the girls are sexually educated and conditioned at a very early age to respond orgastically to deep internal stimulation.(18) An Islamic poet once wrote that

> Bananas, long and round, smoothly shaped
> > Are loved by all little girls
> Who are anxious to be raped.

Little Arab girls masturbate as intensely as little Arab boys. In Muslim Africa and Arabia, female children force bananas, cucumbers, corncobs, wax or tallow candles, and other phallic

---

more realistic than the outrage of an American husband who has caught his wife flagrante delicto with a sausage.

Needless to say, any indignation at female masturbation is even less justified when the case is that of a woman whose husband is frequently away from home during which times she is supposed to remain erotically ascetic while he, his behavior sanctioned by the traditional double standard, fornicates as abundantly as his virility, sex appeal, and/or bankroll will allow.

(18) It is generally held to be the case that the American female most commonly stimulates her external genitals when masturbating, while only a minority regularly employ vaginal stimulation—with the widest possible variety of objects. The European woman is perhaps somewhere in between the Oriental and the American in this respect. She has for many centuries made use of the dildo, an artificial penis fashioned of materials including hard rubber, wood, and, more recently, plastic; but she also, probably in the majority of cases, prefers manual stimulation of her clitoris, labia minora, and vaginal vestibule.

284

objects large and small into their little vaginas. When these are not available, the most common method is to poke one or more pushing and probing fingers into the orifice. Digital excitation of the clitoris is less frequent in small girls than it is in those who are past the age of puberty. Urchins habitually force their fingers between their thighs in order to stretch the vagina and prepare it for the penis' penetration. Fingertip titillation of the uterus is also ordinary, acclimatizing the child to deep internal stimulation. Anal masturbation with the fingers or with some object such as a pencil is said to be rife among little Jewish girls, whom the Arabs use for sodomy and who often orgastically identify the rectum with the vagina. In Morocco, Muslim boys bugger Jewish girls as they would donkeys and other domestic animals.

Masturbation in very small girls is rarely refined or deliberately localized, owing to their mental and physical immaturity. One merely sees the child pressing her garment against her little vulva, squeezing her thighs together with her fingers or hand between them, and impulsively pushing in or rubbing up and down. Often she will stop short of the orgasm, not anticipating it amid all the acute titillation and keen sensation; or if distracted, will go off completely oblivious of what she was doing. Many learn to masturbate quite spontaneously as a result of retaining urine by flexing their pubic muscles, squeezing their thighs close together, and firmly holding the vulva. This is an extremely common sight. With her fingers the little girl tightly presses her dress and panties in between the labia, closes her legs, squeezes hard again and again, and holds her hand (or hands) fast against her cunnus. When she has stemmed the flow, and in order to retain the pleasant feeling and intensify the urethral tickling, she will now slowly or quickly move her hand or pull her panties up and down over her vulvar lips and clitoris.

Tots ordinarily manipulate their genitals only a few seconds, sometimes compulsively or unconsciously—as when anxious, excited, or frightened—for their little hands seem instinctively to dart down and press between their legs, perhaps as a means of psychic pacification, withdrawal, or distraction. The innocent and incidental habit or impulse does not become intense and refined until its nature is first understood, or when the child is instructed or seduced by other and ofttimes older girls. General friction of the labia in childhood eventually leads to a discovery and localized rubbing of the clitoris toward adolescence, when many females pinch, pluck at, and attempt to elongate their little "tickler," perhaps wishing to make a full-sized penis of it. Aside from use of the fingers or hands, Eastern girls rapidly and repeatedly rub and tickle their vulvas to orgasm against such objects as bolsters and bedposts, also employing such items as towels, blankets, and panties to produce the pleasurable friction.

For centuries Islamic physicians have related the prevalence of female masturbation and lesbianism to the remarkable size of the clitoris (*zembūr*, hornet) in little girls. Burton observed that even in the babe it protrudes beyond the labia, and genital manipulation in girl babies is a spontaneous phenomenon. Because so many female children tend to become "clitorized," preferring masturbation and cunnilingus to vaginal intercourse, many Muslims have their daughters declitorized shortly after birth, hoping by this means to insure vaginal responsiveness.

But as is the case with countless male babies, excision of the clitoris or merely circumcision of the clitoral prepuce is commonly the cause of active masturbation in female infants and little girls. Excision of the glans clitoris and incision or resection of the clitoral hood, although operations performed in a trice as compared with amputation and suture of the male prepuce, nonetheless lay bare an entire network of hypersensitive nerves around or at the root of the clitoris. In simple resection or incision, the small area where the clitoral foreskin or upper juncture of the *nymphae* was severed to expose the glans is extremely tender and responsive to the slightest friction and irritation. Frequent erections of the clitoris are the result; and the infant or little child constantly rubs and squeezes her thighs together, presses and frictionizes her fingers between them, or tightly and sharply pulls her panties against her vulva in an effort to ease the intense and at times almost intolerable titillation. This activity frequently inflames the clitoris, and numerous orgasms are experienced. In the case of excision, a half-burning half-itching sensation prevails where the head of the clitoris was cut off; the whole area throbs and sometimes swells with an unbearable tickling and stinging which result in compulsive genital rubbing and repeated orgastic spasms. Male circumcision likewise produces a tingling around the corona and lays the sensitive glans bare to chance friction, which results in numerous erections and impulsive fondling or rubbing.

Van de Velde writes that "girls who habitually practice self-relief (masturbation) acquire enlargement of the labia and clitoris, but not increased all-round development." The small breasts and large vulva of the Oriental girl present quite a contrast, but the factors involved in this genital prominence are primarily genetic and possibly also climatic. While the body may be very slight and slender, and the breasts and buttocks relatively flat and fleshless, the outer lips of the vulva arc plump and protuberant and the tip of the clitoris exposed.

Felix Bryk found that all East African girls masturbate, persistently plucking *nymphae* and clitoris till the orgasm is induced. He writes:

> Because it is considered unclean by them to touch the vulva with the hand, many Hamito-Negro girls masturbate with the skinned, unripe fruits of the banana. If they are surprised by the boys while at this pastime, they are copulated without

287

further ado. But onanistic manipulations are indispensable in the very formation of the Hottentot apron. Let it not be thought that the Hottentot apron is the exception, produced only by women erotically free and loose. Just as declitorization is a mark of every married woman, there is hardly a female to be found among the Swahili without a Hottentot apron since her youth. Men and women assured me: women without a Hottentot apron are simply boycotted by men; marriage itself would be annulled if the woman decided to retain her natural clitoris and refused to elongate her *labia minora*.

Even before the girl reaches the age of puberty, her mother says to her: "Go, make yourself a cock's crest." Instructed by older friends, the child busily plucks both *labia minora*. With regular treatment, the "cock's crest" is ready inside of a week. It is considered ready when it has reached the length prescribed as standard [at least two inches, but preferably three]. For this the girl takes a leaf, places it along her little finger, and tears off the part reaching above it. The measure is now ready. She then places the leaf against the lengthened lips to see whether the required length has been attained. If not, the plucking is continued. Girls know another method for producing the Hottentot apron. They bind together the plucked labia with a string and have a small stone hang down as a sinker to stretch them properly. "Then the lips become like the crop of a turkey," added a woman who was unaffectedly telling me about the operation in the presence of other women.

The origin of the Hottentot apron is to be found in masturbation. It was noticed that the little labia became elongated [by repeated pulling and jerking]; what had been a necessity became a virtue. A man was pleased with such a woman, especially since continual masturbation had intensified her sex instinct and her sensuousness. As a matter of fact, masturbation is very widespread among the Swahili women. Married women often find pleasure in it, repeatedly plucking the india-rubber bands of their elongated labia until the orgasm finally sets in. In fact, the woman with her Hottentot apron makes great demands of her husband's capabilities; she is hardly ever satisfied.

We read in the Babylonian Talmud:

> Said Rabbi Nahman: "Tamar exercised friction with her finger; for Rabbi Isaac said, 'All women of the House of Rabbi who exercise friction are designated *Tamar.*' And why are they designated *Tamar*? Because Tamar exercised friction with her finger."

The sight of a little Jewish girl rubbing her clitoris under her clothes or lifting her skirt and poking her finger (or fingers) into her vagina is quite common. Among the daughters of rabbis, "Tamar" is a general nickname, just as every Jewish boy of a rabbinical family is an "Onan" or masturbator. Eastern Jews believe that Onan and Tamar, both between twelve and thirteen years of age, practiced mutual masturbation to achieve orgasm and prevent impregnation. Western scholars have concocted a theory of *coitus interruptus* or "withdrawal." But when the ancient Cabalist tells us that "he [Onan] spilled [his semen] on the ground," he means exactly that; and when the modern Talmudist tells us that "Tamar exercised friction with her finger," he means masturbation and nothing else. In Hebrew, *ma'sēh 'Ōnān* (the act of Onan) is a polite term for manual masturbation; and to call one an "Onan" is to call him a masturbator. Serious scholarship becomes the silliest when it ignores these facts; moreover, our Biblical scribe would have laughed at the preposterous assumption that a thirteen-year-old Israeli boy practiced *coitus interruptus.*(19)

ת
----

(19) *Nonetheless, sympathies should be extended to all those sexologists who may now have to stop rebuking their predecessors for using the term "onanism" as a synonym for masturbation.*

289

To discourage vaginal masturbation in their prepubescent girls, middle- and upper-class Sephardic Jews are wont to swathe them in skin-tight Occidental panties. Little Arab girls are always thrusting their fingers in their vaginas; and lest little Jewish girls should follow their example, the parents try to keep their daughters "safe" in close-fitting underpants. Masturbation still occurs, but it is vulvar or clitoral rather than vaginal—unless the little girl, sitting or standing alone, pulls down her panties and parts her legs to introduce one or two fingers all the way in between them. To facilitate the experiment, she sometimes wets her fingers with saliva. The hymen (if she has been born with one) is rarely broken but is gradually stretched out of existence as the excited child tries to probe as far in as possible and makes circular boring movements with as many fingers as will fit. Arab children, who commonly masturbate vaginally, have little difficulty achieving orgasm in vaginal copulation as compared with Jewish children who are clitorally oriented in their sexuality.(20)

The Japanese female is predominantly vaginally orientated

---

(20) We cannot, of course, regard it as conclusively demonstrated that vaginal masturbation in childhood necessarily makes for vaginal responsiveness in the mature female. But let us suppose that the fact is proved: what then?

This would indeed be a sore dilemma for the rigid moralists of the West, who deplore masturbation, but who also have a powerful interest in vaginal responsiveness since it makes for more stable marriages. Should they encourage (by some devious means, of course) our little girls to masturbate vaginally? Or should they not?

We will have to leave it to those moralists to answer the questions; but it is likely that little girls vaginally masturbating would present so horrendously unsettling a picture to the "mind's eye" that the stability of home and family would be left to sink or swim in preference to salvaging it by such a means.

in her capacity for orgastic response. We find a marked development in size and sensitivity of the *labia minora* rather than of the clitoris. These hypertrophied *nymphae* are often serrated or saw-toothed in shape, and projecting beyond the *labia majora* they constantly irritate the clitoris and increase both vulvar and vaginal esthesia. A strong *sphincter cunni* encircles the wide orifice which, despite its width, is capable of intense voluntary contraction; and a general smoothness (i.e., a lack of delicate folds or corrugation of tissue) characterizes the vaginal walls which, however, are reinforced by powerful *constrictor vaginae* muscles. About a minute or two of vigorous deep internal friction is all that is needed to kick off the venereal climax, although in some highly spiced women a sustained orgasm starts the very moment a man's penis penetrates her vagina. The firm, tight little vulva of a young girl is called a *hamaguri* or "clam"; while the well-used organ of a woman is dubbed *akagai* or "shellfish," alluding to its fullness and width.

Vaginal masturbation with fingers or an artificial phallus is extremely widespread among Japanese girls. It often happens that extravagant onanism produces a certain looseness or lack of elasticity in the vagina of a young female, especially if she does not bother to develop her pubic muscles by voluntary constriction and compression during each masturbation. Many females force a very thick rubber phallus or all four fingers into their canals, submitting themselves to a prolonged and violent stimulation, and sometimes they become slack and wide like a woman after childbirth; but a maximum development of the enclosing muscles means that she can voluntarily compress and constrict upon and literally milk the virile member, thus controlling and increasing mutual sensations far better than a girl could possibly do without assiduous internal exercise.

Shaykh 'Omar en-Nefzawi observes that "there are women and young girls who love coition only on the edges of their cunnus; and when a man tries to introduce his member all the way in, they take it out with their hand and place the glans penis between the lips of their vulva." The standard and traditional Islamic lawbook, *El-Hhidāyeh* (The Guidance), states that "if a man commits any amorous act with a strange woman which does not involve complete penetration of the penis into the vagina, but only the insertion of the glans between the labia such as in *tekhfīdz* [planing, polishing: the practice of pressing down upon and applying friction to the lips of the cunnus with the head of the penis] or the simple procedure of rubbing the male member externally between the thighs of a female until the two orgasms occur, he is to be corrected by *ta'zīr* or reproof." This injunction generally refers to forcible contact with a strange woman or a little girl; in legal Latin, *penem fricatum inter femorum* (rubbing the penis between the thighs). Interfemoral rape is superficial and in many cases pleasurable, hence there is no punishment save verbal reproof. Moreover, the Muslims add: *En-na'jeh dhebīhh mā khāyif es-selkh* (The slaughtered sheep [the deflowered female] has no fear of being skinned [is not afraid of interfemoral rape]).

Tekhfīdz, as a prevalent and extremely popular form of mutual onanism, is commonly called *mik'hhāl fī mekāhhil* (the stick in the box, the pencil in the kohl pot; so named because the glans penis stirs between the labia like the tip of an eyelid stick in a mascara box) and, in Turkish, *badana* (whitewashing; so named because the glans penis brushes up and down the labia and "whitewashes" them with prostatic and seminal fluids). Dr. Jacobus writes:

> *Badana* is done by rubbing the big lips of the vulva with the head of the penis, the shaft of which the woman holds in her hands or which the man guides manually himself, until the spermatic ejaculation is produced. Men often rape little girls in this manner, owing to the great disproportion between the adult penis and the infantile vagina, and thus incur no punishment if caught in the act; for rather than harming

292

these girls they please them immensely with the vigorous rubbing applied to their little vulvas by the big glans penis.

Dr. Stern writes that "in Alexandria the *badana* is engaged in with small Negresses who have not yet attained the age of puberty but who, in spite of their delicate age, go along to coffee parties in order to acquire knowledge." In noting the mechanism of this extracoital contact between Arab men and Negro girls, Stern adds: "The maiden takes the penis in her hands and rubs its tip against her sexual organ." Since such girls are usually given to habitual masturbation, the result rather than the cause of their peculiar trade, the following Egyptian phrase arose: *Sehhq kelbet el-mes'hhūq* (Skinning the skinned bitch). This is commonly applied to the process of suffering a second time what one has suffered once already. "To skin [rub vigorously] a skinned bitch" is to frictionize with the glans penis the cunnus and clitoris of a female who has just finished masturbating herself in the same manner by fingers or hand. Conversely, little girls seized and raped in this fashion (by having energetic friction repeatedly applied to their vulvas) frequently become addicted to the habit which before the attack they knew virtually nothing about.

The Babylonian Talmud notes that *tekhfidz* (pressing) "may be compared to a man who puts his finger to his mouth; it is impossible for him not to press down the flesh." Moreover:

> When Rabbah ben Bar Hana came from Palestine to Babylon, he stated in the name of Rabbi Johanan: "Consummation is constituted by the insertion of the corona." Rabbi Shesheth raised an objection: "*Carnally* [re Lev. 19:20] implies when intercourse is accompanied by friction [Heb. *merōk*, rubbing of the penial shaft, as in masturbation]. Does this not refer to friction of the member [complete penetration or rubbing of the penial shaft by the walls of the vagina]?" Said Bar Hana: "No; friction of the corona."

293

Unlike the Arabs, who regard legal consummation as rupture of the hymen or complete penetration of the penis into the vagina, the Sephardic Jews accept the mere insertion and friction of the glans between the labia or in the vulvar vestibule. This is a common "contraceptive measure" adopted by newlyweds, and one which brings sexual satisfaction to both partners because mutual stimulation is thereby centered in the most sensitive areas of the genitalia. During heavy petting sessions, Muslim and Jewish boys and girls are wont to enjoy *tekhfidz*, especially if the preservation of virginity is to be desired until marriage. It is estimated that unmarried females achieve orgasm through interfemoral copulation at least once a week, many as often as two or three times depending upon individual opportunity. Among the Jews of North Africa, betrothal by copulation (wherein a little child is served *à la droit du seigneur* by her new father) is customarily carried out by *coitus intrafemoris* or external rubbing. Conversely, while insertion of the corona does not constitute legal rape among the Muslims, a mere pressing of the vulvar lips by the tip of the glans is punishable under rabbinical law.

Just as many fathers throughout the East have for centuries set their sons up in sodomy, especially in Iran where they have a saying *Khākh-i-pāi kāhū* (There's lettuce in the dirt at your feet), so also many pimping mothers set their daughters up as fricatrices and, with the money they earn, marry them off to well-to-do boys; whence the stock witticism:

> *Daughter:* "Mother, there's a man at the door who wants to have intercourse with you!"
> *Mother:* "Tell him to wait; I won't be long!"
> *Daughter:* "But Mother, he's rubbing up his penis in his right hand and with his left hand offers me twenty pieces of silver! I think he wants to start on me first!"
> *Mother:* "Nonsense; you're too young. Anyhow, you'll only freeze his penis and make it flag!"

294

>*Daughter* (lifting her skirt, holding the man's penis in her hand, and rubbing it against her little cunnus): "I may be young, but I'll heat his penis and get him warmed up for you!"

Hence the proverbial expressions exchanged by two rival sisters over the same boy:

>*Eldest girl* (raising her dress to reveal a gaping vulva): "You're too young; you'll leave him cold!"
>
>*Youngest girl* (raising her dress and rubbing a tight little vulva): "I'm young; I'll make him hot!"
>
>*Boy:* "I'll prime the cannon on the little one first, then I'll open fire in the big one!"

A popular parallel to the aforementioned Persian proverb concerning the sexual usefulness of sons for monetary gain is found in the following Japanese saying: "The debt hole is filled with the daughter's hole!" From about the age of ten, North African Muslim and Jewish girls traditionally aid and increase the family income by way of lucrative promiscuity; and even little children are often sold into prostitution by their luxury-loving parents.

Many prepubescent Muslim, Jewish, and Negro girls between the ages of seven and eleven are amateur and professional *sehhīqāt* (cunnus rubbers). In Arabia, for example, little brown and black females congregate outside the bathhouses to offer their erotic favors. It is a favorite male trick to smuggle small Negro girls dressed as boys into the *hhemmām*, where they are entertained and titillated as at private parties and hashish orgies. Arabian women, occupying the public bath in the morning after the menfolk have left, have testified that they found the unemptied and unrefilled pool in the hot room literally filled with seminal fluid. Sperm, spattered all over the tile floor, told of a bacchanalia of mutual masturbation, fellation, analism, and interfemoral copulation. There are numerous authenticated cases on record of women and girls, both married and unmarried, becoming accidentally impregnated while bathing in pools wherein men and boys had spilled their sperm a short time before. In fact, Muslim and Jewish law allows for this; and any female, virgin or nonvirgin, who can prove that she was impregnated in a public bathing pool adulterated with male ejaculate is immediately exempted from charges of fornication or adultery.

7. ORAL INTERCOURSE

Women who like to lick the penis are lustful.

JAPANESE PROVERB

Historians charge the Phoenician and Egyptian women and girls of the ancient world with commercializing fellatio and cunnilingus, or with making of the female mouth a popular vehicle of voluptuousness. They were the inventors of lipstick, the original significance of which would surprise many modern women. For the fellatrices of Egypt and Phoenicia, being the first to employ red lip paint or rouge, did so merely to make the mouth appear like the vulva and thereby indicate their profession. Consequently, any female who painted or rouged her upper lips so that they resembled her lower labia was at once recognized as one who specializes in oral stimulation of the penis. Records also reveal that this bright red color was exactly the same as that of the *nymphae* and the vulvar vestibule.

Cleopatra of Egypt set the nonprofessional fashion for fellatio and, next to Sappho, was perhaps the most famous freelove fellatrice of the ancient Eastern world. Cleopatra, who

297

wore lip paint like all fashionable and promiscuous ladies, is said to have sucked a thousand men. The Greeks called her *Meriochane* (Gaper), meaning "she who gapes wide for ten thousand men; the wide-mouthed one; the ten-thousand-mouthed woman." Cleopatra, who allegedly fellated a hundred Roman noblemen in one night, was also known as *Cheilon* (Thick-Lipped).

The ancient Egyptians, like the modern Muslims, were notorious for their sexual abuse of strangers and especially Jews. Lucian, in his *Pseudologistae*, notes the fellatory rape of the Syrian Timarchus by an Egyptian seaman:

> In Syria you are known as "rose-laurel" [cunnus licker], but in Palestine as "the hedge"—on account of the prickles of your beard, I suppose. In Egypt, on the other hand, they called you "sore throat"—and this is a well-known business. It must have been a close thing with you not to be choked, that time you came across the sailor of a three-master, who fell upon you and stopped up your mouth for you!

To ask facetiously a home-coming traveler whether or not he had experienced an attack of "sore throat" while in Egypt was the same as asking him whether or not he had become the victim of an Egyptian sexual custom and been orally ravished by a big Egyptian penis.

Arab eroticists claim that the genital kiss forms an integral part of copulation; hence the common saying, "A wet kiss is better than a hasty coitus!", or:

> One warm wet kiss, by definition,
> Is worth far more than a fast coition!

The Arabs say: *"Bus el-miftāhh ila kus!"* (Kiss is the key to coynte). They also have a little sex riddle: "How is a woman's coynte like a cooking pot?" Answer: "You have to heat it before you put the meat in!" The Iranis own a saying: *Kih wājib bōsīden* (What best deserves kissing)? *Kus-i-nao peshm* (A crack with a new bush)! In verse form:

> What claims the kiss that wins renown?
> A tender young coynte with silky down!

By way of contrast, however, a common Muslim curse is: "You son of a dog! do you lick your wife between her legs, where her beard grows?" Other oft-heard execrations include "O cunnus licker!" and "O sucker of your wife's oversized clitoris!"

Lip-and-tongue stimulation of the genitals is common and customary among all classes and races in Asia and Africa. It is traditional both heterosexually and homosexually. Mutual fellatio and cunnilingus is deemed even more intimate and enrapturing than genital union, perhaps because oral excitation yields the most acute and intense pleasure. The sensations produced by the caressing mouth of one's beloved seem more ardent and enravishing than those produced by the penis or vagina. The early Arabs and Jews, for example, learned oral eroticism in the most natural manner: by observing nature. Few there be who have not seen dogs, cats, hyenas, and other domesticated or wild animals licking each other's genitals. Thus, from natural observation, investigation, and experimentation, emerge the arts of love.

Muslim and Negro women have for centuries been purported to be passionate and adept at erotic refinements. In many North and East African cities there are places of prostitution wherein *qerdz* (mouthing, sucking) is principally practiced by Arab, Indian, and Negro females, many of them young girls who are just learning the trade of love. Jewish women are also quite famous after this fashion (*metzītzāh*, sucking) both at home and abroad. They are commonly called *serāfōth* or "penis swallowers," the plural of *serāfāh* (hot-mouth, she-sucker), from the root *sāref* meaning "to suck in, to swallow down, to burn with passionate thirst."

It was found by Dr. Jacobus that a prime reason for Oriental females becoming fellatrices is their "early addiction to oral activities." Traumatic childhood experiences are also influential, for fellatory rape perpetrated by older boys upon small girls is very common among the Arabs. Such a rape may have a lasting effect on the young girl's libido, yielding intensification of oral eroticism. But even when force is not involved, an early and repeated introduction to active fellatio is unquestionably instrumental in the exaggerated development of buccal sexuality. Moreover, the unlimited explorations and experimentations of Eastern children insure that this development will take place in countless numbers of females. For a little sister to take her little brother's penis into her mouth is but one phase in a vast and continuing variety of prepubertal sex play fashioned and fostered by environmental factors.

According to Jacobus' investigations, four out of five North African Muslim and Jewish women recalled having been coaxed or forced into fellatio by their older brothers and/or other boys, including cousins and other male relatives. Most of the girls were between the ages of three and five at the time of their first oral experience. The oldest was six; none could remember below the age of three. The average age range of the boys involved was between six and twelve, although a few were between thirteen and fifteen. Only a third of the women admitted or remembered having performed the act without previous provocation on the boy's part. They said that during genital exhibition and handling, the impulse suddenly struck them to put the boy's penis into their mouth. However, that was apparently the limit of their activity, for the boy himself moved it around therein to produce the desired titillation, or there was little or no movement at all. The pleasure was then more psychic than physical.

300

Mutual fellatio is a prevalent form of innocent play between little Eastern boys of from three to five years old. It is also a spontaneous sex phenomenon, arising from genital games and the powerful lactation complex. Among the Jews, for example, small children will crawl under the covers at night and each contentedly suck the other's penis until they fall asleep. Often they bicker over who will "milk" whom, one wishing to hold the other's "teat" in his mouth, until they come to lie contraposed on their sides for simultaneous suckling. Girls are frequently involved in these genital games, holding and sucking their little brothers' penises to their heart's content, but cunnilingus rarely if ever occurs unless the female child initiates it. In other words, she has no "teat" for the male tots to "milk"; so she is automatically excluded as a passive partner in their bedtime play.(1)

---

(1) *While information concerning the sexual behavior of children in the United States is inadequate and piecemeal, it seems safe to say that childish cunnilingus is rare in this country also. Probably the fellatio of boys by girls is quite rare, too, running a poor second to such experiments between pre-adolescent males.*

A great many boys undoubtedly at one time or another, on a dare or as an outgrowth of mutual inspection of genitals, have the experience of taking another boy's penis into the mouth. To call this fellatio is probably to stretch things a bit. The act is likely to be very hastily performed, perhaps with a slight amount of sucking, and much less often with any tongue stimulation or up and down movement of the mouth on the penis.

Behavior of this kind probably most commonly occurs at a much later age than is the case in the East. The participating boys are more likely to be ten to twelve than three to five. Of course, older boys sometimes induce small children to perform an approximation of fellatio; but that is a different matter from the behavior of small contemporaries.

301

In doorways, hallways, alleyways, bathrooms, and other con-
venient or secluded places such as empty chambers and clumps
of trees, little orthodox or middle- and upper-class Jewish girls
of North Africa lift their dresses, pull their panties down to
their knees, and allow boys to finger and tongue their little
vulvas. Then, when the boy pulls his erect penis out of his
pants, the girl will clasp it in her hands and place it in her
mouth, holding it there and making "chewing" motions. Sometimes the child does not pull down her underpants, recalling
her parents' warnings and afraid lest the boy should poke his
fingers or indeed his penis into her vagina, for as long as her
panties are drawn up tight around her waist complete penetration is impossible; so the boy rubs or licks her cunnus outside
her underclothing. When she has been sufficiently tickled, she
then touches his penis.

In Arabia, Negro boys will perform repeated cunnilingus on
little Arab girls, then induce them to "eat" their "banana"
(perform fellatio). The Negro boy will sexually excite the Arab
girl by saying: "If I lick your peach, will you suck my banana?"
or "I have a banana for you to chew if you let me nibble your
fig." He will thrust his hand up her skirt and touch her smooth
little vulva, pressing and rubbing it with his fingers to excite
her even more. She will reach into the open fly of his pants and
catch hold of his stiff little penis, yanking it to and fro. He will
then drop to his knees, grip her little bottom as she separates
her legs, and bury his face between her thighs. Cunnilingus is
enacted by ravenously and repeatedly licking up and down or
forcing the tongue in and out of the labia, sometimes even
kissing and sucking the clitoris if it protrudes. When she begins to squirm and tries to push him away, it is his signal that
she has had enough and is now anxious to lick and suckle his
own organ. Because dogs and cats commonly lick each other's
genitals, Arabian children call mutual fellatio and cunnilingus
el-kulaybī (puppy play) or *el-qutaytī* (pussy play). The little

302

ones learn much from their animal pets, including coitus, which the youngsters perform in kneeling or squatting positions.

It is said full many a time that cunnilingus, fellatio, and other so-called "homosexual" pleasures are epidemic at Mecca and Medina, where all the men are bisexual and three out of five women active lesbians. Once introduced to the practice by older playmates, be they male or female, little Arab girls become so passionate for cunnilingus that they often induce dogs and other domestic animals to lick them between the legs.(2)

We have previously observed how adultery and divorce are as rampant and rife in "orthodox" Sa'udi Arabia as they are elsewhere in the general unorthodox East. Males and females mate and separate at least a half dozen times, many a dozen, and some even more. In the great cities and towns of the Arabian peninsula, wives and daughters practice a predatory form of sexual hospitality that dates back to pre-Islamic times. In order to live in luxury and have some fun, Arabian females are adept at extracoital activities. When their husbands are away at work, Muslim wives prostitute themselves to pilgrims, travelers, neighbors, and anyone else who attracts their fancy. Most of them will engage in any manner of erotic contact except vaginal intercourse, wishing to avoid possible pregnancy. But since vaginal intercourse is such a cheap and easy-to-come-by commodity, few male partners object to by-passing it for what seem more fascinating and provocative pleasures. Fella-

---

(2) *This particular practice has been known in the West for centuries and is far from rare today. If accurate data could be obtained, the results would surely be shocking to most persons, for both the masturbation of dogs and the enticing of those animals (and cats) to perform cunnilingus, is surely a very common experience—much more common, we think, than Kinsey's data on female practices indicate.*

303

tio and cunnilingus hold the highest charm; then comes mutual masturbation, next anal copulation, and finally *coitus intra femora. Coitus interruptus* is common in marital relations, but never trusted in adulterous liaisons. However, those fashionable females who equip themselves with diaphragms, condoms, and other contraceptive devices usually indulge in vaginal intercourse to their heart's content.

Colonel Dickson found that the women of Kuwait, while their husbands are off on business, will fit their personal financial ends together by practicing "unnatural forms of intercourse" or extracoital activities with both strange and familiar men. Sucking of the penis is the usual stock-in-trade, followed by friction of the phallus between the thighs and penile rubbing of the buttocks or penetration of the anus. Arab, Irani, African, Indian and other traders, travelers, pilgrims, seamen, etc., arriving in the port cities of Arabia, will find thousands of promiscuous women and girls anxiously waiting to provide them with the manifold pleasures of "love." Muslim, Jewish, Negro, and Indian fornicatresses and adulteresses teem in Jiddah and other coastal towns when the pilgrim ships and caravans arrive and depart. They invade the inns and motels, swarming all over the urban and suburban areas, which are ordinarily well-stocked with black concubines and servant girls —Sudani, Somali, Ethiopian, and Swahili whores—who are much prized "because their skins are always cool even in the hottest weather."

Men of taste look for the *elmā* or "brown-lipped beauty," for *lumā* (dark reddish-brown of the lips and labia) is admired by the Arabs. The dusky belles of Araby become passionately wild in fellatio, whence their renown. They love to handle a man's genitals, massaging and manipulating them with delirious delight, then pressing them feverishly to their flushed and burning cheeks. They ravenously suck the glans penis, forcing the entire organ in and out of their mouths as far as possible,

304

kissing and squeezing and agitating and biting and licking it in a veritable frenzy of lust, until it is red all over with *hhamreh* or lipstick. Kissing, licking, and sucking of the male member is followed by caressing, rubbing, and shaking. The skillful female executes an elaborate masturbation. She smears nondrying vegetable oil or fat, or vaseline or some other lotion, over her hands and, firmly clasping the man's penis, slips and slides rapidly up and down. Saliva is rarely used because it evaporates too quickly. The woman squeezes, wrenches, and rotatively rubs the glans penis in her fist until the man experiences an ejaculation. She will fellate and masturbate him repeatedly and raveningly until he loses his erection.

Among the women and girls of Mecca and El-Medina are great numbers of free-lance fellatrices and fricatrices. All middle- and upper-class Arabian males fill their households with dark-skinned mistresses or concubines, nursemaids, servant girls, and other feminine domestic help whom they are wont to employ in the bedroom for fellatio, anal intercourse, and other erotic specialties which appeal to their amatory tastes. Arabian females likewise delight in these lustful servant girls, who are avidly addicted to sapphic sports and who are connoisseurs of cunnilingus. The taste for lesbian practices is widespread throughout Arabia, and is early acquired. It begins in infancy, when the female baby's genitals are kissed and orally caressed by her nurse or some other family servant. Negresses are notorious for masturbating and practicing cunnilingus upon infant as well as older Arab girls. They will entice a little child, finger her vulva affectionately, kiss it, then touch their tongue to her clitoris and lick the smooth delicate labia until she squirms and squeezes her legs together in reaction to the acute titillation. These early experiences, repeated again and again, have a lasting effect on the sensuality of the Muslim female. Countless girls become bisexual and/or fixed upon oral gratifications in this way, having the clitoris tickled to orgasm by

305

the tongue of another girl, and they do not exaggerate when they say that to them cunnilingus is ten times more enrapturing, thrilling, and soul-stirring than vaginal coition.(3)

The *funduq* (inn) of Morocco is like our proverbial motel or hotel, a place of promiscuous pleasure. In Marrakesh, for example, the word *kāshēr* (kosher, orthodox) is written on the hostelries of whoredom in the Jewish quarter, meaning that the females therein will serve only circumcised Jews. Nevertheless, what goes on inside such a *funduq* is not exactly "kosher" according to rabbinical standards of sexual conduct. Prepubescent girls ranging in age from three to nine years are available to fellate and masturbate the "orthodox" male, while female adolescents and women eagerly await anal and vaginal intercourse. Sexual stimulation is generally free of charge in keeping with ancient codes of erotic hospitality, although a decent and deserving man is traditionally expected or even obliged to give the girl baksheesh, and no one is allowed to enter unless he desires refreshments and entertainment for which there is a small fee. One of the specialties of the house is the conventional *reqs es-surreh* or "belly dance," which a lithe and lovely Jewess performs for one's private amusement or as a means of finding a part-time lover amid a circle of admirers. The playful *sehhīqeh* will sometimes approach a likely lover who is seated and straddle herself in his lap, making coital movements

—————————————

(3) *It would not be difficult to speculate at volume length about why the Easterner is so often bisexual in his inclinations and activities, while the Westerner has so often tended to become exclusively heterosexual or exclusively homosexual.*

The either/or values system traditional to the Christian West undoubtedly has much to do with such results. And it is surely no accident that just now, when an ethical relativism is particularly noticeable in the United States, we are producing bisexuals to an extent far beyond anything hitherto experienced in this country.

back and forth until she feels his erection and he buys her off. Most of these young and accomplished Jewesses are sexually deviated, preferring masturbation and cunnilingus to vaginal copulation, but if they find an attractive man who fervidly and unselfishly satisfies their luxurious senses they will not want to let him go. They will love him and return his affection with equal fervor, passionately handling and mouthing his penis, which is almost an amorous obsession with them.

Jacobus was completely convinced that the average Muslim male lives only to have his penis suckled by a beautiful female or a handsome male. Indeed, fellatio is to the Muslim the most exquisite voluptuous experience in all the world, ranking far above anal or vaginal coition. To watch Arabs being fellated will verify this belief. The woman need only run her tongue up and down the sensitive underside of the glans penis, and the man's erection is dynamic and ecstatic. Jacobus observed in North Africa:

> What the woman calls "swallowing it" consists in continuing the operation until all the sperm has been ejaculated into her mouth, then she lets go of the penis and spits the semen out.
>
> If, when she observes the voluptuous contractions of the urethral canal, the woman withdraws her mouth at the precise moment when the sperm begins to spout out, and then merely masturbates the penis, ejaculation takes place but the physiological pleasure is diminished to a very great degree. This is so true that most men are excessively angry when a woman breaks her word and withdraws her mouth at the moment when ejaculation begins, and often abuse her violently. The man seizes hold of the woman's head with both his hands and forces her to swallow every last drop of his ejaculation.(4)

'I'

---

(4) Among American homosexuals, and probably among homosexuals everywhere, the same reaction is to be observed. It is of con-

This mouth coition affords a keener pleasure than vaginal coition, thus explaining its universal popularity, but the consequent nervous exhaustion is greater. If the woman continues to caress the glans with her lips and tongue during orgasm, the sensation is so keen and shooting as to be near to pain. The man, panting passionate cries of "*Ah! ah! Allah! Allah!*," seizes hold of the woman's head with both his hands in order to stop the movement of her mouth and tongue until the orgasm is over.

Some Arab women will, as it were, "swallow" the entire penis of their lovers; that is to say, especially at the approach of the venereal climax, they will press the penis as far as possible into their mouths, plunging full length up and down so as to simulate vaginal coition. These women invariably swallow the semen. Others, however, merely apply their lips and tongue to the glans, kissing and licking it, tickling the orifice, and sucking the corona. While they move the head of the virile member around in their mouths, they also squeeze and stroke the shaft of the penis with their hands—a combined fellatio and masturbation. Most Arabs whom I questioned on the subject preferred having the shaft of their penis manipulated by hand at the same time they enjoyed a sucking of the glans. However, not one of them wished their partner to

siderable importance to the fellated that the fellator swallow his semen; and this requirement is all the more powerful when the emotional bond between the participants is intense. The spitting out of the semen implies a rejection of the fellated by the fellator; and such a rejection is also implied when the fellator gags on the ejaculate, and especially if the fellator vomits. Scientific findings confirm that the chances of gagging diminish as the degree of erotic arousal increases, with the fully aroused fellator (or fellatrice) able to perform violent up and down movements upon the full length of a large penis, something that would surely provoke gagging under any other circumstance than intense sexual excitement.

remove her mouth at the critical moment and produce the emission manually; for each of them expressed an ineffable desire that the woman receive their sperm into her mouth and, as proof of affection and love, drink every last drop of it. Indeed, many Arab females have told me that they delight in drinking the semen of the males they love, not only as a token of their devotion, but because the absorption of seminal fluid is deemed most beneficial in both a physical and supernatural sense.(5)

When a girl receives a boy's semen into her mouth, it is a sign of special love. She says to him: "I love you so much, I will swallow it all!" His glans is so unbearably supersensitive at the moment of orgasm that he holds her head or presses her cheeks in his hands and cries: "Oh, stop; I'm coming!" She makes a final movement and he ejaculates, then he sighs in severe nervous exhaustion, having been drained of all his desire. Next to anal intercourse, mouth coition is perhaps the most prevalent and popular contraceptive practice in the East. It is safe and, in view of Muslim cleanliness, quite sanitary. It is certainly esteemed above vaginal intercourse, especially

---

(5) Western prostitutes have a different thought about this: their professional lore includes a belief that drinking the semen is likely to cause their teeth to rot or fall out. (Just one more strange fruit of an antisexual society!) Dentists who work with prostitutes often encounter this curious notion, and many harlots bitterly blame all of their dental difficulties on beastly males who demand fellatio in spite of what it surely does to a girl.

Worthy of note, too, is the belief frequently found among the lower economic classes in the United States that ingesting the semen may result in pregnancy. Many uneducated women have indicated that they would engage in fellatio with their husbands as a contraceptive device if it were not for the fact that some friend had become pregnant in that way. Physicians are by no means always able to convince them that this is not possible.

309

when the woman's organ is too large or loose, and man may assume either an active or passive role depending upon his mood. Moreover, fellatio allows greater variety and subtler nuances of pleasure than vaginal or anal activity, which are more or less restricted in their execution and effect. In a word, as the Turks say, "Penis sucking is better than fucking!" (6)

While in Istanbul, Bernhard Stern noted:

> The Turkish woman rarely engages in onanism with a man. In order to please her husband she sometimes acts as an object for pederasty, but she draws the line at rubbing his penis with her hand or sucking it in her mouth. Only the prostitutes in Algiers, Muslim women who must be numbered among the most accomplished courtesans of the whole world, indulge in such practices.

Turkish women have long been renowned for their addiction to anal intercourse, perhaps in answer to the extravagant needs of their bisexual menfolk, who bear a predilection for pederasty. The Turkish females with whom Stern came into erotic contact doubtless refused to practice masturbation and fellatio for purely esthetic reasons, wishing to save these extremely intimate acts for those they love. When in bed with her lover, the Turkish woman is remarkable for the vigor and violence of her manipulating and sucking, delighting to drink the semen and drain the cup of bliss. A line from an old folk song reads:

'I'
_____

(6) *The idea that fellatio allows of a greater variety of execution than coitus is an unusual one, and in particular it is surprising to find it attributed to the East where hundreds of coital variations have been described by erotologists. It is probably true, on the other hand, that with teeth, tongue, and lips brought artfully into play, more distinct sensations may be provided.*

310

"Hey," says the boy to the girl, "you're biting the head off my penis!" Needless to say, Turkish females love cunnilingus.

In Iran, *perdeh-zerdeh* (huggermugger mouthful) alludes to "the secret indulgence in oral intercourse with strange males." This hole-and-corner work (*zerd*, swallowing) is done by a great many females, both married and unmarried, for pleasurable and contraceptive purposes.

Fellatio has for centuries been the specialty of a particular breed of men and boys who frequent the bathhouses, the cafés, and private parties. The professional fellator is commonly called a *jinq* or *ginq* (jerk), a Turkish word contracted from the Arabic *jennāq* (jerker) and literally meaning "one who jerks off." These *jinqīn*—mostly Jews, Arabs, Negroes, and Turks—are usually boys and young men who are by nature transvestites, effeminate male homosexuals who masquerade as females. The *jinq*, as his name implies, is by habit a masturbator. In fact, his addiction to solitary and mutual manipulation amounts to a kind of autoerotic frenzy. In this respect he is not so much anoerotic as he is the victim of compulsive masturbation; for although these effeminates abandon themselves to anal intercourse, their supreme pleasure lies in their being simultaneously masturbated by their active partner. The famous motto of the *jinq* is: "Mutual jerking is sweeter than ferking!" *Elish-tekish* (give and take) is what Irani boys are wont to call mutual masturbation. Its technique is clearly indicated in the terms *jenq* (jerking), *jelq* (flipping), *jerq* (jiggling), and *musht-zenī* (fist beating) or "to hold the phallus in the fist and pound it up and down." The pederastic poet Abu Nowas writes of the *jinqīn*:

> Are not this child's eyes all fire?
>   O desire,
> Feel the first flush of the eggs
>   Between his legs!

311

> Dearest, seize what you can seize,
>> If you please;
> Fill your boyish fist with me
>> And then see
> Will it go a little way,
>> Just in play? *

And:

> I told three youths, for joyance sake,
> To shake it with their hands, you see,
> And have each other, give and take,
> A-rubbing this, my rod, for me.

Burton translates "And have each other, turn by turn, shampooing this my tool you see!"

The "vulgar" name for the professional practice of the "jerk" is *qerdz or qirādzeh* (mouthing, chewing, nibbling), which means fellatio as well as cunnilingus. Stern notes that "in Algiers there are brothels where only oral coitus is practiced, mostly by Arabs." This is also true of the other seaport cities from Morocco to Egypt and down the East African Coast. In Morocco, for example, the *Maricónes* or "Fairies" reign supreme. The *Maricón* is a male prostitute of Spanish and Moorish extraction. He is a Sephardic Jew, and although he is unorthodox he is nonetheless circumcised in the modern tradition: for "hygienic motives." These Jewish *Maricónes*, many of whom are transvestites, have their own houses and districts like their sisters the *sehhīqāt*. They are passionate masturbators, fellators, and passive analists. Some of them are fastidious in the extreme, refusing to serve any male who is uncircumcised, for they seem to possess a peculiar fascination toward handling and mouthing the circumcised penis. Hence

* Mardrus & Mathers, *op. cit.*

312

kāshēr often appears over their door, and both Muslim and Jew enter therein.

The *qerrādz* (penis swallower) is ofttimes regarded with humorous scorn, and *yā qerrādz* (O prickle eater) or *yā qerrādzeh* (O clitoris nibbler) are common curses hurled at "those who browse upon the female bush" and "those who gnaw away at the glans penis." They belong in the same category with such time-honored expressions as *yā menyūk* (O beferked, fem. *menyūkeh*), *yā mezlūq* (O bejerked, fem. *mes'hhūq*, berubbed), and *yā d'wer* (O one-eye, O prick).(7)

A typically Egyptian fellatory anecdote is told of the Cairene wit and buffoon, 'Ali Goheri, who lived in the time of Tamerlane:

> One day, when Goheri was on a visit to his sister-in-law, the woman asked him to mind her baby while she went to the hammam. As soon as she had gone, the little one began to mule and pule with all his strength. So Goheri pulled out his Turkish Delight and let the child suck it until he went to sleep. When the mother returned and found her bantling in a calm slumber, she thanked Goheri for his care, but he replied: "That is nothing at all, nothing at all. If you had but

(7) In the United States, the term "prick," when applied to a person, is one of opprobrium and its connotations are roughly the equivalent of those attached to "son-of-a-bitch" and "bastard." One expects to find a term for the organ of copulation so used in our society, but it is rather surprising that the Arab, noted for his "penis pride," should denounce his adversary as a "prick."

Or it might seem surprising at first blink. Actually, the Arab reveals in innumerable ways his erotic ambivalence. This was true of the Prophet, and it has always been true of Muslims generally.

The reader will note that most of the other Arab epithets mentioned in this book are also to be found—albeit they are usually less colorful—in the various languages of the West.

313

seen my sleeping draught you would have fallen head over heels at once." *

'Ali Goheri is thus reminiscent of that sinister joker Tiberius, Emperor of Rome, whom Suetonius wrote about:

> He would take infants not yet weaned and put them to his member as to a mother's teat, their being indeed both by natural disposition and time of life more apt for this form of indulgence.

The old Arab belief that sexual connection with a Negress is a sure cure for temporary impotence may be attributed to the fact that African and Arabian Negro women are famous for fellatio, perhaps the most effective means of provoking an erection. Hindu females have always employed mouth coitus for the purpose of arousing or rearousing their bedmates; hence it is highly recommended in Indian erotic treatises.

Bryk writes that "the black woman feels no disgust at semen." She represents quite a contrast in this respect to the Muslim or Jewish female affected by Koranic and Talmudic taboos. Many an Arab or Israeli fellatrice, anticipating the seminal ejaculation, will remove her partner's penis from her mouth and then manually masturbate it and catch the emission in a piece of cloth. But Negroes and Hindus, who derive an ineffable thrill out of receiving a man's vital essence in their oral cavity, continue to suck the glans until all the processes of orgasm and ejaculation are ended. They either swallow the semen or secretly spit it out into a towel. When nearing his climax, the usual impulse is for the man to hold the woman's head to make certain that she does not withdraw and thus break the acute current of sensation; and even if she deliberately stops the suction, the man makes the motions of coition by moving her head up and down and in a rotative fashion

* Mardrus & Mathers, *op. cit.*

314

from side to side. Sometimes, if he is frantic enough, the man will lock his legs around the woman's shoulders, roll her over until he sits on top of her, and then thrust his penis forcefully in her mouth. Several Algerian girls, orally raped by older boys, told Dr. Jacobus that their attackers when offered resistance said: "By Allah, as I plunge it down your throat a thousand times, you will drink my sperm until you drown!" Biting the penis left their cheeks black and blue from a sound beating.

Promiscuous Muslim girls of East Africa will do almost anything for money. Numerous cases are on record of Arab prostitutes allowing themselves to be straddled and enfiladed by donkeys, dogs, goats, and other large animals. Many Muslim and Indian females are extremely vicious, abusing their bodies in the most extravagant manner. They masturbate and copulate as often as possible, indulging also in sapphic and tribadic diversions, and they are said to experience from ten to twenty orgasms every day. In Zanzibar, for instance, these supersexual women are wont to kidnap little girls and cause them to perform repeated cunnilingus upon them. They will then ravenously finger and tongue each child, exciting her to orgasm after orgasm. The young males of Zanzibar will seize little girls in the streets at night and, holding their heads between their legs, thrust their penises furiously into their mouths until the ejaculation is produced. The little Negresses are then made to swallow the semen. Others are brutally raped in the anus and vagina besides, for nothing pleases the frenetic lecher more than to force his erect phallus into the smallest possible receptacle.

"To lick a lotus blossom," in Sanskrit, is to enact cunnilingus; and *padmachātī* (lotus-blossom licking) is common and customary throughout India. The Hindus have several words coinciding with "licking of the lotus bud" to express the act of fellatio. Perhaps the most scientific are *mukhamēthūna* (oral churning) and *ōparishtaka* (mouth congress), while the literary appellation for fellatio is *āmbārchūsī* (mango-fruit sucking). It

315

is so named because the ripe mango fruit closely resembles the glans penis, which the *āmbārchūsā* (mango sucker) mouths, in both shape and color. The feminine counterpart of this word is *vāmbhagābhachūsī* (sucking a bamboo sprout) or *padma-kōmpalachātī* (licking a lotus stamen), signifying oral excitation of the clitoris.

In the immortal *Kāmasūtra* of Pandit Mallinaga Vatsyayana, an entire chapter is devoted to oral coitus, which he says is extremely common and customary in India and performed by all classes of males and females. Let us now explore the activities of the Indian "flute player" as they are revealed to us in the *Kāmasūtra*:

Ōparishtaka or Mouth Coition

Under the pretense of massaging, a Negro of the *ōparishtaka* or fellatory class embraces and draws towards himself the thighs of the man whom he is handling; and after this he touches his groins and his belly, slowly feeling his way around the *jāghana* or central portion of the man's body.

Then, if he finds the *lingam* of the man erect, he presses it with his hands and teases him for getting into such a state. But while he chaffs the man, the Negro continues to squeeze the *lingam* in his hands and rubs it to keep it in a condition of erection.

If after this, and after knowing his intention, the man does not tell the Negro to proceed, then the latter does it of his own accord and begins the oral congress. If, however, he is ordered by the man to do it, then he disputes with him and only consents at last with difficulty. But even during all this wrangling the Negro continues to clasp and rub the man's *lingam*.

The following eight things, one right after the other, are now done by the Negro. At the end of each of these the Negro expresses his wish to stop, but when one of them is finished the man desires him to do another—and after that

316

is done, then the one that follows it—and so on till all eight are finally accomplished:

(1) When, holding the man's *lingam* with his hand and placing it between his lips, the Negro moves his mouth up and down and round and round in a churning manner, it is called *jhūthamēthūna* or "counterfeit coition."

(2) When, covering the head of the *lingam* with his fingers collected or joined together like the bud of a lotus flower, the Negro presses the sides of it with his lips, using his teeth also, it is called *bāharadāntakarma* or "biting the sides."

(3) When, being desired to proceed, the Negro presses the head of the *lingam* with his lips closed together, and kisses it as if he were drawing it out, it is called *bāharatīpa* or "outside pressing."

(4) When, being asked to go on, he puts the *lingam* further into his mouth and presses it with his lips, then takes it out, it is called *bhītaratīpa* or "inside pressing."

(5) When, holding the *lingam* in his hand, the Negro kisses it, as if he were kissing the lower lip, it is called *chūma* or "kissing."

(6) When, after kissing it, he touches it everywhere with his tongue and then passes the flat of his tongue over the head of the *lingam*, it is called *chāta* or "licking."

(7) When, in the same way, he puts the half of it into his mouth and forcibly kisses and sucks it, this is called *āmvārchūsa* or "sucking a mango fruit."

(8) And lastly when, with the consent of the man, the Negro puts the whole *lingam* into his mouth and presses it to the very end, as if he were going to swallow it up, it is called *lingabhakōsa* or "devouring the penis."

The "swallowing-up" plunge of the man's penis all the way into the Negro's mouth is supposed by the force of the shock to produce the ejaculation, which would serve to explain why the ancient Greek and Roman satirists portray the fellator as a chronic sufferer from sore throat. Vatsyayana adds that "when the Negro holds the man's *lingam* in his hand, then squeezes and strokes it, it is called *pānīmathāna* or 'hand churning.'"

Koka Pandit, who composed the *Ratīrahasya* (Secrets of Sex), tells us that "the women of Bengal are widely known and adored for beginning with their mouths the task of man's serving the *yōnī* with his *lingam*; and they do this to enkindle their lovers' desires, owing to their excessive and ravenous craving for the joys of love." The Hindu men of Bengal hold the same philosophy as Martial: 'No one, Thais, is too old a man for irrumation [passive fellatio]!" (*Nemo est, Thai, senex ad irrumandum*).

Every Indian boy in Southeast Asia whom Dr. Jacobus had occasion to examine was a "compulsive fellator" or, in native parlance, a "sucker of the mango." The Muslims call them "banana eaters"; and at a private sex party in Malaya, Jacobus witnessed little Indian boys fellating Muslim men:

> The scene is the same all over the room. While the man lies at full length on a couch or sits reclined in a chair, the boy—kneeling or stooping—holds and kisses his penis, sucks it, and receives the emission of semen in his mouth, right up to the very last drop.
>
> The Indian, one of the oldest of civilized beings, is as lascivious as a monkey. His genitals are very small, not exceeding the size of an ape's, but his erotic appetite is excessive. The youths are called "boy-monkeys" because they masturbate incessantly, rapidly and repeatedly shaking their stiff little penises (which are no longer and not much thicker than one's little finger) like masturbating monkeys. The Muslims frequent them for sodomy, and they are much in demand as house servants. Fellatio is their specialty. This depraved taste becomes a pressing need with them. They will suck, for absolutely nothing, any man who offers his penis to them; and while doing so they will masturbate.

318

Jacobus compares the average Chinese woman with Sappho, who was aptly described by Ausonius: "She jerks, she sucks, she futters by either orifice, that she may not leave anything untried and so have lived in vain!" It is said in Southeast Asia that Chinese females love "to peel and eat the yellow bamboo stick," *huang-li* (whangee) or "a long, slender, very hard yellow bamboo rod" being a classic appellation for the erect male organ. "To peel and chew a bamboo cane" is to practice masturbation and fellation upon a man. In the *Arabian Nights* we find an erotic sentence which reads: "She began to peel the man's sugarcane and press it" (i.e., she began to shake his penis with her hand and squeeze it). "Stripping a sugarcane shoot," in Sanskritic parlance, refers to the manual manipulation of little boys and monkeys.

Taoist Chinese believe that impotence can be cured if the man will apply his lips and tongue to a highly passionate girl's vulva, perform cunnilingus until she experiences an orgasm, then "lap up and swallow down her vital secretions." Although little mention is made of it in Chinese erotica, cunnilingus was and still is very prevalent among the free Chinese. Empress Wu Hu, who ruled during the great T'ang Dynasty, created a peculiar sexual custom designed symbolically to elevate the female and humble the male. Since fellatio was such a widespread and popular heterosexual and homoerotic practice when she came to power, and since it represented (to her) masculine supremacy, lustful Wu Hu devised a means whereby "licking of the lotus stamen" could be exalted into prime extracoital importance and thus symbolize the advent of feminine domination. Consequently, all governmental officials and visiting dignitaries were obliged by royal decree to pay homage to her Imperial Highness by performing cunnilingus upon her. Old paintings depict the beautiful empress standing and holding her ornate robe open, while a high official or *kuan* is shown kneel-

319

ing humbly before her and lavishly applying his lips and tongue to her protruding clitoris.

In *Chin P'ing Mei* we encounter a delicate description of cunnilingus, which the classic people of the Celestial Kingdom cleverly called "Carrying fire over the mountains" (inflaming the vulva lips with the tongue). In Japanese, *yama-san* (mountain man) means "he who kisses and orally caresses a woman's cunnus."

> Through the light silk skirt, Hsi-men could see her crimson trousers; the sun's rays made them so transparent that he could clearly distinguish the cool flesh beneath them. The sight aroused his passion, and finding that they were alone, he carried the Lady of the Vase to a long summer couch. He pulled aside her skirt, took down the crimson trousers, and played with her the game which is called "Carrying fire over the mountains." They played for a long time. Hsi-men Ch'ing was delighted beyond all measure. He set both hands upon her legs, and the woman beneath him raised herself to welcome it.

Frequent mention is made of fellatio in Chinese erotica, which exemplifies its wide acceptance and popularity, as evidenced by these excerpts from *Chin P'ing Mei:*

> Hsi-men sat on the bed and made the Lady of the Vase place herself upon the cushions and play the flute for him. Grasping Hsi-men's treasure, she wished she could suckle it the whole night through. She tickled the jade-scepter with her lips and fondled it for hours, ever unsatisfied. She held it firmly in her mouth, drawing in and out continuously. Hsi-men was delighted and cried, "Let the essence flow," and she sucked as it shot into her mouth. She was not able to drink it quickly enough.

> The red lips open wide; the slender fingers
> Play their part daintily.
> Deep in, deep out. Their hearts are wild with passion.
> There are no words to tell the ecstasy that thrills their
>   souls.

Hsi-men lay down on the bed, took down his trousers, lifted his limpo, and told the woman to take it into her mouth while he himself enjoyed some wine. "Suck this well for me," he said, "and I'll give you a gorgeous gown to wear on the next festival day."

"To be sure," answered the woman; "I wish to suck it all night long."

Her slender fingers were playing with the drooping warrior between his legs, pressing it to her cheeks, fondling it with her hands; and finally she put it between her lips and kissed its head. Instantly the warrior was inflamed with fury and arose; its head was as hard as a nail, its eye was wide open, its jowls bristled with bushy hair, and its body stood perfectly stiff.

Neither of them wasted any words. His lust for the woman was great; and she spread her legs, opened her yellow blossom with her fingers, and let the man invade her to the furthest recess. Warm liquid flowed out of her and wet his clothes. Hsi-men placed a considerable amount of red powder upon the head of his member, and then holding fast to the bedsides with both his hands, he thrust so vigorously that the woman opened her eyes wide and called him "Darling."

When he finally withdrew, he wished to wipe his weapon on his trousers; but the woman stopped him and said: "I don't want you to wipe it. I will suck it for you." Hsi-men wishing for nothing sweeter, she bent over, seized his treasure in both her hands, and sucked it until it was clean. Then the man put it back in his trousers.

Hsi-men wished to enjoy the delights of love with his new lady. He knew that she played the flute exquisitely. With tender fingers she opened his trousers, took out his treasure,

321

and stroked it passionately until it rose up rigid and became a superb purple color. The man asked her to mouth it.

She lay back upon the bed and put his jade-scepter between her ruby-red lips. "It's so enormous," she said, "it hurts my mouth." Then she suckled, and tickled the head with her tongue, and began licking up and down. His giant became longer and thicker. With smooth fingers she seized it and entirely devoured it, soon letting it drop dead from her mouth.

At dawn, Golden Lotus and Hsi-men Ch'ing awoke. Golden Lotus saw that his weapon stood upright like a ramrod. "Darling," she said, "you must forgive me, but I can stand it no longer. I want to suckle it!"

"Suckle it," said Hsi-men. "If you can soften it, good for you." The woman seized and received his member between her lips. She sucked for a whole hour, but it did not die. Hsi-men, placing his hands on her dazzling white neck, began to move his weapon about, now pushing it in and anon pulling it out of her mouth with all his might. Soon her lips were dripping, and she slowly drank it down.(8)

***

(8) *Oral intercourse has until lately been rare in American literature. Henry Miller's novels, long banned in the U.S. but much smuggled into the country after publication in Paris, were a famous exception. Erskine Caldwell's God's Little Acre undoubtedly owed much of its fantastic popularity to the presence in the book of a female who inspired in males the desire to perform cunnilingus on her.*

Recently, however, oral intercourse has become commonplace in American fiction—particularly in popular paperbacks, but also in serious creative works. Other previously tabooed sexual practices are also being dealt with; and in many novels the individual who prefers heterosexual coitus, or who is content with coitus alone, is the abnormal one.

There is little question that the acceptance of such material reflects changes in the sexual standards and practices of Americans.

When Golden Lotus, in the act of fellating Hsi-men Ch'ing, states that his penis (or the glans thereof) is so large that it hurts her mouth, she seeks to inflate his ego. In both Chinese and Japanese art work portraying the heterosexual practice of fellatio, the head of the male organ is rarely if ever shown completely in the woman's mouth. In fact, the penis is often depicted in such exaggerated proportions that it would appear never to fit between the feminine lips which approach or kiss it. The reason for this artistic stylization is that Oriental notions of decency and estheticism demand that the female mouth should not be represented as wide enough to receive the virile member. When a court artist was ordered to paint the Emperor Yang Wang being fellated by his chief concubine, he drew the concubine's mouth so small that it seemed unable to absorb even the equally small glans of his Imperial Highness' long slender penis. What would otherwise have been an "obscene" picture was thus given the traditional touch of tasteful delicacy and finesse.

Wilhelm Stekel noted that, next to masturbation, the pleasure of sucking is the first and the strongest gratification known to male and female. This powerful desire for oral stimulation of the genitals is doubtless at least partially a throwback to the paradisaic contentment experienced by the nursling. Moreover, fellatio and cunnilingus are more superexciting to many persons than vaginal coitus.

Heterosexual fellatio and cunnilingus, previously for the most part the property of the better educated, are becoming the rule rather than the exception on most levels of our society.

Moralists lament the trend, and give tongue to their perennial complaint that we are falling into depravity, but the plain fact is that the American people are simply beginning to behave sexually as most other people have always behaved, and as a good many of the more intelligent members of our own society have long behaved.

323

In the classical Japanese Yoshiwara or Whores' Quarter, little girls were kept for fellatio; and their motto was: "I'm not old enough to fuck, but I know how to suck!" They called their erotic trick "fluting" or "playing the pipes." Since mature or full-fledged geishas refused to practical sexual "deviations" and were available only for vaginal coitus, fellatio was therefore restricted to small apprentices who were paid only what the customer wished to give them in return for their oral services. Hence Japanese erotologists recommended that "If a man wishes to make love to a geisha girl he should first get her worked up with wine, kiss her tenderly, caress her passionately, touch his hand to her vulva, rub her clitoris with his fingers, spread her thighs wide apart, and then thrust in violently with his penis." The following advice is given to a young man who is anxious to seduce a budding geisha:

> If one wishes to stretch the sheath, probe the mouth of the vagina continuously and vigorously with the fingers. Ply round and round with two or three fingers together for as long as possible. Continue the forceful rotative motions and the poking in and out until such a time as all four fingers are able to enter the entranceway.
>
> Although they are easily excited by external friction of the labia and clitoris, little girls cannot accommodate a complete penetration of the penis because their narrow and shallow sheaths are not yet adapted thereto. At about the age of puberty they become long and wide. These girls can take it full-length. The walls of the canal are smooth and even, and when the head of the penis rubs against the lips they pout and produce liquid. After constant intercourse, the vagina is gaping and the *labia minora* lengthened. When the opening is rubbed and the womb rammed several times, orgasm is inevitable and instantaneous.

The natural absence or rudimentary state of the hymen facilitates self-gratification and sexual intercourse in little Japanese girls, and the act of coition need entail very little or no pain. The only matter here to be considered is the extreme narrowness and shallowness of the vaginal canal. For stretching or elongating the vagina, the artificial penis (*harigata*, cunnus beater) is recommended. This instrument measures six inches in length and is fairly thick, and for purposes of dilation it is forced in and out several hundred times until the vagina becomes perfectly adapted to its conformation. Some girls masturbate over and over again in this manner, thrusting the *harigata* to and fro more than five thousand times or for several hours, enjoying one orgasm after another. When they are thoroughly exhausted, they go to sleep.

Numerous colored prints, found in Japanese books on sexual instruction, depict the acts of heterosexual fellatio and cunnilingus. Characteristic of Japanese erotic art, the penis is generally shown in enormous proportions; the short prepuce is in all cases fully retracted, and the exposed glans is huge and red. The woman is barely able to clutch the shaft with her small hand, but the wrinkles in the skin of the penis reveal that she is flipping it with her clamping fingers in order to retain the erection and impart stimulation. Her mouth is unable to receive the gigantic glans all the way, for it is at least as large as her fist. While she strokes and kisses his Herculean *hara*, the man fondles her hairy and exceedingly protuberant *hari* with his hand.

In other scenes the woman, her legs wrapped about the man's shoulders, is taking an active role by gripping his penis and fellating it while he, lying beneath her, is ardently caressing her cunnus with his tongue in the so-called *soixante-neuf* or "69" position. This act of simultaneous fellatio and cunnilingus is commonly called *ai-name* (mutual love-licking, reciprocal sucking) in Japanese. The woman, exciting the shaft with her hand and lavishing caresses upon the glans with her lips, is saying: "When I suck your penis it swells up big and

325

tremendously tall. Since I'm as true to you as this, you shouldn't cheat on me." Repeated sucking sounds are then written in Japanese at the top of the picture. The man, his legs tense and toes flexed as he approaches his ejaculation, replies: "Oh! oh! The inside of your cunnus is pink and scarlet, and when I lick it I will lengthen my life three thousand years." Repeated licking sounds are then given in Japanese.(9)

Soixante-neuf or *ai-name* is the most sacred expression of mutual love and devotion known to the traditional Japanese. Ovid's *dulce opus* (sweet task) was fellatio and cunnilingus, which he described as a masculine-feminine secret for winning mutual affection. For a wife orally to absorb her husband's semen is deemed a most blessed and beneficial deed, and a husband's absorption of his wife's secretions is thought to have a rejuvenating effect upon his entire system.

The ways of the world are a wonder to behold and to contemplate!

---

(9) *These are not, to the Japanese, obscene or pornographic books. They sound rather like the "eight-page bibles" of U.S. fame, but the point is irrelevant; what is significant is the attitude of the reader, and the very concept of "pornography" is rejected by the Japanese.*

It is otherwise with the Chinese, who like ourselves are given to labeling books pornographic and then selling them on an under-the-counter basis. Even the immensely popular Chin P'ing Mei, from which we have frequently quoted, has often been banned in China. But an idea of the resistance to such censorship may be gleaned from the fact that when Emperor K'ang Hsi sought to suppress Chin P'ing Mei, his own brother helped bring out a new edition.

8. EAST AND WEST:

Concluding Remarks

We run carelessly to the precipice, after we have put some-
thing before us to prevent us seeing it.

PASCAL

Improved transportation and media of communications, the activities of the United Nations and the threat of nuclear war, have made the world's peoples aware of one another as never before. Even the hundreds of millions of savages and illiterates are to some degree affected, whether they know it or not, by the global shrinkage. And there seems to be taking place a not always comprehensible interpenetration of ideas and attitudes, and of unconscious as well as conscious needs and yearnings, even between peoples separated by gulfs traditionally regarded as unbridgeable.

It is no longer possible plausibly to assert that East is East, and West is West, and never the twain shall meet. On the contrary, there has been for a long time a "Westernizing" trend apparent in the East; and more recently it has been possible to discern what would seem to be "Easternizing," and even "Africanizing," tendencies at work in the West.

Those who seek hope and security in the one-world ideal

may find little in the spurt and flow of events to promise them that nationalism is perishing; but they may find much evidence that the peoples of the world, in spite of their national boundaries, are becoming increasingly alike.

The dramatic loosening of sexual morals in the United States is in part a product of this over-all trend to alikeness. Both the "animal sexuality" of the less developed peoples, from below, and the greater sophistication of Europe, from above, chipping and sucking at the "puritanism" of America, have bludgeoned and drained off traditional rigidities and certainties, filling the gaps, when not leaving them yawning, with still undigestible substance, and so spawning confusion.

The sophisticates have largely, and in the main rightly, convinced us that much of what we once thought to be vice, in the area of sex, was not vicious after all; and those who have always been largely unfettered by sexual restrictions hold out to us an example that is more and more tempting as our punctured and eroded absolutism becomes increasingly useless as a shield against the temptation and as an alternative gratification.

There will surely be some who will say that this is an immoral book, that such a book can only give further encouragement to the drift to demoralization already so apparent in the United States and throughout much of the rest of the world. But the careful reader will know better.

Even the most rigid moralist of the "old school"—which has had, in any case, its day—should find something in these pages to applaud. For what is perhaps the main lesson to be learned from this study of Asian and African sexual behavior? Surely it is that sexual freedom alone is not a good remedy for the psycho-sexual or any other problems of the mainly Christian West.

It has become customary to regard the West as materialistic, and the East as idealistic—both to a fault. But in sexual matters, exactly the reverse has often been the case. What is most commendable in the Oriental approach to sexual relationships is the clear realistic understanding that the needs of the flesh must and should be met. What is most commendable in the Western approach is the recognition that sexual intercourse need not be *just* a physical experience, that it may also involve mind and emotions, blending selfless benevolence with self-interest, to the enrichment of the participants.

The materialistic-egoistic approach of the Muslim leads to coarseness and brutality, and so necessarily fails to realize the potential value of the sexual experience. The Christian Westerner, attempting to largely or totally psychologize or mentalize the experience, minimizes and finally denies the legitimate needs of the flesh with the result that he, too, impoverishes the experience he had sought to enrich; and more, by going against his nature, he sickens both his body and his mind.

There is a widespread, though less than fully understood, recognition in the United States today that we have ideologically fouled our sexual nest. Even while paying lip-service to the old fundamentalist and absolutist doctrines, the people are in full-fledged rebellion against them. The vague understanding that we have overvalued the psychical content of the sexual experience—and, concomitantly, undervalued the physical content—has led to a too total rejection of the psychical elements. Consequently, our behavior comes increasingly to resemble that of the Muslim in its loveless promiscuity, its untempered sensuality, and often in its brutality.

Unconsciously, or only very hazily, people understand that their sexual values have been at fault. Lacking insight into the nature of their difficulties, conscious only of their misery, they tend to abandon all sexual values—restrained only by tradition, the disapproval of their elders and, to some extent, by fear of legal consequences. Sexual intercourse in the United States, in becoming more free, becomes less discriminating. The incidence of rape increases drastically, especially among the young —those most in revolt (or most noticeably and dramatically in

329

revolt) against the old, inadequate, and ever more widely rejected values. The breakdown in the area of values leaves a void covered over by what is often misunderstood as psychopathy.

The Eastern world, under the influence of Western ideas, gathering up like some half-crazed beachcomber the flotsam and jetsam of dead and dying Western values, fares little better.

The West fails to give to the East what is best in the Western tradition: the enhancement of the erotic experience by inclusion of the mutual affection and esteem of one lover for the other. The East gives to the West not a realistic emphasis upon the physical aspects of the erotic experience, but an example which the West is only able to understand as the grossest sort of sensuality and license. The two draw closer, but with little benefit to either and with damage to both. Hopefully the condition is transitional and each will eventually receive from the other what is most beneficial.

The detailed accounts of the sexual practices of children may be particularly jarring to some sensibilities. But they should stimulate thought among those whose business it is to ponder and decide the advantages and disadvantages of restraining the sexual impulses of the young; and who must determine the proper degree of such restraints, and how to impose them. As a great many Western scientists now understand, the attempt to defer sexual intercourse beyond the time when it is desired and the individual is competent to engage in it is fraught with grave risks.

In general, the longer normal sexual fulfillment is denied, the greater are the chances that a satisfactory sexual life will be impossible later on. Sexual and mental disorders are much more likely to beset those who live in sex starvation over a long period of time than those who experience sexual gratification at sufficient intervals. However, it must also be kept in mind that a system of morals which condemns much of our

330

sexual behavior may largely negate the benefits of regular gratification, and even make full gratification impossible. The individual who abides by the prohibitions has to suffer both frustration and guilt—the last because, while he or she may remain
physically chaste (and frustrated), desire will be strongly present, phantasy indulgence will multiply and intensify, and self-
condemnation will result. The individual who ignores the
prohibitions may avoid the frustration; but he will not be able
to avoid the guilt.

As the store of collective knowledge increases, more and
more individual knowledge is needed to "get ahead" in society.
This means that more and more education is required, which
in turn means that a greater number of years must be spent in
acquiring the education. And during all of those years, income
is slight, not at all sufficient to allow for marriage (with reasonable expectancy of permanence), much less for raising a
family. Thus we unrealistically demand ever-longer periods of
sexual deprivation for those who do not wish to engage in
premarital intercourse while requiring open defiance of the official morality from those who are unable or unwilling to deny
their legitimate biological and psychological requirements.
This last-mentioned group is now a clear majority of the young
people in the United States, and their activities extend chrono-
logically downward to involve those still younger.

Since the official morality has proved itself so resistant to
change, while also proving itself unrealistic, efforts to alter it
are abandoned. The idol is permitted to stand on its pedestal:
sincere oldsters and middle-aged hypocrites still come to genu-
flect; more and more of the young pass by without a glance.
Later, they learn to their misery that this ugly and rusty old
god, so impotent in consciousness, may still exact a grim unconscious toll from those who offend against him.

Of course, not only the young are in revolt. Science is in
head-on collision with law—which is to say that scientific find-

ings in the area of human sexual behavior increasingly result in recommendations running counter to the laws on the statute books as well as to the official morality. Marriage counselors, obeying the dictates of conscience, recommend unlawful acts; legislators decline to revise laws they regard as outmoded for fear of being accused of encouraging vice; judges sentence individuals to prison or otherwise penalize them for acts the judges not only privately condone but also personally engage in; and among the masses of the people there is an understandable confusion.

The two main "practical" objections to premarital and extramarital intercourse are no longer valid. Venereal diseases could be readily and rapidly conquered by a program of sex education to supplement medical advances. Unwanted pregnancies could be easily prevented by making available to all who wanted them the oral contraceptives presently on the market. And in the offing are contraceptive immunizations, which could be administered to both teenagers and adults who wanted them just as smallpox and polio shots, etc., are provided now.

We are faced, then, with the reality that the "practical" objections to premarital intercourse have lost their validity. What remain are mostly arbitrary and irrational moralistic objections, rooted in superstition and prejudice, and sometimes cloaked in psychological and sociological jargon. These objections no longer deter sexual intercourse; they only thwart efforts to revise our way of thinking, and so encourage chaos.

Many highly responsible and intelligent persons, after arduous study and lengthy reflection, have concluded that we must permit premarital relationships. However, no responsible person would suggest that such relationships ought to be entirely promiscuous and sensual—as now is so often the case. What we urgently need are new values which will condone the sexual relationships of those who enter into them affectionately and with mutual respect. All human experience instructs us that we will have to allow too for very transient relationships (a Westernized "futtering") if they are not merely brutal and sordid. And most importantly our sexual values must encourage a proper blending of physical and psychical elements, giving society's blessing to the sexual encounter as a mentally and emotionally enriching experience, and encouraging everyone to make of the sex act something more than a vehicle for the discharging of tensions accompanied by momentary pleasure.

It seems plain that an expanded sexual freedom (which we already have and which will increase), unless accompanied by new and realistic moral values, will result among the young in behavior increasingly like that of the Arab, African and some other children described in this book. There will be limitless sexual exploitation—and there is already a great deal of such exploitation in our larger cities. Our values, while holding out the reward of sexual fulfillment, will have to condemn what is truly exploitative and otherwise damaging.

As premarital intercourse becomes ever more common, as inevitably it will do, we are going to be faced with the problem that the age at which such intercourse begins will sink gradually or rapidly lower. And the younger the child participating in sexual activities, the greater will be the tendency to introduce other, still younger, children to such activities—as we see evidenced in the rapes and seductions of very small children by somewhat older children in the Muslim world. These tendencies and processes, presently at work and gaining impetus with startling rapidity, would seem to be irreversible and unmanageable unless by a drastic overhaul of the sex-moral structure. Police action is ineffective, even if it were desirable, in dealing with adolescents and still younger children of all social classes; while parents, caught up in the same maelstrom of confusion and shifting standards, are manifestly unable to exert control or effect a reversal.

333

Obviously the time will come when we will feel that we must draw a line at all costs. If we are logical, we will draw it at the place where the sexually immature and the irresponsible are exploited by those who have attained sexual maturity. If it is possible to draw such a line, and to make it effective, we will have to provide for the needs of the mature, so diminishing the incentive to exploit while affirming the positive values inherent in what is allowed. This book makes plain enough the alternatives to such a reasonable course, and they are not alternatives likely to prove acceptable to Western peoples.

As remarked earlier, the East has something to teach the West about tolerance in the area of sexual and other individual peculiarities. Human beings of the future will surely both ridicule and deplore the obsessive Western preoccupation with who puts what into which orifice of whom. And this remarkable concern would indeed be altogether ludicrous if it were not so catastrophically neurotogenic.

Magical ideas about the sexual organs still permeate Western civilization. Those organs are no longer deified, nor are they (by the majority) considered the particular province of the Devil as in the Middle Ages and up into the eighteenth century; but the prohibitions based upon such beliefs, even though deprived of their faulty foundations, irrationally persist and govern our thinking to a calamitous extent.

The sex statutes of the United States, in particular, are a source of wonder and amusement to the rest of the world. Theologians who debated the number of angels able to dance on the head of a pin, or who devoted their time and energy to calculating the velocity at which the fallen angels fell, were no more nigglingly disputatious or bizarrely credulous and naïve than are those American moralists who would deny a husband the right to orally caress his wife's genitals, or who would allow such caresses, but only for so long as they do not

334

result in a climax, and are followed up by the insertion of the penis into the vagina.

The "practical" objection to erotic refinements—that they do not result in the procreation of children—has long since lost whatever small legitimacy it may once have possessed; and in fact the need to control reproduction is now among the most pressing (and the least adequately dealt with) of all human problems.

In much of the East, if a girl prefers to fellate her lover rather than copulate with him, and if he is agreeable, then no one finds anything much to condemn in that. Society does not suffer, the participants are made happy, and anyone who objected would be recognized for the reprehensible meddler that he or she certainly is. But in the West, and in the United States especially, it is the meddling that is taken for granted, socially approved, and often backed up by the full weight of the statutes, the police, and the courts.

The homosexual, who neither chooses his condition nor is able to change it or (except rarely) have it changed, has relations with another homosexual or bisexual to the benefit of both and without harm to society. In the East, that is likely to be considered his affair; and in Europe it is considered less than a menace to the security of the state. In the U.S., however, such hapless individuals are publicly branded as damnable "cocksuckers" and "queers" and are ostracized by society, hounded and hunted by the police, and sent to prison whenever possible or practicable. While crimes of violence increase, an irrational public policy dictates that police forces maintain vice squads to carry out espionage activities in toilet booths.

It is small wonder that an increasingly well-educated and sophisticated people, sickened at what is said and done in the name of morality, should abandon a sex code productive of such stupidities and evils.

Yet, as we have pointed out, such abandonment *in toto* of

335

sexual restraints, without an attempt to replace with something sound and workable the unsound and unworkable principles abandoned, must lead when the process is sufficiently advanced to an African-like license and finally to exploitation and brutality on the mass behavior level. It is not such a sexual freedom, or sexual anarchy, that we ought to desire or that we may permit to develop and flourish except at our peril.

To say the obvious: Stripped of all restraints, freedom of speech becomes freedom to libel and slander; freedom of action becomes freedom to murder and pillage; sexual freedom becomes freedom to rape and to victimize. And all such freedoms are illusory, because total freedom will swiftly be overwhelmed by a tyranny of total terror.

A reasonable sexual freedom will never tolerate assault or the victimization of the irresponsible. It will be merely a freedom similar to the freedoms already enjoyed in other areas of human life, with males and females, from a realistic minimum age upward, permitted to choose and act freely so long as they do not infringe unduly upon the freedom of others. Such sexual freedom combines the tolerance of the East with the rationalism (in its best sense) of the West. It is what we must aim for if we are to avoid dangerous disorder on the one hand and the wholesale manufacture of neurotics on the other.

Also discussed in this book is the havoc presently being wrought in some parts of the East by the movement toward "feminine equality." The movement is world-wide, not just limited to the East, and everywhere its consequences are unfortunate in the area of sexual relationships.

The equality of the female has meant, in practice, not just political and economic, but also sexual equality. This sexual equality, so desirable in theory, has had a crippling effect upon the male, who by nature or through centuries-long conditioning has accustomed himself to the role of aggressor and initiator of erotic activities. The male fear of the female, deriving in

336

part from the ancient belief that the female, because unhampered by the tumescence-detumescence mechanism, is sexually insatiable, is intensified by confrontation with the new and more aggressive woman.

In other ways, too, as a result of her politically and economically competitive situation in the world, woman becomes "masculinized." The male reacts to this not by becoming more masculine, but by becoming less masculine, at least by comparison. Differences between the sexes are diminished, bisexuality becomes (in the West) more prevalent, and potency problems increase. The female, still used to male domination, loses respect for and often comes to despise the male who is no longer able to dominate. Her obvious course of action, since it is clear that male sexual dominance is bound up with male dominance in other areas, is to retreat into traditional feminine passivity and pretense of subjugation; but instead she reacts by becoming still more bold and aggressive. Yet another unmanning retreat is forced upon the male. We are presently in the midst of this process and where it will end is impossible to say.

It is certain, however, that sexual equality for the female imposes almost intolerable stresses and strains upon the institution of monogamous marriage and the family as it has developed in Christian countries. This institution, firmly based upon a double sexual standard weighted in behalf of the male, owed such success as it enjoyed to a variety of factors. Among these, the most important was probably the economic dependency of the female, which forced her into marriage and made it exceedingly difficult for her to terminate a marriage once entered into. The same economic dependency made it possible for her to remain sexually faithful, because the consequences of infidelity were so disastrous. Meanwhile, monogamy was made endurable for the economically independent male by his greater sexual freedom and by the ready accessibility of prosti-

337

tutes. Prostitution also provided, for many women, the only real alternative to wretchedness in wedlock.

Prostitution, as is well known, is the invariable concomitant of the kind of monogamous marriage with an insistence upon wifely fidelity that we have had in the West. The decline of prostitution is therefore an ominous sign for the future (and present) of marriage and the family. It is a decline (most dramatic in the smaller cities and towns) made possible only by increasing divorce rates and frequency of both premarital and extramarital intercourse. In the Muslim world, where society has always been quite differently organized, prostitution has suffered no similar fate. The equality of women has probably increased rather than diminished the incidence of prostitution —a fact made possible by the greater freedom of movement and action now accorded women in a prosexual culture where self-interest is admittedly paramount.

Depending upon definitions, it might also be said that prostitution has increased, and similarly, in the West. But this would be to include all of those girls and women who now barter, rather than honestly sell, their sexual services—in exchange for gifts, automobile rides, night-club entertainment, etc.; and always with the understanding that the female is giving, not selling, her favors. Such new free females operate not in a prosexual culture, as do their Eastern counterparts, but in a culture where antisexual values have collapsed.

In attempting to understand the sexual behavior of the African and of the Asian, and perhaps especially of the Muslim Arab who seems more comparable to ourselves, it will be very difficult for the Westerner to grasp the almost exclusively physical approach to many sexual acts. Both our traditional values and our psychoanalytic orientation lead us to reject the idea that an adult male may copulate with a little girl merely or mainly because of the superior friction afforded to his penis,

338

or that masturbation or anal intercourse may be preferred to coitus on similar grounds.

Our emphasis upon the psychical elements of sexual relationships leads us again and again to overlook or deny physical aspects which are also of great importance, so that the question, for example, of disparity of size of the male and female organs is seldom treated with appropriate respect. Love is expected to conquer all, but alas even love is not always able to overcome the problems presented by a slender penis or a slack vagina; and it is also the case that the sexual passions of husbands and wives are seldom, save in the case of newlyweds, sufficient to blind the sex partners to a variety of practical considerations.

The idea of "futtering" is so alien to our theory, and so cheapening and guilt-provoking to our practice, because we have overweighted the scales on the side of the psyche. Futtering—intercourse that is based primarily upon physical attraction and appetites, though it need not be unesthetic or without tenderness and respect for the other—has a legitimate, and certainly an inevitable, place in the sexual relations of mankind. To deny this would be altogether unrealistic. At the same time, we should recognize futtering for what it is—a "second-class" or "second-rate" kind of relationship, offering rewards which are substantial, and which ought not to be minimized, but still a relationship inferior to one characterized also by affection or love for the sex partner. It makes no more sense for the desiring man or woman to reject sexual intercourse just because the partner is not loved than it would for a starving man to reject hamburger because, under the best of circumstances, he laudably prefers a gourmet's fare.

The objection will surely be raised that sexual intercourse without love is degrading to both participants. But that is true only if one first arbitrarily declares that all sexual intercourse except that of lovers is degrading. And such a declaration condemns to degradation not only all of mankind throughout much of our past, and much of mankind throughout all of our past, it also assigns degraded status to the vast majority of sexual acts engaged in by married couples in our own country today, which will not be what such a moralist intended.

To this particular objection it is also possible to respond by demanding that the alternatives be examined. Sexual frustration, whether in the name of chastity or whatever, is scarcely ennobling. On the contrary, and as saints and other celibates have especially well demonstrated, it results in an excessive preoccupation with the erotic, manifested in phantasies and worse—and neurosis is often the end product (when it is not, as may be more common, the cause). The probable fact that only a minority of human beings are ever erotically in love at any given time means that at all times a majority of persons would be doomed to frustration by any (enforceable) insistence upon loving intercourse.

Thus, the Easterner, with his awareness and acceptance of sexual needs quite apart from love, recognizes the realities of the human condition in this particular phase of his existence and behaves accordingly. The Westerner often behaves in much the same way, but denying the realities the Easterner recognizes, with the consequent guilt so well known to us all.

It is his superior mental equipment, his mind, that has given man a dominant status among the animals of which he is one. Western-Christian man's crucial error in the area of sexuality has resulted from his pride in this dominant status. Although belief in God as the creator of the world implies that God created man as both body and mind, man has equated mind with God and body with the beasts. He has striven to be God-like by exalting his own mind or spirit; and he has striven to sever his connection with the other animals by denying his body.

This arbitrary mind-body division and separation, ironically

340

coming out of Persia, resulted in a hatred of the flesh (which could not be successfully denied) that manifested itself primarily in an attempt first to reject and then to spiritualize the sexual experience. By way of this error, which the Muslim never made, the Christian went against his nature and paid a terrible price in mental and emotional and physical illness; but he also brought something valuable into the world—psychical elements which, properly blended with physical ones, proved capable of greatly enriching human sexual relationships.

It is this great discovery that the Muslim has never fully grasped and that the West has to offer to him and to many other Africans and Easterners (and to most of our own Western peoples as well). On the other hand, as we have courted boredom to emphasize by repetition, it is appropriate regard for what is physical in man and for what is properly carnal in the sexual relationship that the Muslim has to offer to the West.

When the Sudani girl, just married, spends her wedding night copulating with the friends of her new husband, much or all that is mentally and emotionally enriching in the union of male and female is entirely wanting. She will have no more to offer her husband sexually, and he will have no more to offer her, than was available in the orgiastic celebration in the brush.

But when the terrified, sobbing, frigid bride lies down with the anxious, impotent groom, then we have an extreme example of just the opposite emphasis, and it is one largely peculiar to the Western (Christian) world.

Somewhere in between lies the coming together of healthy, desiring, loving human beings—and in the area of human sexuality it is just here that East and West must and some day shall meet.

341

SELECTED BIBLIOGRAPHY

Abu Nowas el-Hasan bin Hani. *Dīwān* (Poetry Collection).

Apocrypha, The Old Testament.

Babylonian Talmud, The. 35 vols. London: Soncino Press.

Brantôme, Pierre de. *Lives of Fair and Gallant Ladies.* Paris: Carrington, 1900.

Bryk, Felix. *Voodoo-Eros.* New York: Ethnological Press, 1933.

Burton, Sir Richard F. *Personal Narrative of a Pilgrimage to El-Medina & Mecca.* 2 vols. London: Bell, 1898.

Carlson, John Roy. *Cairo to Damascus.* New York: Knopf, 1951.

Dickson, Colonel H. R. P. *The Arab of the Desert.* London: Allen & Unwin, 1951.

Edwardes, Allen. *The Jewel in the Lotus.* New York: Julian Press, 1959.

Ferezdek, Hemmam bin Ghalib el-. *Dīwān* (Poetry Collection).

Gichner, Lawrence E. *Erotic Aspects of Hindu Sculpture.* Washington, D.C.: 1949.

    Erotic Aspects of Japanese Culture. Washington, D.C.: 1953.

    Erotic Aspects of Chinese Culture. Washington, D.C.: 1957.

343

Halebi, Khojeh 'Omar (Abu 'Othman). *El-Kitāb Sherī'et el-Khabbeh fī 'Ilm el-Muhhabbeh* (Book of the Secret Laws of Love).

Herbert, Lord George. *A Night in a Moorish Harem.*

Heriri, Abu Muhammed bin Qasim el-. *El-Meqāmāt* (The Assemblies).

Hezm, Abu 'Ali bin Sa'id Ibn. *El-Kitāb Tōq el-Hhemāmeh* (Book of the Ring of the Dove).

Hhidāyeh, El- (The Guidance).

Isfahani, Shaykh Sadiq bin Tebib el-. *Bāh Nāmeh* (Book of Lust).

Jacobus, Dr. *(nom de plume). L'Ethnologie du Sens Génitale.* 5 vols. Paris: 1935.

Kalyanamalla, Pandit. *Anangaranga* (Code of Cupid).

Kemal Pasha, Shemseddin Ahmed bin Sulayman Ibn. *El-Kitāb Rujū' esh-Shaykh ila Sebāhh fī Qūwet el-Bāh* (Book of Male Rejuvenescence in the Power of Concupiscence).

Khaiyam, 'Omar-i-. *Er-Rubā'īyāt* (The Quatrains). Edward FitzGerald translation, in numerous editions.

Khatefa, Jerir bin el-. *Dīwān* (Poetry Collection).

Kitāb Elf Layleh wa-Layleh, El- (Book of the Thousand Nights and a Night).

Koka Pandit. *Ratīrahasya* (Secrets of Sex).

Lane, Edward William. *Notes on the Arabian Nights.* London: 1898.

Leeuw, Hendrik de. *Sinful Cities of the Western World.* New York: Citadel Press, 1949.

Mahābhārata (The Great Story).

Mantegazza, Dr. Paolo. *L'Amour dans l'Humanité.* Paris: 1886.

Mirabeau, Honoré Gabriel Riquetti, Comte de. *Erotika Biblion.* Bruxelles: 1890.

Montaigne, Michel de. *Essays.* In numerous editions.

Nefzawi, Shaykh 'Omar bin Sidi en-. *Kitāb Rōdzet el-'Ātir fī Nuzhet el-Khātir* (Book of the Scented Garden Site for Heart Delight).

Old Man Young Again, The. Paris: Carrington, 1908.

Old Testament, The (Tōrāh, Nebī'īm, Kethūbīm).

Qurān, El- (The Scriptures).

Ring of the Dove, The (Ibn Hezm). Translated by Dr. A. J. Arberry. London: Luzac, 1953.

Riza Bey. *Darkest Orient*. London: Arco, 1953.

Rosenbaum, Dr. Julius. *The Plague of Lust*. Paris: Carrington, 1910.

Seyuti, Gelaleddin es-. *Kitāb el-Īdzāhh fī 'Ilm en-Nikāhh* (Book of Revelation in the Science of Copulation).

Siddiqi, Muhammad Mazheruddin. *Women in Islam*. Lahore: Institute of Islamic Culture, 1959.

Stekel, Dr. Wilhelm. *Auto-Erotism*. New York: Liveright, 1950.

Stern, Dr. Bernhard. *Medizin, Aberglaube und Geschlechtsleben in der Türkei*. 2 vols. Berlin: 1933.

Thomas, P. *Kāma Kalpa*. Bombay: Taraporevala, 1958.

Thousand Nights and a Night, The Book of the. Translated by Richard F. Burton. 17 vols. London: Burton Club, 1885–88.

Thousand Nights and One Night, The Book of the. Translated by Dr. J. C. Mardrus and Powys Mathers. 4 vols. London: Routledge, 1947.

Van de Velde, Dr. T. H. *Ideal Marriage*. New York: Random House, 1947.

Vatsyayana, Pandit. *Kāmasūtra* (Laws of Love).

Wang Shih-cheng. *The Golden Lotus* (*Chin P'ing Mei*). Translated by Clement Egerton. 4 vols. London: Routledge & Kegan Paul, 1957.

Yezdi, Haji 'Abdu'l- (Sir R. F. Burton). *El-Qesīdeh* (A Lay of the Higher Law). In numerous editions.

INDEX

347

art (*cont.*)
  Japanese, portraying fellatio
    and cunnilingus, 325–326
asceticism, 113–114, 115; *see also*
  coitus reservatus
Ashref Khan, 36
atrocities, sexual, of Arabs on
  battlefield, 211–212
atropine, *see* aphrodisiacs
Attila the Hun, 103n
Auto-Eroticism, 271
Avicenna, 173–174
avisodomy, 16n

Baal, penis of, 242
badana, see onanism, mutual
Bāh Nāmeh, 122, 157–158
baksheesh, payment, 306
banana, in masturbation, 284,
  287–288
Bar Hana, Rabbah ben, 293
bathhouse, masturbators and
  pederasts in, 280
Bathsheba, 110–111
Bedawin, 175, 178
  modesty of, 7, 193
  rapists, 210–211
  women, make condoms, 190
belly dance (*reqs es-surreh*), 306
Benjamin ben Hiyya, Rabbi, 257
Berber child prostitutes, 135–136
Berserkers, The
  homoerotic sex club, 246
  masturbation and sodomy, men
    with boys, boys in turn with
    men, 246
bestiality, 16
  cure for satyriasis, nympho-
    mania, 242n

improvement of potency by,
  243n
Moors of Maghreb, 210
remedy for venereal disease,
  242n
taught to children of Moroccan
  Muslims, 242
Bodin, Jean, 124n
Book of Lust, 122
*Book of Male Rejuvenescence in
  the Power of Concupiscence*,
  57
*Book of Revelation in the Science
  of Copulation*, 8–9
Book of the Ring of the Dove, 8,
  28
*Book of the Scented Garden Site
  for Heart Delight*, 9
Book of the Secret Laws of Love,
  3
*Book of the Thousand Nights and
  One Night*, 7, 8, 9, 16
Bowles, Paul, 71
boy, Indian
  fellator, 318
  masturbator, 318
  semen swallower, 318
  sodomy and, 318
Brantôme, 105
bride
  child, 120–121, 123, 127–128
  copulation with all males at
    wedding, 238, 341
  droit du seigneur, 131–133, 294
  frigid, 341
brothel, special
  ancient Rome, babies as penis
    suckers, 222
  boy and eunuch, 216, 217

348